POET IN THE MAKING

THE NOTEBOOKS OF DYLAN THOMAS

BY DYLAN THOMAS

Poet
in the Making

THE NOTEBOOKS OF
DYLAN THOMAS

EDITED BY

RALPH MAUD

LONDON
J. M. DENT & SONS LTD

SBN: 460 03829 X

Five of the poems in this volume were first published with notes by Ralph Maud, in *Mademoiselle* for June 1966, to which grateful acknowledgment is here made. Approximately forty of the poems are early versions of poems in *The Collected Poems*, *1934–1952*, of Dylan Thomas, Copyright 1939, 1942 by New Directions Publishing Corporation; Copyright 1952, 1953 by Dylan Thomas. The publishers are particularly grateful to the Lockwood Memorial Library of The State University of New York at Buffalo, where originals of the Four Notebooks of Dylan Thomas are preserved, and to Professor Oscar A. Silverman, formerly Chairman of the English Department and now Director of Libraries at the University of Buffalo.

CONTENTS

INTRODUCTION

THE AIM OF THIS EDITION is to provide a pleasant reading text of the four manuscript exercise books[1] in which Dylan Thomas copied approximately two hundred poems as he finished them during the crucial years of his youth, 1930 to 1934.

The sense in which they are finished poems is indicated by Thomas in a letter dated February 1935 to his friend Charles Fisher:

> my method is this: I write a poem on innumerable sheets of scrap paper, write it on both sides of the paper, often upside down and criss cross ways unpunctuated, surrounded by drawings of lamp posts and boiled eggs, in a very dirty mess; bit by bit I copy out the slowly developing poem into an exercise book; and, when it is completed, I type it out. The scrap sheets I burn. . . .[2]

However, Thomas later came to think of these Notebook poems as first drafts. He wrote to Henry Treece in July 1938: "I have a great deal of material still, in MSS books, to shape into proper poems; and these I will include . . . in future published books."[3] Thomas had already gone back to the early Notebooks, revising poems for inclusion in *Twenty-five Poems* (1936), and was to use the Notebooks in this way until he relinquished them in 1941.[4]

An attempt has been made in this edition to provide the reader with the poet's second thoughts without obliterating his first. Where Thomas simply crossed out his early lines, the words and passages are enclosed in square brackets in the text; where he altered or

[9]

added, a footnote in the text directs the reader to the textual notes at the end of the volume, where revisions and other idiosyncracies of the manuscript are dealt with.

This edition, then, reveals for the first time the extent of Thomas' poetic output from his fifteenth to his nineteenth year. It also confounds previous assumptions about the poet's later development by showing, also for the first time, how much of the poetry printed up to his twenty-sixth year was really a reworking of early poems.[5] We might regret the absence of a notebook for the period July 1932 to January 1933, a gap that interrupts the sequence;[6] but a student concerned with Thomas' obscurities can be happy that in these remains are illuminating first drafts of over forty of Thomas' published poems, including some of the most famous; and a student of the poetic process has here apprenticeship material enough to match the bulky worksheets of Thomas' later years.

And if it should be feared that we are fussing over stuff that the poet·himself discarded as worthless, we can be assured of the contrary. Thomas cherished these exercise books as trophies of his energetic youth and as inspiration for new poems. He also realized their potential interest to the student of poetry in writing of the last two Notebooks:

> they show the growth of poems over a period of just more than a year, one extremely creative, productive year, in all their stages and alternations, and—in many instances—show how a quite different poem emerges, years later, from the original.[7]

It is hoped that this volume, by its fidelity to the Notebooks, reflects the poet's nostalgic care and pragmatic concern.

I. THE POET AS SCHOOLBOY

These poems of the inner life are a contrast to what we know of Thomas' external world at the time. Born on 27 October 1914, he was a struggling fifteen and a half when he started the first of the Notebooks—struggling within himself, that is; for his actions in the outer world were astonishingly decisive. At school he paid little attention in any class (with the exception of English, which his father taught) and failed all his examinations (again with the exception of English, in which he got 98% in the Central Welsh Board Senior Certificate).[8] What he chose to do he did with aplomb. In the brooding 1930 Notebook there is no indication that at the previous Sports Day D. M. Thomas had come in first in the quarter mile (under fifteen);[9] or that, three months before, he had played the lead in Drinkwater's *Oliver Cromwell,* "a meritorious performance, which reached real brilliancy in the third scene";[10] or that he was editing the *Swansea Grammar School Magazine* and writing most of it in order to simplify decisions and insure style. But, since Dylan Thomas from the age of six or seven was nothing if not a poet, his real personal history is rather to be found in the secret Notebooks, whose poems were not for the profane pages of the school magazine. P. E. Smart, co-editor of the magazine during 1929–1930, has described Thomas' double standard:

> He was writing at the time some delightful light verse, sparkling, bright and clear, but he was of course already producing verse of the kind which many people can't understand, and I remember asking him why he did it: what was the point of writing "privately" in this way. But he couldn't really understand the question: he wrote, he said, what was in him, and it was really quite irrelevant whether anyone else even read it.[11]

The light, schoolboy verse can be found elsewhere;[12] this edition finally brings to light the obscure, private verse the young Thomas wrote up to the unveiling of his first volume, *18 Poems.*

2. THE 1930 NOTEBOOK AND INFLUENCES

You want to know why and how I first began to write poetry, and which poets or kinds of poetry I was first moved and influenced by.

To answer the first part of this question, I should say I wanted to write poetry in the beginning because I had fallen in love with words. The first poems I knew were nursery rhymes, and before I could read them for myself I had come to love just the words of them, the words alone.

Thomas is here answering questions put to him in later life; and his "Poetic Manifesto"[13] begins with this early falling in love with words, an experience he tried to express in such poems as *Especially when the October wind*. Next, Thomas recalls his earliest contacts with literature:

> Let me say that the things that first made me love language and want to work *in* it and *for* it were nursery rhymes and folk tales, the Scottish Ballads, a few lines of hymns, the most famous Bible stories and the rhythms of the Bible, Blake's Songs of Innocence, and the quite incomprehensible magical majesty and nonsense of Shakespeare heard, read, and near-murdered in the first forms of my school.

We are given a picture of the newly self-conscious poet-to-be:

> It was when I was very young, and just at school, that, in my father's study, before homework that was never done, I began to know one kind of writing from another, and one kind of goodness, one kind of badness. My first, and greatest, liberty was that of being able to read everything and anything I cared to. I read indiscriminately, and with my eyes hanging out.

What he read he imitated in his own writing efforts: Sir Thomas Browne, de Quincey, Henry Newbolt, the Ballads, Blake, Baroness Orczy, Marlowe, Chums, the Imagists, the Bible, Poe, Keats, Lawrence, Anon., and Shakespeare.[14] These were "the primary influences upon my very first and forever unpublishable juvenilia." From some points of view it is a good thing that the earliest notebooks do not exist and that Thomas in 1941 chose out the four which might not be forever unpublishable. For by 1930 a more serious apprenticeship was under way.

The clue to the new development is given by the heading to the 1930 Notebook: "Mainly Free Verse Poems" (repeated on the 1930–1932 Notebook). Indications are that up to this point Thomas' poems had been derivative, the borrowed forms dictating the subject and keeping the compositions essentially, albeit enthusiastically, artificial. The poems of this self-assigned homework appeared in the school magazine from 1925, first as precocious buddings, later as deftly turned parodies. In April 1930, at the same time as he began

the extant Notebooks with *Osiris, Come to Isis,* a serious poem in
the early Yeatsian manner, Thomas was actually ribbing Yeats in
the school magazine with a parody entitled *In Borrowed Plumes*:

> There was a pearl-pale moon that slid
> Down oceans of ambrosial sky,
> Under the drooping of the day's dusk-lid
> Where darkness and her wine-waves lie . . .[15]

Clearly Thomas could handle himself in the Celtic twilight. But he
left the Oisin style forever as an apprentice task accomplished, and
pushed on into free verse and a new stage of *self*-expression.

The kind of free verse he began to write was not, of course,
without precedent. His friend Daniel Jones was in a position to see
the influences at work in the decade 1924 to 1934:

> [Thomas'] poetry passed in ten years from simple lyricism, remi-
> niscent of W. H. Davies or De La Mare, to the violent imagery of
> the poems that first appeared in Victor Neuburg's corner of the
> *Sunday Referee*; on the way he came more or less under the in-
> fluence of early Yeats, Aldington, Sacheverell Sitwell, Lawrence, and
> Hopkins, in that order; but of course there were many others.[16]

Aldington and Sacheverell Sitwell were singled out for special
praise by Thomas in his pert survey of "Modern Poetry" in the
Swansea Grammar School Magazine (December 1929):

> Richard Aldington, the best known Imagist of to-day, has adopted
> the original method of accentuating the image and making it first
> in importance in the poem, but has modified it and made it more
> intelligible.

> Sacheverell is the most difficult [of the Sitwells] to become intimate
> with. His difficulty is genuine, the strangeness of the picture he sees
> and wishes to explain, justifying the strangeness of the magic he
> employs.

This last remark is exactly what one might want to say of Thomas'
own work and, probably, what Thomas himself wanted to have said
of it. In any event, it is hard to distinguish the Thomas of 1930
from the two poets praised in 1929, as a glance at the following
specimens will show:

(1) At last, after years, I am saturated
With pity and agony and tears;
At last I have reached indifference;
Now I am almost free—
A gold pellet of sunlight
Dropped, curdling, into green water.

(2) My love is deep night
Caught from the tops of towers,
A pomp of delicious light
Snared under the tips of each stalk,
Dew balanced to perfection
On the grass delicate beyond water.

(3) Grant peace;
For a space let there be no roar
Of wheels and voices, no din
Of steel and stone and fire.
Let us cleanse ourselves from sweat and dirt,
Let us be hushed, let us breathe
The cold sterile wind from colourless space.

(4) Let me escape,
Be free, (wind for my tree and water for my flower),
Live self for self,
And drown the gods in me,
Or crush their viper heads beneath my foot.

(5) A wall of cactus guards the virgin sound—
Dripping through the sword-edged leaves
The wayward milking
Of your mental stalactites
On the strung bells of music,
Arrests the moment,
Petrifies the air.

(6) Each silver moment chimes
in steps of sound,
And I, caught in mid-air perhaps,
Hear and am still the little bird.

(1) and (3) are Richard Aldington; (5) is Sitwell; and (2), (4), and (6) are from Thomas' 1930 Notebook.[17]

Thomas is perhaps distinguished by his lust for the obscure, unglossed image; already one finds the kind of assertion entirely through imagery for which he was to become famous:

> How shall the animal
> Whose way I trace
> Into the dark recesses,
> Be durable
> Under such weight as bows me down,
> The bitter certainty of waste,
> The knowing that I hatch a thought
> To see it crushed
> Beneath your foot, my bantering Philistine.

This last poem of the 1930 Notebook, a remote ancestor of the published *How shall my animal,* falls into mere exposition with "The bitter certainty of waste"; but for the most part the image of the "animal" moves through the poem, evoking, not explaining, its meaning. Thomas' later revision of such early poems invariably involved the further *imagification* of what explanatory seams had been left showing. In this case, the straight statement about "waste" became a scissors image: "sly scissors ground in frost / Clack through the thicket of strength."

Daniel Jones' list of influences on Thomas contains one name, Hopkins, whose effect on Thomas it has not been customary to doubt. Yet doubt we must, on the evidence of a letter to Henry Treece, who had sent Thomas the chapter of his projected book called "The Debt to Hopkins",[18] and on 16 May 1938 received this reply:

> I've never been conscious of Hopkins's influence. As a boy of 15 or 16, writing in all sorts of ways false to myself, composing all sorts of academic imitations, borrowing sometimes shamelessly and sometimes with the well-suppressed knowledge of a pretence to originality, I find—from looking over many hundreds of those very early poems—that there was, and still is, to me, not a sign of Hopkins anywhere. (And I *had* read him, then, as I had read a great deal of poetry, good and bad, or, rather, I had read *through* his book.)

"The people most to be found in those early poems were," Thomas judges:

the Elizabethans and George Peele, Webster and, later, Beddoes, some Clare (his hard, country sonnets), Lawrence (animal poems, and the verse extracts from the Plumed Serpent), a bit of Tennyson, some very bad Flecker and, of course, a lot of bits from whatever fashionable poetry—Imagists, Sitwells—I'd been reading lately.

"But out of all that muddle," he adds, "I see no Hopkins."

The poet's disclaimer puts great onus on those who would illustrate his debt to Hopkins. A few isolated lines from poem *41* of the 1930 Notebook have a Hopkins ring:

> I lift to look, to see,
> Ah, it is fair I more than glance at,
> And, clever wish, I long to kill,
> Or kill—

but, if indebtedness, it is momentary. Thomas rather disapproved of Hopkins in the "Modern Poetry" essay (*Swansea Grammar School Magazine*, December 1929), referring to the obscurity of Hopkins' lyrics "where, though more often than not common metres were recognized, the language was violated and estranged by the efforts of compressing the already unfamiliar imagery." In spite of surface appearances, Thomas certainly did not intend to model himself on Hopkins; and prolonged acquaintance with the works of the two poets seems to confirm that their obscurities are essentially dissimilar.

Hopkins aside, then, Thomas' list of poets "to be found" in his early poems provides large scope for scholars; and no doubt the influences will be found. Some are easy to find: poem *8* in the 1930 Notebook, for instance, is a Lawrentian lion poem, and *Admit the Sun* (poem *28*) smacks of Quetzalcoatl. Flecker provides at least the name and journey motif for *Hassan's Journey into the World* (poem *29*). Similarities to Tennyson can be found. But all who enjoy this kind of literary exercise might well ponder the passage in "The Fight" where young Dylan (aged 14¾ in the story) recites his poem *Frivolous is my hate* (pre-1930 Notebook) to Mr. Bevan, a brother poet:

> Now could I wake
> To passion after death, and taste
> The rapture of her hating, tear the waste
> Of body. Break, her dead, dark body, break.

To which finale Mr. Bevan rejoins: "The influence is obvious, of course. 'Break, break, break, on thy cold, grey stones, O sea.'" Mrs. Bevan adds: "Hubert knows Tennyson backwards . . . backwards."[19] And we should take this parable as a warning, who know our Tennyson, our Lawrence, our Flecker, our Beddoes, our Clare, our Webster, or our Peele, backwards.

3. THE 1930−1932 NOTEBOOK : A CRISIS

It would be useful if we could at least find some literary source for the sudden leap that these poems of self-expression make in the middle of the 1930–1932 Notebook. Poems XXIII (10 June 1931) and XXIV (16 June 1931) seem to be automatic writing, especially the second with its disregard for initial capitals to the lines, its many slips of the pen, and its flashes of comment on the chaotic stream of consciousness: "I'll in a moment but my version's sane / space is too small." One is reminded, with perhaps good reason, of the ending of poem *38* in the first Notebook:

> so I am getting drunk
> sense she has wings
> and   is just as sane.

Poem XXV (3 July 1931) begins: "Through sober to the truth." And a new sober note has crept in after the orgy of words, a soberness connected with death:

> I have a friend in death,
> Daywise, the grave's inertia
> Mending my head that needs its hour's pain
> Under the arc-lamp,
> Or between my skull and me.

B

Not that death, despair, and disgust were not found before; but the tone here is more heartfelt. The next poem (XXVI, 28 July 1931) has a passage typical of what is to come:

> And whose affections aren't corrupt?—
> Listen and lie;
> The head's vacuity can breed no truth
> Out of its sensible tedium,
>
> .   .   .
>
> For I shall turn the strongest stomach up
> With filth I gather . . .

And within the next few poems of the 1930–1932 Notebook he gathers: "scabrous," "cankered," "pollution," "lipless," "itch," "weariness," "coarsened," "emetic," "cancer," "spewing," "nightmare," "poison," "corrupted," "vermin," and "hideous."

This list sufficiently sums up the depressing mood. If the answer were to be found in literary precedent, one could quickly make a similar compilation of delirious terms in Webster or, given the hint by Thomas, in Beddoes. "Pity's dead," says the Duke in *Death's Jest-Book* (Act II, Scene 2):

> Under the green-sod are your coffins packed,
> So thick they break each other. The days come
> When scarce a lover, for his maiden's hair,
> Can pluck a stalk whose rose draws not its hue
> Out of a hate-killed heart. Nature's polluted,
> There's a man in every secret corner of her,
> Doing damned wicked deeds. Thou art old, world,
> A hoary atheistic murderous star. . . .

Compare Thomas, newly entering this world with poem XLVIX (26 October 1931):

> This pus runs deep.
> There's poison in your red wine, drinker,
> Which spreads down to the dregs
> Leaving a corrupted vein of colour,
> Sawdust beneath the skirts;
> On every hand the evil's positive . . .

The despondency is sublime; but the true explanation for Thomas' condition is probably not a spate of Jacobean or nineteenth-century Jacobean drama—rather something not at all literary. *He had just left school and had been forced to go to work*. Romantic only in myth, the job as copyholder with the *South Wales Daily Post* was merely irksome. Hardly an improvement was his transfer to the reporting staff. Not only the enforced routine but also the disagreeable discoveries made in the morgue and other seamy stages of his beat disaffected the schoolboy who had been spoiled by a liberal education. The dockside company and drunkenness described in the story "Old Garbo" surely contributed some of the *Walpurgisnacht* imagery to the poetry. Early in February 1932 Thomas told Trevor Hughes, a Swansea friend recently moved to London, that he "managed to become drunk at least four nights of the week." He intimated a coming crisis:

> My purple is turning, I think, into a dull gray. I am at the most transitional period now. So whatever talent I possess may suddenly diminish or may suddenly increase. I can, with great ease, become an ordinary fool. I may be one, now.

Here we detect the fear that all clever schoolboys feel when they see their skills count for little in the outside world. With Thomas there was the further fear of what hard work and suffering his genius for words might demand of him if he gave it its due; and fear of the self-treason waiting in the steady job and the evening pub. The surrealist or drunken poems of June 1931 were probably a reaction against the first oncoming of what in a later letter he called "reporter's decadence"; and the remaining half of the Notebook can be seen as resistance to "the slow but sure stamping out of individuality." He finished the Notebook by throwing in a few unnumbered poems with the date, 2 July 1932, and a footnote: "This has taken a hell of a time."

We do not know what poetic output, if any, immediately followed during that summer. The next Notebook we have began seven months later on 1 February 1933; and by this time he was a new man. His answer to the suicide of the steady job was to leave. After January 1933 he did nothing: nothing, that is, but work at his own poems and stories. This was the beginning of the great gestation period of his life. The transition, which he feared might be to pubs and mediocrity, became a worthier one, to literary heights and the deserved success of *18 Poems*.

4. THEMES IN THE FEBRUARY 1933 NOTEBOOK

If the first two Notebooks strike one as a medley, a collection of free responses to the rising and falling of adolescent spirits, the last two Notebooks offer more cohesion, the steady development of a style and of a subject matter. The confessional and hortatory free verse gives way to the more regular, packed stanza, with its antithetical presentation of the processes of life and death. Morbidity is still dominant: the young man who in poem XXIX (12 August 1931) was nightly troubled by those "who have no talk but that of death" has, by the time of the first poem in the February 1933 Notebook, heard the voices many times:

> Companionship with night has turned
> Each ugly corpse into a friend,
> And there are more friends if you wish:
> The maggots feasting on dead flesh,
> The vulture with appraising beak,
> The redcheeked vampire at the neck,
> There is the skeleton and the naked ghost.

Thomas may very well have suffered from insomnia, but again this is rather an inner vision than a response to any dire circumstance in his material existence. In a letter to Trevor Hughes of late January 1933 Thomas could still say, "I have known little physical suffering and no actual hardships or heartbreaks." Then, dramatically, seeming to challenge this statement of immunity, an opportunity for personal bereavement broke in upon the letter:

> As I am writing, a telegram arrives. Mother's sister, who is in the Carmarthen Infirmary suffering from cancer of the womb, is dying. There is much lamentation in the family and Mother leaves. The old aunt will be dead by the time she arrives. This is a well-worn incident in fiction, and one that has happened time after time in real

life. The odour of death stinks through a thousand books and in a thousand homes. I have rarely encountered it (apart from journalistic enquiries), and find it rather pleasant. It lends a little welcome melodrama to the drawing room tragicomedy of my most uneventful life. After Mother's departure I am left alone in the house, feeling slightly theatrical. Telegrams, dying aunts, cancer, especially of such a private part as the womb, distraught mothers and unpremeditated train-journeys, come rarely. They must be savoured properly and relished in the right spirit. Many summer weeks I spent happily with the cancered aunt on her insanitary farm. She loved me quite inordinately, gave me sweets and money, though she could little afford it, petted, patted, and spoiled me. She writes—is it, I wonder, a past tense yet—regularly. Her postscripts are endearing. She still loves—or loved—me, though I don't know why. And now she is dying, or dead, and you will pardon the theatrical writing. Allow me my moments of drama.

But the foul thing is I feel utterly unmoved, apart, as I said, from the pleasant death-reek at my negroid nostrils. I haven't, really, the faintest interest in her or her womb. She is dying. She is dead. She is alive. It is all the same thing. I shall miss her bi-annual postal orders. That's all. And yet I like—liked—her. She loves—loved—me. Am I, he said, with the diarist's unctuous, egotistic preoccupation with his own blasted psychological reactions to his own trivial affairs, callous and nasty? Should I weep? Should I pity the old thing? For a moment, I feel, I should. There must be something lacking in me. I don't feel worried, or hardly ever, about other people. It's self, self, all the time. I'm rarely interested in other people's emotions, except those of my pasteboard characters. I prefer (this is one of the thousand contradictory devils speaking) style to life, my own reactions to emotions rather than the emotions themselves. Is this, he pondered, a lack of soul?

This letter is quoted at length partly because it shows well the self-dramatizing, anesthetized state Thomas was in as he began the February 1933 Notebook, and partly because it directly relates to one of the Notebook's most famous poems, and in turn to one of its main themes. The aunt is Ann Jones, who died 7 February 1933; and the poem is number Six, written three days afterward, presumably on the day of the funeral. Thomas, a veteran graveyard poet, here reacts very strangely to an actual burial. In keeping with the letter, the poem in the Notebook version is a coldly generalized refusal to mourn:

Death has rewarded him or her for living,
With generous hands has slain with little pain,
Wounded with a sharp sword,
And let the ancient face die with a smile.

Another gossips' toy has lost its use,
Broken lies buried amid broken toys,
Of flesh and bone lies hungry for the flies,
Waits for the natron and the mummy paint.
With dead lips pursed and dry bright eyes,
Another well of rumours and cold lies
Has dried, and one more joke has lost its point.

The dead person is a mere "him or her"; the personal sentiment of the later *After the funeral* dates from 1938 when Thomas went back to the poem.[20] The boy in 1933 was anything but "desolate"; rather than slitting his own throat he sliced at everyone else with his irony. Thus, in an unexpected setting, we come upon one of the basic themes of the February 1933 Notebook: a satirical world-weariness.

Thomas' poetry of social complaint hardly matches that of W. H. Auden, whose *Poems* (1930) Thomas had on his bookshelf. But poem Four (6 February 1933), for instance, shows that Thomas could write about "the century," "the state," "civilization," and "man's manmade sparetime" (i.e. unemployment) with the rest of the thirties poets. Poem Seven describes sick youth in a sick society; continued as poem Nine, it expresses the "world's curse" in figures such as

Young men with fallen chests and old men's breath,
Women with cancer at their sides
And cancerous speaking dripping from their mouths,
And lovers turning on the gas,
Exsoldiers with horrors for a face,
A pig's snout for a nose,
The lost in doubt, the nearly mad, the young
Who, undeserving, have suffered the earth's wrong,
The living dead left over from the war . . .

Poem Thirteen, which appears to be subtitled "In Hyde Park," sums up the passing show with: "The suicides parade again, now ripe for dying." Poem Fourteen, the published *I have longed to move away,* is the poet's reaction to a world of conventions and lies; poem Eighteen (*O make me a mask*) the same. Poem Twenty laments that the world is taken over by machines. Thomas' answer to all this chaos seems to be concentrated in the word "faith," a word repeated to the point of incantation in poem Nine, for instance, but rather offset by the last line: "Believe, believe and be saved, we cry, who have no faith." This dichotomy of despair and faith, and the groping for a synthesis, is a dominant thread through the poems of this period.

That this theme has a social as well as a mystical side to it should not surprise anyone aware of the Thomas family's position, newly arrived in the middle class: "the transition from farm-house and railwaymen standards to schoolmaster in a semi-detached suburban matchbox," as Caitlin Thomas bluntly put it. "From lavish rough comforts to pinched penny-pricing gentility."[21] No self-satisfaction in this situation, there could only be burning class consciousness, with pressures to maintain a tedious hypocrisy. "My only sister," wrote Dylan in a letter about this time, "passed through the stages of longlegged schoolgirlishness, shortfrocked flappery and social snobbery into a comfortable married life." This class pattern was the tendency that Thomas himself had to fight: he longs to move away from it; to live in it at all he needs a mask to cover his constant rebellion. His poems are, in a sense, the mask he was making; he looks out from them with a cold, often satirical stare.

Not that there are a great number of poems of social consciousness, just enough to show that *18 Poems* did not come from a political hermit. *The hand that signed the paper,* his acknowledged political poem (the first poem in the August 1933 Notebook), is appropriately dedicated to "A.E.T."—Bert Trick, Thomas' Labour Party friend. But it is more a tribute to the friend than to the subject;[22] a month before, he had quite clearly condemned the social poem, likening it to radio and poster advertising:

> Praise to the architects;
> A pome's a building on a page;
> Keatings is good for lice,
> A pinch of Auden is the lion's feast;
> Praise to the architects;
> Empty, To Let, are signs on this new house . . .

This poem Forty One in the February 1933 Notebook can be glossed by a letter to Trevor Hughes of January 1934:

> Do we need "New styles of architecture, a change of heart"? Does one not need a new consciousness of the old universal architecture and a tearing away from the old heart of the things that have clogged it?

With this dismissal of "public" poetry, he presents in the same letter his current notion of what kind of poetry is valid, not the social but the mystical:

> I become a greater introvert day by day, though, day by day again, I am conscious of more external wonders in the world. It is my aim as an artist . . . to bring those wonders into myself, to prove beyond doubt to myself that the flesh that covers me is the flesh that covers the sun, that the blood in my lungs is the blood that goes up and down in a tree. It is the simplicity of religion.

By this time, then, Thomas is already established in the kind of religious outlook that pervades the *18 Poems,* the concern with "the very many lives and deaths . . . in the tumultuous world of my own being" (*Quite Early One Morning:* Dent edition, p. 137; New Directions edition, pp. 174–175). If we look for a poem which seems definitely to mark the inception of this outlook (or *inlooking*), poem Forty Six (15 July 1933) suggests itself, an early version of the published *Find meat on bones.* Poems before that in the February 1933 Notebook do not seem to draw on the same enduring organic cosmos. They are essentially occasional poems. Poem Ten, for instance, portrays the poet's feelings on leaving an all-night talking session such as were held every Wednesday at 5 Cwmdonkin Drive and every Sunday at Bert Trick's house. Poem Eleven is a "conceit": the idea that one can waste oneself in wrong love and have nothing left when real love arrives. Poem Sixteen (22 March 1933) bears a similar relation to his sister's marriage as poem Six did to his aunt's funeral: again the impersonal attitude and the use of a conceit—the husband is replacing the sun as the lover. Even in the poems of faith and despair Thomas is really trying out feelings or testing ideas as the mood strikes him. So that poem Twenty Three, the early *And death shall have no dominion,* is not, no more than *After the funeral,* a poem of life and death in the cosmic process that was soon to become Thomas' poetic universe. It should rather be thought of as a poem on the topic of death, trying out the thesis that death shall have no dominion, a thesis running counter to adjacent doubt poems such as Twenty Four with its forlorn refrain, "Where, what's my God?"

If the February 1933 Notebook can be viewed as moving from a fairly conventional agnosticism toward a personal religion of the organic processes, poem Twenty Four is notable in drawing on the specifically Christian. Seeking an ultimate expression of doubt, Thomas echoes Christ's "why hast thou forsaken me?" and has his protagonist endure crucifixion:

> So crying, he was pushed into the Jordan.
> He, too, has known the agony in the Garden,
> And felt a skewer enter at his side.
> He, too, has seen the world as bottom rotten . . .

In discussing the religious elements in these poems, one best begins with the premise that Thomas' pessimism owes more to Mr. Thomas, Sr., than to literary precedents. Thomas once spoke of his father's atheism, an atheism which

> had nothing to do with whether there was a god or not, but was a violent and personal dislike for God. He would glare out of the window and growl: "It's raining, blast Him!" or, "The sun is shining—Lord, what foolishness!"[23]

Dylan imitates his father's scorn in a letter to Trevor Hughes of August 1933: "God was deposed years ago, before the loin-cloth in the garden. Now the Old Boy reigns . . . Here's to him." This blasphemous mood is found in *Incarnate devil,* entitled *Before We Sinned* in the February 1933 Notebook; and in poem Thirty Three:

> . . . No man believes
> Who curses not what makes and saves,
> No man upon this cyst of earth
> Believes who does not lance his faith . . .

If the devils that Thomas saw were inherited, at least they were not borrowed from James Thomson (nor his angels from Francis Thompson, for that matter).[24] He is too clumsy in these poems to be imitating. "Let for one moment a faith statement," he begins to plead (in poem Two of the August 1933 Notebook); but these poems really are statements about, rather than expressions of, faith. His lyric powers were still unequal to the job of making poetry of his new discoveries about the internal world. In a letter to Trevor Hughes in January 1933 he was conscious that his philosophy had not found poetic form, though he was able to explain it in prose:

> You must live in the outer world, suffer in it and with it, enjoy its changes, despair at them, carry on ordinarily with moneymaking routines, fall in love, mate, and die. You have to do that. Where the true artist differs from his fellows is that that for him is not the only world. He has the inner splendour (which sounds like a piece of Lawrence or a fribble of Dean Inge). The outer and inner worlds are not, I admit, entirely separate. Suffering colours the inner places, and probably adds beauty to them. So does happiness.
>
> You may think this philosophy . . . strange for me to believe in. I have always believed in it. My poems rarely contain any of it. That is why they are not satisfactory to me. Most of them are outer poems. Three quarters of the world's literature deals with the outer world. Most modern fiction does. Some of it is purely reporting outer incidents. Not that that need condemn it. Perhaps the greatest works of art are those that reconcile, perfectly, inner and outer.

Using the terminology of this letter we can say that the poems of the first half of the February 1933 Notebook were still in the "outer world," reporting incidents and occasional ideas. By poem Twenty Six (22 April 1933) Thomas is expressing the need for "a modern synthesis":

> Five years found no hope
> Of harmony, no cure, till this year,
> For bridging white and black,
> The left and right sock, light and dark,
> Pansy and piston, klaxon horn
> And owl addressing moon.
>
> .   .   .
>
> Twenty years; and now this year
> Has found a cure.
> New music, from new and loud, sounds on the air.

This is an allegory of his renewed confidence in his own poetry. At the time he was certainly beginning to write more, and more substantial, poems. As we have already conjectured, it seems that by July 1933, with poem Forty Six (*Find meat on bones*) and the half-dozen poems that end the February 1933 Notebook, he had really begun to express lyrically his philosophy, bringing the living inner world successfully onto the living page.

5. THE AUGUST 1933 NOTEBOOK: PROCESS POEMS

It might be thought that in the August 1933 Notebook Thomas finds too much meat on his bones. One of his correspondents apparently thought so, Pamela Hansford Johnson, then a newly published poetess ready to congratulate and challenge her contemporary in Swansea immediately his voice was heard on the London scene in September 1933. In a letter to her of October 1933, Thomas defends his preoccupations:

> I fail to see how the emphasizing of the body can, in any way, be regarded as hideous. The body, its appearance, death, and diseases, is a fact, sure as the fact of a tree. It has roots in the same earth as the tree. The greatest description I know of our "earthiness" is to be found in John Donne's *Devotions,* where he describes man as earth of the earth, his body earth, his hair a wild shrub growing out of the land. All thoughts and actions emanate from the body. Therefore the description of a thought or action—however abstruse it may be—can be beaten home by bringing it on to a physical level. Every idea, intuitive or intellectual, can be imaged and translated in terms of the body, its flesh, skin, blood, sinews, veins, glands, organs, cells, or senses.

Echoing *Ears in the turrets hear* (Forty Seven in the February 1933 Notebook) with its "island, bound / By a thin sea of flesh / And a bone coast," he continues:

> Through my small, bonebound island I have learnt all I know, experienced all, and sensed all. All I write is inseparable from the island. As much as possible, therefore, I employ the scenery of the island to describe the scenery of my thoughts, the earthquakes of the body to describe the earthquakes of the heart.

In other words, the body is not necessarily his subject but almost always the source of the imagery by which he speaks of all other things. Sending Trevor Hughes in January 1934 copies of the poems *Before I knocked, My hero bares his nerves, Light breaks where no sun shines, I fellowed sleep,* and the unpublished *See, says the lime,* all from the August 1933 Notebook, he commented:

> They are, I admit, unpretty things, with their imagery almost totally anatomical. But I defend the diction, the perhaps wearisome succession of blood and bones, the never ending similes of the streams of the veins and the lights in the eyes, by saying that, for the time at least, I realise that it is impossible for me to raise myself to the altitude of the stars, and that I am forced, therefore, to bring down the stars to my own level and to incorporate them in my own physical universe.[25]

The "stars" seem to be used as an image for beliefs (or "faiths") difficult to talk about without imagery. Thomas consciously presumed to be a mystical poet. "I am in the path of Blake," he wrote to Pamela Hansford Johnson in a letter which also contained a copy of *Before I knocked,* a Christian poem as oblique as any of Blake's. Blake's "The Everlasting Gospel" could very well have given Thomas precedent for "standing by when Jesus died," and for a vision of a True Jesus and a False Jesus. Surely it was after reading Blake's epigram "On the virginity of the Virgin and Johanna Southcott" that Thomas wrote poem Six on 29 August 1933—we are indebted to the poet for his footnote—saying that Christ is not to be born to one person but everywhere:

> From the meadow where lambs frolic
> Rises every blade the Lamb,
>
> . . .
>
> Not in the fanatic womb
> Shall the jelly mix and form
> That shall be the three in One,
> God and Ghost, Anointed Son.

Before I knocked, the next poem in the Notebook, is even more audacious, depicting the gestation and birth of the actual Christ. Thomas utilizes the Biblical "Get thee behind me, Satan," in four interesting lines left out of the published poem:

> A virgin was my sad-faced dam,
> My sire was of wind and water.
> Get thee behind me, my blood's tempter,
> I cried out when the blood was dumb.

The spiritual ("wind and water") joins the animal ("dam") to make a Christ in conflict with his own physique, a conflict climaxed by the temptation in the wilderness. Perhaps another literary ancestor D. H. Lawrence (of "The Man Who Died" and "The Risen Lord") is behind this concept: that Christ was wrong to starve his physical body. His "blood was dumb"—implying that the body wanted to respond fully to the temptation. Thus, Christ is to be pitied in that, taking on a body, he did not really become a man. It is the man whom he didn't become (and in this respect he "double-crossed" [betrayed] his mother's womb) that we are being asked to remember in the last few lines of the poem:

> You who bow down at cross and altar,
> Remember me and pity him
> Who took my flesh and bone for armour,
> And double-crossed his mother's womb.

In order to make a similar point Lawrence did not find it necessary to go back to the womb; but Thomas begins the body's story with its earliest prenatal stage and spends six stanzas within the "small, bonebound island." The narrator is the body-Christ, who has received none of the rewards and all the pains of incarnation: it is poignant, then, to have the unformed body in the womb prefigure the blows to come. The stage is set for Thomas' distinctive organic imagery.

If these poems deal rather violently with the traditional view of Christ it is not that we have gone without warning. On the page of the Notebook opposite *Before I knocked* there is the illuminating quatrain:

> If God is praised in poem one
> Show no surprise when in the next
> I worship wood or sun or none:
> I'm hundred-heavened and countless sexed.

God is hardly being praised in *Before I knocked;* in the next, however, poem Eight, Thomas hymns a "city godhead" with "a steel gospel" and a hopeful message:

> Over the electric godhead grows
> One God, more mighty than the sun.
> The cities have not robbed our eyes.

A serious attempt to praise. And with body imagery even here (the city gospel heard as a "secret wind behind the brain"), Thomas is gradually maneuvering the god inside the body. Poem Nine approaches this concept of the body's God in:

> Take the scissors to this globe,
> Firmament of flesh and bone
> Lawed and ordered from on high
> By a godhead of my own.

And poem Ten:

> Not forever shall the lord of the red hail
> Hold in his velvet hand the can of blood

where the "red hail" (blood) in the "can" (the body) is ruled by the body's own Lord.

These poems lead up to *My hero bares his nerves* (poem Thirteen, 17 September 1933) and help us to understand what "the hero" might signify. Perhaps most helpful is poem Three:

> You are the ruler of this realm of flesh,
> And this hill of bone and hair
> Moves to the Mahomet of your hand.
>
> .   .   .
>
> You are my flesh's ruler whom I treason,
> Housing death in your kingdom,
> Paying heed to the thirsty voice.

"Thirsty voice": this act of self-destructive treason against the body's god could be lust in general, or one lust in particular, that for drink! There is a similar act of treason against the "hero" as god of the body in *My hero bares his nerves.* The doublecross may not be too clear in the printed version, which lacks the Notebook's final stanza:

Jack my father let the knaves steal off
Their little swag, the gems of life and death,
The lightest bubbles that we breathe
  Out of the living grave
And let my hero show his double strength
And all his laughter hidden up my sleeve.

When "knaves" are "jacks" and therefore "jack off," this stanza is
clearly concerned with onanism—or, if not *clearly,* then we have to
consider the phraseology in several other poems that makes the pres-
ence of this theme here more clear. Poem Twenty Four, continued
as poem Twenty Six, describes the biological development of the
individual from conception to adolescence, symbolized by increasing
numbers: one, two, four, twenty, and then a million. The last line as
published glances back at an imagined single source of life power:
"One sun, one manna, warmed and fed." The Notebook poem goes
further:

Now that drugged youth is waking from its stupor,
The nervous hand rehearsing on the thigh
Acts with a woman, one sum remains in cipher:
Five senses and the frozen brain
Are one with wind, and itching in the sun.

A nervous hand on the thigh rehearsing acts with a woman—this
can only be interpreted as onanism. The nullity of the act is repre-
sented in the juggling of the numbers, and the enervated questions
that follow the above lines and end the poem in the Notebook. We
should not forget that it was an adolescent who wrote these poems;
but an adolescent not concerned with hiding any truths, rather with
a commitment to revealing things hidden too long. Within a year
he was to write his much-quoted answer to a question concerning
the influence of Freud; it is in the context of the very poems we are
discussing that his answer on that occasion can be judged.

Have you been influenced by Freud and how do you regard him?

Yes. Whatever is hidden should be made naked. To be stripped of
darkness is to be clean, to strip of darkness is to make clean. Poetry,
recording the stripping of the individual darkness, must, inevitably,
cast light upon what has been hidden for too long, and by so doing,
make clean the naked exposure. Freud cast light on a little of the

darkness he had exposed. Benefitting by the sight of the light and the knowledge of the hidden nakedness, poetry must drag further into the clean nakedness of light more even of the hidden causes than Freud could realise.[26]

We should suspect from this that the "stripping" of the loin in *My hero bares his nerves* is less erotic than part of the process of making clean "the naked exposure." These poems shed light—though perhaps not in so blunt a manner as the boy's reference in the story "A Prospect of the Sea" to "death from playing with yourself." Perhaps no less succinct an expression of Thomas' apparent feeling that onanism is equivalent to death is *My hero bares his nerves*: "the gems of life" are wasted and become "gems of death" out of a body which has thus become a "living grave." All the graveyard figures in these poems are associated with the physical waste involved in sexual dreams and nocturnal emission. This death-bringing, nightly sex has the horror of nightmare, accounting for such lines as poem Twenty Nine's

> Crow on my heap, O living deaths;
> There is no horror death bequeaths
> I cannot number on this sleepy hand . . .

In another sleep poem, Thirty One, the sleeper "fathered dreams as races from the loins," and "fellowed sleep who drained me with a kiss." The dreams in poem Thirty Seven "whack their boys' limbs"; but they are "eunuch dreams," unfertile, thus "no children break, all flavoured into light." Of the varying responses to this basic fact of adolescence *Our eunuch dreams* is perhaps the most positive, with its ending:

> For we shall be a shouter like the cock,
> Blowing the old dead back . . .
>
> . . .
>
> And we shall be fit fellows for a life,
> And who remain shall flower as they love,
> Praise to our faring hearts.

In *My hero bares his nerves* one feels a mood of affirmation tempered with resignation. The undeniable existence of "cistern sex" (a phrase from poem Twenty Seven of the February 1933 Notebook in its typescript form) is ruefully acknowledged and the theft of the life fluid is allowed; but the hero, the lord of the body, will assert his pride nevertheless, and laugh in secret knowledge of extra, reserve strength.[27]

The themes we chiefly find in the two later Notebooks, faith vs. despair, love vs. sexual waste, waking action vs. dream world, can all be seen as part of a universal antithesis of growth vs. decay. It is on such an abstract plane that Thomas ultimately conceived them. When "the cistern moves" in *My hero bares his nerves,* a whole range of bodily functions besides sex is implied. Poem Thirty Five has the sexual theme in the lines:

> The seed that makes a forest of the loin
> Forks half its fruit; and half drops down,
> Slow in a sleeping wind.

But the poem (published as *A process in the weather of the heart*) incorporates several themes in a number of images of process, and is about process in general. The inscription Thomas wrote on the front of the August 1933 Notebook expresses the duality of the process world in its simplest terms:

> To others caught
> Between black and white.

Thus the contents of the Notebook can be thought of as a series of poems utilizing a wide range of imagery in order to reiterate the predicament of being in the grip of forces of darkness and light, life and death, black and white. The most notable of such "process poems" is *The force that through the green fuse drives the flower,* which, after an interesting draft of the first stanza, appears in the Notebook (poem Twenty Three, 12 October 1933) practically as published in the *Sunday Referee* on 29 October 1933. This time we can turn specifically to a Blake poem, "The Sick Rose":

> O Rose, thou art sick!
> The invisible worm,
> That flies in the night
> In the howling storm,

C

> Has found out thy bed
> Of crimson joy;
> And his dark secret love
> Does thy life destroy.

Compare the lines from the first draft of Thomas' poem as found in the Notebook:

> And I am dumb to tell the eaten rose
> How at my sheet goes the same crookèd worm,
> And dumb to holla thunder to the skies
> How at my cloths flies the same central storm.

It would not be far wrong to say that Blake's notions of "Heaven and Hell" and of "Innocence and Experience" have acted as authority for Thomas' dualistic view of the world and his antithetical mode of expressing it.

"The Sick Rose" may have had special significance for Thomas: he was himself sick, and at the time of writing *The force that through the green fuse drives the flower* thought himself dangerously infected with tuberculosis. During the week in which the poem appeared Thomas wrote "A Touching Autobiography" to Pamela Hansford Johnson, mentioning his illness, but in a jocular manner, which could only leave his new correspondent incredulous:

> A misanthropic doctor, who apparently did not like the way I did my eyebrows, has given me four years to live.

If we want to deny the seriousness of this death knell, we have to face the fact that Thomas came back to it again and again, for instance, in the next reply, apparently written after twelve days without sleep:

> Four years, my sweet. 1340 days and nights. And thank you for the optimistic remarks. I don't believe it either, but then it would be very odd if I did. You should hear me cough, though—a most pleasing sound, exactly like a sea-lion peeved.
> No, I don't think consumption has very much effect on what I write (Oh my bravery with that not-quite-polite word). I can't help what I write. It is part of me, however unpleasant a part it may be,

and however necessary it should be to cauterize and castrate that part. Your belief in my power to write is one of the few things that makes me deny that twice-damned, diabetic doctor.

In the next letter of the correspondence, Thomas talks of his father's illness:

> . . . the last three months he has spent in the London University Hospital, undergoing treatment for cancer of the throat. He is home now, partially cured and exceedingly despondent. His time limit is even shorter than mine.

He refers to these circumstances in the letter to Trevor Hughes of 12 January 1934:

> Today [my father] went back to school, weak and uncured. And only a little while ago I learnt the truth of my own health. But the statement of Dad's disease and the warning of mine have left me horribly unmoved; I become a greater introvert day by day.

The father did recover and lived for twenty years after; the son the same. But if Thomas at this vital moment of his development had suddenly had thrust upon him in some convincing and frightening manner the precariousness of his physical existence, it might to some extent explain the depth of feeling in his poetry about mortality.[28] The universally acknowledged poignancy of such poems as *The force that through the green fuse drives the flower* can be thought to bear some relation to the young poet's effort to absorb the conviction, however gained, that death was immediately threatening. The poetry shows that he was not, as he claimed in the above letter, "horribly unmoved." Later in the same letter he put it better: "If only I could say with Blake, Death to me is no more than going into another room." The poems are an attempt to say what he *can* say death is to him—or, at first, what he is dumb to say death is:

> And I am dumb to tell the lover's tomb
> How at my sheet goes the same crookèd worm.

Death now has dominion; and Thomas continually imagines the literal entering of the grave and its rotting community:

> All night and day I eye the ragged globe
> Through periscopes rightsighted from the grave . . .
> (Twenty Seven)

> Here lies the beast of man and here his angels,
> The dead man said,
> And silently I milk the buried flowers.
> (Twenty Eight)

> See, says the lime, my wicked milks
> I put round ribs that packed their heart . . .
> (Thirty Two)

When he entitles the draft of poem Thirty Three *Breakfast before Execution* (published as *This bread I break*), not only the date, 24 December, gives the poem special significance but also the poet's personal feeling of being condemned to early dissolution.

On the other hand, we should bear in mind that these poems are not really wails of anguish, as his earlier poems might be considered wails of love and frustration. They are artificed, and sometimes metaphysically witty—witness the use of "breakfast" in relation to the sacramental theme of *This bread I break*. The "ruin" of the "boys of summer" may have been felt by Thomas to be his own; but *I see the boys of summer,* the climactic poem of the August 1933 Notebook, is a most intricately ordered and imaged poem. The very architecture of the poems stands, as it were, at the positive pole from the negative pole of the poet's physical condition: they are the "light" that "breaks where no sun shines." *Light breaks where no sun shines* itself illustrates the point; subject to misinterpretation as lazy surrealism, it is traditionally metaphysical in the disparate images used to express the ebb and flow of process. When the poem (Thirty, 20 November 1933) was published in the *Listener* (14 March 1934) readers apparently complained about the lines

> Nor fenced, nor staked, the gushers of the sky
> Spout to the rod
> Divining in a smile the oil of tears.

"The little smut-hounds thought I was writing a copulatory anthem," expostulated Thomas in a letter to Miss Johnson. "In reality, of course, it was a metaphysical image of rain and grief." As a metaphysical poet, Thomas was too busy turning and reworking phrases to be despairingly morbid; and the product, the poem, is tense with the effort. "So many modern poets," Thomas continued to his correspondent, "take the *living* flesh as their object, and, by their clever dissecting, turn it into a carcase. I prefer to take the *dead* flesh, and, by any positivity of faith and belief that is in me, build up a *living* flesh from it." If "positivity" is not very extensively defined in the dictionary, we have a long and lofty Christmas letter to Miss Johnson, which in part constitutes a definition:

> I want to forget all that I have ever written and start again, informed with a new wonder, empty of all my old dreariness, and rid of the sophistication which is disease . . . I want to read the headlines in the sky: birth of a star, death of a comet. I want to believe, to believe forever, that heaven is *being,* a state of being, and that the only hell is the hell of myself. I want to burn hell with its own flames.
>
>   .   .   .
>
> And if I can bring myself to know, not to think, that nothing is uninteresting, I can broaden my own outlook and believe once more, as I so passionately believed and so passionately *want* to believe, in the magic of this burning and bewildering universe, in the meaning and the power of symbols, in the miracle of myself and of all mortals, in the divinity that is so near us and so longing to be nearer, in the staggering, bloody, starry wonder of the sky I can see above and the sky I can think of below.

These ecstatic resolutions—even if he failed to maintain exactly that height of pitch beyond the new year—are good to bear in mind when we read the final poems of the August 1933 Notebook, especially Thirty Six (23 February 1934), *Foster the light, nor veil the bushy sun,* which in this Notebook version, at least, should not be interpreted as other than a poem of praise.[29] We have already looked at the "positivity" of the last lines of Thirty Seven, *Our eunuch dreams.* Thirty Eight, *Where once the waters of your face,* has a similarly hopeful ending. The inspirational summation of Thirty Nine, *I see the boys of summer,* should be felt in the final line to each of the three parts of the poem:

> Oh see the the pulse of summer in the ice.
>
> Oh see the poles of promise in the boys.
>
> Oh see the poles are kissing as they cross.

Forty, *In the beginning,* rewrites poem Fifteen, giving it a more beneficent aura: the last word of the poem is now "love." Forty One, *If I were tickled by the rub of love,* is a final—final for these Notebooks anyway—settlement of the adolescent worrying over sex and death; the cry is for liberation, liberation from "bad blood" into reality and manhood:

> I would be tickled by the rub that is:
> Man be my metaphor.

The process poems, which one expects to be merely morbidly descriptive, turn out to be, on the whole, moral and manly. The poet and his subject matter may dwell in the domain of death; but the poetry itself has a buoyancy which seems to assert that death shall have no dominion over it.

6. THOMAS' USE OF THE NOTEBOOKS

The British Museum has typed copies, with some corrections in Thomas' hand, of eighteen of the forty-six poems in the 1930 Notebook. Perhaps some of these typed copies constituted the "batch of early poems" that Robert Graves received from the sixteen-year-old Swansea youth:

> I wrote back [says Graves] that they were irreproachable, but that he would eventually learn to dislike them . . . Even experts would have been deceived by the virtuosity of Dylan Thomas's conventional, and wholly artificial, early poems.[30]

In addition to those from the 1930 Notebook, the British Museum has copies of eleven of the poems in the 1930–1932 Notebook, and seven of the poems in the February 1933 Notebook. These are manuscripts that Thomas left at the home of Trevor Hughes in Harrow when he went off with other manuscript poems, his hurried selection from the larger mass, to see Sir Richard Rees, editor of the

Adelphi, in Chelsea in August 1933. In a letter of January 1934 he asked, "Lie my old poems unremoved?" But, such was his chaotic existence, he never retrieved them on subsequent visits. Thus Mr. Hughes still had them and was able to present them to the British Museum at the time of the poet's death in 1953. Along with those mentioned are five poems from the August 1933 Notebook typed and sent by Thomas to Trevor Hughes with the letter of January 1934. Sixteen poems in the British Museum collection but not in the Notebooks appear in the Appendix (pages 337–349).

Thomas gave typescripts to several other friends. Glyn Jones, over from Cardiff in April 1934, was given typescripts of two or three early stories and six poems from the August 1933 Notebook, three of them (poems Seventeen, Eighteen, and Nineteen) typed under one title, *Jack of Christ.* These manuscripts are now in the collection of Charles E. Feinberg of Detroit. Another collector, T. E. Hanley of Bradford, Pennsylvania, has fourteen typescripts from the February and August 1933 Notebooks, given to Margaret Taylor in 1947.[31]

Thomas began sending out his poems to London magazines probably around January 1933 when he left his job on the Swansea newspaper. It is known that he submitted a nonextant poem, *The Romantic Isle,* for a BBC Competition in February 1933; he won a broadcasting of it on 28 June 1933. By that time he had appeared in the London *New English Weekly* with poem Twenty Three (an early version of *And death shall have no dominion*), written in the Notebook in April 1933 and published 18 May 1933. It is clear that the Notebook poems were the ammunition with which he began his assault on London, on the *Sunday Referee* "Poets' Corner" in particular. The acceptance of *Light breaks where no sun shines* by Janet Adam Smith for the *Listener* (14 March 1934) proved the crucial move; it prompted requests from the two leading poetry editors, T. S. Eliot and Geoffrey Grigson, requests met from the Notebooks.[32] Thomas turned to this store of poems again when Victor Neuburg, who had published five Thomas poems in the "Poets' Corner" since September 1933, announced on 22 April 1934 that Thomas had won the Book Prize, i.e. the *Sunday Referee's* sponsorship of a first volume of poems. Within a couple of days Thomas wrote to Pamela Hansford Johnson, who had won the Book Prize the previous year, that he had started "typing and revising stuff for Vicky." His next letter, 2 May 1934, under the heading "Referee Poets. No. 2," gave his view of Miss Johnson's attempt to make a selection of his poems. He is referring (with one or two noted exceptions) to poems in the August 1933 Notebook, which he had just that week filled with the copying in of *If I were tickled by the rub of love:*

> Thank you for your abortive list of poems. I disagree heartily with you. "We See Rise The Secret Wind" [Eight], "In Me Ten Paradoxes" [Thirty Nine, February 1933 Notebook], "The Eye of Sleep" [Twenty Two] and "Thy Breath Was Shed" [33] are all very bad indeed. I have rewritten "The Eye of Sleep" almost entirely, and it is now a little better, though still shaky on its rhythms and very woolly as to its intention (if any). But I know how hard it is to make any sort of comprehensive list for anyone else. I am going to include some poems which have been printed, so "Boys of Summer" [Thirty Nine], though altered and double the length, is to open the book.[34] Other poems are: "Light Breaks Where No Sun Shines" [Thirty]. "Before I Knocked And Flesh Let Enter" [Seven]. "No Food Suffices" (revised) [Forty Eight, February 1933 Notebook]. "When Once The Twilight Locks" (revised) [Twenty Nine]. "Our Eunuch Dreams" [Thirty Seven]. "A Process In The Weather" [Thirty Five]. "The Force That Through The Green Fuse" [Twenty Three]. "Where Once The Waters Of Your Face" [Thirty Eight]. "That The Sum Sanity" (revised) [Four]. "Not Forever Shall The Lord Of The Red Hail" (revised) [Ten]. And about six or seven others. I am still in the process of pruning and cutting about.

Thomas had plenty of time to change his list; for the production of the book was delayed through the summer, and only announced on 11 November 1934. In the end *18 Poems* was, in effect, compiled from his most recent poems: thirteen from the August 1933 Notebook; four written after the Notebook was filled; and only one of earlier vintage, *Especially when the October wind,* and that one revised considerably from the undated typescript in the British Museum.

The proposal for a second volume came so close upon the heels of the first that Thomas, now writing new poems more slowly, had no alternative but to go back and pick up some of the Notebook poems he had passed over for *18 Poems*. He revised poem Five of the August 1933 Notebook, and perhaps others, while on vacation in Donegal in the summer of 1935. During the autumn he revised at least two more poems for immediate publication. It was on returning to Swansea for the Christmas season, which appears to have extended into February 1936, that Thomas applied himself intensively to revising old poems for the volume.[35] At least sixteen of *Twenty-five Poems*, published 10 September 1936, can be traced back before 1934.

It is the same story with *The Map of Love* (1939). In the two and a half years between volumes Thomas finished only five new poems. Already in a letter to Pamela Hansford Johnson of May 1934 he had confessed that "the old fertile days are gone, and now a poem is the hardest and most thankless act of creation." Much of what appeared to be current output now came from "the old fertile days," even days as old as 9 December 1930. Actually this poem 42 of the 1930 Notebook, a remote ancestor of *How shall my animal,* was completely rewritten. "I had worked on it for months," he told Vernon Watkins in a letter of 1 April 1938 (*Letters to Vernon Watkins,* p. 40). More typical of his use of a Notebook poem is the case of *The spire cranes* (poem IX, 27 January 1931), which, from the evidence of the letters to Vernon Watkins, was revised in November 1937:

> I've done another little poem: nothing at all important or even (probably) much good: just a curious thought said quickly. I think it will be good for me to write some short poems, not bothering about them too much, between my long exhausters (*Letters to Vernon Watkins,* p. 31).

He had cut down the Notebook poem by half, regularizing the lines, but retaining the thought and much of the wording. This kind of revision (sometimes taking place in the Notebooks, sometimes not) accounts for about half of the sixteen poems of *The Map of Love.*

That *Twenty-five Poems* and *The Map of Love* contain two basically different kinds of poems is one of the important additions these Notebooks make to a discussion of Thomas' poetic development. Critics have noted the fact,[36] but the Notebooks explain it. Responding to Henry Treece's detection of the two styles of writing, Thomas said in a letter that the "straight" poems were not "a calculated escape from the personality-parade of my loud and complex poems." He then revealed what is confirmed by the Notebooks: "I wrote them, most of them anyway, quite a long time before the other poems in the 25 volume. The straight poems in 25 were, indeed, with very few exceptions . . . written before most of the poems in the *18* volume." Thomas was inviting Treece to see the "straight" poems for what they really are: pre-*18 Poems,* pre-*Find meat on bones,* pre-process poems of gentler disposition, created through fairly relaxed revision. The Notebooks allow us to see some of this revising in its true light, though the entire debt of later poems to early versions remains conjectural.[37]

Especially conjectural because at a certain point Thomas began writing shorter, clearer poems not surreptitiously from the Notebooks but in a conscious attempt to eschew massive obscurity. The revising of old poems, not something to be counted in the main stream of Thomas' development, seems to have led into a new line of major yet simpler poems. *Twenty four years* (1938) was built on a single line from an early, nonextant poem (*Letters to Vernon Watkins,* pp. 47-48); but it is a strong poem—with the strength of twenty-four rather than eighteen years. This new mode is found at its most perfect in such poems as *This Side of the Truth* and *In My Craft or Sullen Art,* both written in 1945 without the aid of early versions, when, indeed, the Notebooks were long since in their Buffalo repository.

7. ACKNOWLEDGMENTS

This edition would not have been possible without the commitment to Dylan Thomas' work made long ago by his publishers, James Laughlin and J. M. Dent and Sons; nor without the constant practical encouragement of Robert M. MacGregor of New Directions. The manuscripts themselves might never have been preserved but for the imagination and enterprise of the late Charles D. Abbott of the Lockwood Memorial Library of the University of Buffalo (since 1962, the State University of New York at Buffalo); and it might never have been my good fortune to edit them had not Oscar A. Silverman, formerly Chairman of the Department of English at Buffalo, invited me to join the department in 1958 and made sure I had time and resources to do the necessary research. I am indebted to Dr. Silverman, too, in his current role as Director of Libraries, State University of New York at Buffalo, for permission to publish the Notebooks and to quote from the extensive Dylan Thomas correspondence recently acquired by Lockwood Library. I am indebted to David Higham Associates Ltd. and Harold Ober Associates Inc., representing the Estate of Dylan Thomas, for their approval of this project and for permission to quote from Dylan Thomas' writings. Acknowledgment is made to New Directions and J. M. Dent and Sons, for permission to use copyright material.

All those friends to whom I made acknowledgment in my *Entrances to Dylan Thomas' Poetry*, a small volume in some sense a companion to the present edition, should be mentioned here since they helped a grateful editor to be a better one. But some would feel their contribution embarrassingly remote from the final product, so I repeat my general appreciation and specify only particular indebtedness. First, to the American Council of Learned Societies for a Grant-in-aid, and to the Committee on Allocation of Research Funds, State University of New York at Buffalo. Then, to Donald Tritschler, Herbert Schneidau, Richard Alan Hughes, Jack Dalton, and Jeremy Prynne, whose eyes I have used on the manuscript at various times. To

Thomas' chief correspondents during the period of the Notebooks, Pamela Hansford Johnson, Trevor Hughes, A. E. Trick, Henry Treece, Glyn Jones, and Vernon Watkins; and to the collectors T. E. Hanley, Thomas Taig, Joseph Gold, and Charles E. Feinberg. To the libraries: the British Museum for permission to print the poems in the Appendix; the Houghton Library, Harvard, the Lamont Poetry Room, and John L. Sweeney, who has helped in other ways than as a librarian; the Poetry Room of Lockwood Library, Buffalo, my use of which must have seemed at times over-use; the Swansea Public Library; the Harriet Monroe Collection, University of Chicago Library; the New York Public Library; the National Library of Wales, Aberystwyth; and the Humanities Research Center, University of Texas. Finally, to those scholars in charge of the editor's formal training: Edwin Honig, B. J. Whiting, Harry Levin, Reuben Brower, Douglas Bush, and Alfred Harbage. The late Hyder Rollins might have found the textual notes a little racy; but the level of accuracy aimed at, if not achieved, is his.

RALPH MAUD

Simon Fraser University
Burnaby, British Columbia

1930
NOTEBOOK

1
Osiris, Come to Isis.

He stands at the steaming river's edge
With his soft arms in the air,
And snares the sun among his tangled hair,
And springs upon the wave's thick ledge,
And curls his arms around his hips,
Brushing the hot foam with his lips.
Slowly the river covers him,
The river of the webbed anemone,
The sadr on its leaf-green stem,
The river and the clouds' fair sea,
Until his feet are rested on the bed,
And top-turned plants are spinning on his head
Clutching his face with lean, long nails.

Osiris was the son of Seb[1] and Nut,
A glacial god, a strongly-musled[2] boy,
Who, with one eye open and the other shut,
Caught tears and laughter with an equal joy.
He turned his hands and coiled his thighs,
Watery-handsome like a spotted stoat,
No parhelion in the Egypt skies,
But symbol of the sun's fierce throat
Steering its patriotic note
Out of the air's blue boat,
Among the corals and the sponges,
Wounding the water with his lunges,
So tortuous and dim,
Weaving a tribe over him

Of oval weeds with oval faces,
Symbol of the solace of the Nile,
Of the sun's grimaces,
And the moon's bright smile.

Osiris, Osiris, father of Horus,
Lost in the square houses,
Incarnated in a coal-black taurus,
Famous to the Alexandrian chor[o]us[3]
And Cotta's fine carouses,
You have exemplified the vicissitudinary, the odd
In fate and fortune,
And yet you were as pale as a lily,
You had no morbidity,
[You had no abortion]
Or limpidity,
[Or bad birth-mark, or contortion,]
You were a fair, and a strongly-musled[4] god.
Why were born[5] again in the belly of Apis
Like a bull
Out of reach of the body beautiful,
The firm breasts, and the kiss,
The intercource[6] and regret?

Under the lotus-earth perhaps
With happy stomach and fragrant chaps,
Judging the dead in their absence of vices,
Opening his eye and dreaming of Isis
Lying with Set or the bull, or both,
Side by side on the Nile's white cloth,
(Isis with beautiful breasts and mouth,
With a husband and child, or a cancer and growth)

He parts the water with his patterned knees
And hears the calm song of the waves,

The sadrs in their leaf-green graves,
The lilies and the hard-rock trees,
Moving their supple sounds along,
His hearing is so sweet and strong.
The harmony of grotto-water
Makes him desire Seb's fair daughter,
Earth and sky, with her sacred cow
Who gave her horns for the flat-haired brow.
She sits on a disced and symboled throne,
With a power of love through her skin
Like a sword in the flesh and a saw in the bone,
Fecund with sistrum and sin.

He makes a path with weeds and froth
Out of the river's white cloth,
Further and further down the Nile,
The sun her face, the moon her smile,
Until his body is a balm,
White and calm, white and calm,
Balanced on his shining arm,
Out of harm, out of harm.
He thought of Isis and her lotus-staff,
Pulling the water's wheel in half;
His legs are like her lotus-rod,
His breasts are feminine and white;
He is a happy but a virile god,
Seeking a bull-cow in the night
Under the waters of the Nile,
The sun her face, the moon her smile.

Osiris, Isis, you have made love
A mockery of love.
You have been thigh to thigh,
(Two eyes, one eye),
Breast to breast beneath its milk and heart,

D

But you have always been far apart.
Osiris, Isis, on the Nile's white cloth
You must unite in an Ishah growth,
And one mouth must not touch one mouth.
Apis must come to the cow
(Her horns are poised upon one brow,
While one hand holds the lotus-rod)
Or the cow to Apis
(Coal-black and beautiful,
A re-creating bull,
Half-in-half Serapis),
As the goddess must come to the God,
With her body clean for his.

He weaves the delightful waves with joy,
A glacial god, a strongly musled[7] boy,
Seeking perfection underneath
The river's hot, unwholesome breath,
Weeding the water with his knees,
Twining his body in anemones.

Osiris and Isis, dog-faced,
Even you can acheive[8] beauty
From a sense of duty
And the wells of your straight bodies.

April 27ᵗʰ 1930

2

(Based upon themes from Mother Goose)

The lion-fruit goes from my thumb
And the branches stride from my hand,

Proud and hard. Now I may watch
The wings of the birds snap
Under the air which raises flowers
Over the walls of the brass town,
Near the sun with its dry stream,
Looking down on the turrets
And their gay windows, and their bars
Holding the princess back.
She is a lady of high degree,
Proud and hard, and she wears a coat
Clinging and strident,
Like a net or a basket for berries.
So I consider, I magnetize
With my sunshade up for the sun,
Soaking the sky and the cliffs
That return fury for fury,
My peacock chained to my wrist.

Beat the white sea thin,
Little miss,
Flatten the planted waves,
Plane them fiercely,
Be felt,
Mary, Mary, chop them with your garden-axe.

The boughs stand symbolic
In their stiff truculence
With folded hands folded piously,
Turning away from me,
Avoiding my eyes.
Their leaves shall not frolic
Or throw themselves into buildings
That grow above the traffic

And hold princesses back,
Who with gay coats surrender
Love to the postman or the clown.

Good leaves, where shall we wander
So that we may influence directly
In the fanfare of the sun?
The earth is good for nothing,
The lion fruit refuses,
And the branches shiver at my touch.

If you snatch the flashing snow,
Or the foam of the golden sea,
Or the forests from the brown soil,
You accomplish the great and the good
Like a god from the stars
Flying their angled flags,
Tom, Tom.
What is the body of a pig
Compared with the body of the earth
Which gives you water, and sweet fruits to eat,
Which loves you in return for a little love?

Hammer your verses
On the grounds¹ dark crust,
Print them on the sky's white floor.

The princess from her turret watches,
Clad in her gay net coat,
Not to be refused, please names.

May 2ᵈ 1930

3
Poem Written on the Death
of a Very Dear Illusion

Grant me a period for recuperation,
I have lost my nearest relation,
Let there be tears.
My love is crucified
And split and bled,
Bruised and ravished by commercial travellers.
The lithe girls dance
With bright cloths glittering
And slippery breasts shining.
Oh, I have caused a disaster
Imitating an old master,
Rowing on the standing lakes,
So, I am tolerant,
I respect, I bow down,
My face bleeding in an affectionate smile.
I salute you,
I am a publican like yourself,
Hail, many-coloured Ceres,
I, too, gather and occasionally sow.
The dancing girls are arm-in-arm,
With beautiful thighs and ankles,
Oh, father, is there any harm?

May 2^d 1930

4

You shall not despair
Because I have forsaken you
Or cast your love aside;
There is a greater love than mine
Which can comfort you
And touch you with softer hands.
I am no longer
Friendly and beautiful to you;
Your body cannot gladden me,
Nor the splendour of your dark hair,
But I do not humiliate you;
You shall be taken sweetly again
And soothed with slow tears;
You shall be loved enough.

May 6th 1930.

5

My vitality overwhelms you,
My vigour is too heavy,
My love is a strong burden
That weighs upon your shoulders.
You bear my energy
With your slow fortitude,
Holding it up,
The musles[1] of your arms aching,
And your thighs burning with pressure.
So; you tolerate me;
I am to be tolerated;
Your love for me is lessened,

And has become the love of the animal,
The patient, intense affection of the cow,
The whining, respectful lust of the bitch.
Do not mistake me,
I do not ridicule the animal,
But your breasts and thighs and navel are not enough.
I want something more of you,
Something sexless and unmechanical:
The actions of love are stale,
Let me find a new medium,
A new method of intercourse.
Let me dispense with the animal:
The animal is not enough.

May 10th 1930

6

And so the New Love Came.

And so the new love came at length
Healing and giving strength,
And made the pure love go.
She echoed my laughter
And placed my love upon her,
Bearing the voluptuous burden,
With the pure love coming after.
She led me onto the shore
Carefully by my hand,
Where the wild sea smoothed the sand
And polished the yellow grains.
She took me into the fields
When the moon had risen bitterly,
Into the place of rains
Treading the fine grass

With firm, elaborate feet,
And the old love follows our paths.
I gave my new love a kiss
And her lips were the reddest of berries
Which poison the mouth at a touch,
And her hair was a circle of snakes,
And her delicate eyes were seeds,
So my kiss became twisted
And bitter to my taste,
The new love hard and alive
Like a tree spreading its cruel roots.
"You are too strange" I said
Into the pale shell of her ear,
"You bewilder me with your strength,
You hurt and do not reward."
"I am Lilith" she said,
And placed her savage mouth upon my neck,
And ran into the trees.

I went from the place of rains.

My new love brought me delight,
But my old love brings me her great faith.

May 17ᵗʰ 1930

7
On Watching Goldfish.

You collect such strange shapes
In the cool palm of your hand,
You with long, sinewy limbs
And musles¹ breaking through the skin,
Such close sponges and water flowers,

Fishes, and green-scaled flies,
Each holding its synthetic perfume
Bottled and gay,
That it might sicken with its smell
Or blur at sight.
[The fishes have an envy,
 Like a bill through their fins,
 To ascend, sail, parallel with the sky
 In a motion of adventure.]
You gather the pearls
From the sliding floor
For the necks of girls
To wear, this in the morning
But oh how different in the night.
The fishes in their floral beds,
The fishes in the white under-waves,
Over-bellying jocosely,
Limp and berry-eyed,
Their wet senses swimming faster
Than their clever fins,
The fishes on the sand
Waiting for the beachcomer,[2]
Shy, open-mouthed, pin-teethed,
The fishes in the nets
Making the silly movements of swimming
Without hope or reason,
Bloodwet and beautiful,
How so wrinkled, stealing the fast perfume
From the sea's rose,
Tragedy, tragedy, tragedy, I repeat,
The sea is my enemy.
But there are still the gold-fish,
Slow and double their size,
Their scales are crisp,

They swim sedately because the bowl's palm is cool,
Feed them on seeds,
Change their water.

May 18ᵗʰ 1930

8

The lion, lapping the water,
Moistening his gums
[And restoring his vitality,]
Is a balanced creature
Who lives because he must,
[And eats to live,
And takes, and fights, and loves
The lioness with a hard, bestial love;]
His mind is clean
And he has no unecessary[1] vanity,
But he arouses a jealousy in me
Because of his strength and power
Which are unbreakable.
[Even a lion in a cage
Is a vital, dominant creature,
With his vitality and dominance like a wall.
I cannot become anything but frail,
Asetic,[2] unbalanced,]
My love cannot be anything but a poor return.
[3]The lion and I
Accept the similar gift of death.

[9]

[One has found a delicate power,
Quietly even and sound,

Under the wings of a flower
Raising its head from the ground,
A measure of ease and delight
In the sweet-footed dance of the night.

One has captured an image of joy,
Quietly even and mild,
In the clear-coloured eyes of a boy
Or the beautiful eyes of a child,
In the bird-like rhythm of night
Moving with ease and delight.]

9
I Am Aware

I am aware of the rods
Of the high sun coming down,
Sharply, unwaveringly,
With bright tips to pierce,
Coming down pointed.

Where is the happy rain
That makes no enemies,
That does not cleave the grass
Or hurt the soil
Under its load of vegetation?
This is a harmful rain,
Harder than anything,
Which wounds the ground;
It does not cool as it should,
Ease the sinews of each plant,
Bring a well-oiled movement to each flower;
It pierces, pierces

Beneath the covering.
[I am aware of the sun
Between the rain,
Confident,
With its dignity and loud fastidiousness
Studying the earth.
Why does it stand so urbane?
It is a thing to wonder at,
To stretch back the head and admire,
So much to itself,
So independent and vast,
Like an animal
Living in its freedom,
Or a king
In an alabaster palace,
[Sunday all the week.]]

10

My river, even though it lifts
Ledges of waves high over your head,
Cannot wear your edge away,
Round it so smoothly,
Or rub your bright stone.
You stand a little apart,
Strong enough to tread on the sand
And leave a clear print,
Strong and beautiful enough
To thrust your arm into the earth
And leave a tunnel
Looking up at you.
The metallic rain

Cannot dent your flanks;
The wind cannot blunt
The blade of your long foot,
Nor can the snow
Smoothe the prisms of your breasts.
Sea, do not flow
Against this side.

You stretch out your hands
To touch the hydrangeas,
Then take them away quickly
As the mouth of the tiger-lily
Closes about your clasped fingers
With uneven, spiral teeth.
Your hands are beautiful hands
With [slender]¹ fingers
And milk-white nails.
Your eyes can be the eyes
Of the nightingale,
Or the eyes of the eagle
Rising on black wings.
Your voice can be the voice
Of the sea under the hard sun,
The sea speaking keenly,
Or the voice of the river
Moving in one direction,
In a pattern like a shell
Lying upon the yellow beach.
My river cannot rub your bright stone,
Which cuts into the strength
And takes the heat away.
My river has high waves,
But your stone is many pointed,
And your side is steep.

[12]

[The shepherd blew upon his reed
A strange fragility of notes,
And all the birds and forests freed
The music of their golden throats.

He rose and walked across the grass;
His robe was trailing on the ground;
The birds and forests saw him pass,
And rose and followed without sound.

He led them over hill and glade;
They followed at his feet,
And listened to the sounds he made,
And all the sounds were sweet.]

1 1

The corn blows from side to side lightly,
Tenuous, yellow forest that it is,
And bears the steady wind on its head,
Brushing my two hands.
The flower, under the soil
Rounds its ungainly roots;
Blue flower,
In my continent of strange speech,
Divide and allow the path
Of my warm arm to touch you,
Then touch you again

Not with the drift of voluptuous fingers
But with the possession
That comes from obscure contact.
I must shape the corn
Into a phalanx that satisfies
The eye watching it move,
Mould and round and make mine;
Your tall, straight stalks
Inclining only to the heaviest wind,
Will be my architecture
And my pride above the flower
Whose roots I cannot feel;
I will mount you upon resolute love;
I will raise your columns.
Now flower,
Traveller through the earth,
Spiral and pleasant to the extent
Of your violent, blue way,
Shall I make more of you
Than the ghost from the grave?
Shall I turn you and better you
[Like]¹ I bettered the yellow corn
From one architecture to another?
You move in your island
Like a dark cloud high above the ground,
You circle your stalk
On the night sailing with care and skill.
I know your roots thrust fine, black teeth
Up into the soil,
And swell noislessly.²
In the spire of the top petal
Rings the loud bell of triumph,
As you arch and become longer.

My influence breaks your spell,
And now you can grow,
Now you can cut and hurt the cloud,[3]
[Giant-flower.]

June 18ᵗʰ 30

[1 2]
[The Shepherd to his Lass.]

[He said, "You seem so lovely, Chloe,
  Your pretty body and your hair
  Are smoother than the rose and snowy,
  Soft as a plum and light as air.

I give this garland for your head,
This little flower, and
I give you all I have," he said.
She smiled and took his hand.]

[June 17ᵗʰ 30]

1 2

We will be conscious of our sanctity
That ripens as we develop
Our rods and substantial centres,
Our branches and holy leaves
On the edge beyond your reach;
We will remark upon the size[1]
Our roots,
Beautiful roots
Because they are under the surface

Of our charm.
Give us the pleasure of regret;
Our tears sound wiser
Than our laughter at the air
Or the yellow linnet who does not merit it.
We will be conscious of our divinity
When the time comes,
Unashamed but not with delight,
Making our affections fast;
We will tie you down
To one sense of finality
Like a cave with one thread.
Under this shade
The kingfisher comes
And the fresh-water bird
With his pink beak,
But we do not concern ourselves,
Waiting, waiting,
Waiting for the bird who shall say,
"I have come to elevate you,
To saw through your roots
And let you float."
Then will we rise
Upon broad wings
And go into the air,
Burrow our way upwards into the blue sky;
This shade
Has the dragonfly and the swordfish
Cleaving their own sedges,
The otter
Hand in hand with the mermaid
Creeping catlike under the water.
We will be concious[2]

E

Of a new country
Opening in the blind cloud over our heads;
We will be consious[2] of a great divinity
And a wide sanity

June 6th

13

I have come to catch your voice,
Your constructed notes going out of the throat
With dry, mechanical gestures,
To catch the shaft
Although it is so straight and unbending;
Then, when I open my mouth,
The light will come in an unwavering line.
Then to catch night
Wading through her dark cave on ferocious wings.
Oh, eagle-mouthed,
I have come to pluck you,
And take away your exotic plumage,
Although your anger is not a slight thing,
Take you into my own place
Where the frost can never fall,
Nor the petals of any flower drop.

June 19th

14

My love is deep night
Caught from the tops of towers,
A pomp of delicious light

Snared under the tip of each stalk,
Dew balanced to perfection
On the grass delicate beyond water.
But beauty is a very old friend,
And in the coming and going of the seasons
It is lifted to a high pinnacle
So that we may admire it from a distance,
Not touching it with our cruel fingers
For they might break it into pieces.
We shall regret your delightful arms
Like two clouds,
And your delightful thighs
Like two towers,
Desiring the warmth they have once offered
But which we have once refused
More than the fine gift of sleep
Or the irretreivable[1] gift of death;
We have need of you,
But we cannot touch you with our cruel fingers,
Or make your body a splendid place
For receiving us with more than a clasp of the hand,
More even than a gay laugh full of welcome,
More even than the pressing of your scented lips
On our white and hard skin.
Are we destined to become beautiful
Because we have admired but have not handled,
Allowing you your virginity in cool places,
And the heat of your own love
Where it cannot pierce or endure?
We are too beautiful to die;
All our life is bound to the green trees,
And in the cithern evening
The darkness is insistent,

Loading a pleasure of love upon us
In its great desire to overcome.

1 5

When your furious motion is steadied,
And your clamour[1] stopped,
And when the bright wheel of your turning voice is stilled,
Your step will remain about to fall.
So will your voice vibrate
And its edge cut the surface,
So, then, will the dark cloth of your hair
Flow uneasily behind you.

This ponderous flower,
Which leans one way,
Weighed strangely down upon you
Until you could bear it no longer
And bent under it,
While its violet shells broke and parted.
When you are gone
The scent of the great flower will stay,
Burning its sweet path clearer than before.
Press, press, and clasp steadily;
You shall not let go;
Chain the strong voice
And grip the inexorable song,
Or throw it, stone by stone,
Into the sky.

July 1 1930

16

No thought can trouble my unwholesome pose,
Nor make the stern shell of my spirit move.
You do not hurt, nor can your hand
Touch to remember and be sad.
I take you to myself, sweet pain,
And make you bitter with my cold,
My net that takes to break
The fibres, or the senses' thread.
No love can penetrate
The thick hide covering,
The strong, unturning crust that hides
The flower from the smell,
And does not show the fruit to taste;
No wave comb the sea,
And settle in the steady path.
Here is the thought that comes
Like a bird in its [freshness],[1]
On the sail of each slight wing
White with the rising water.
Come, you are to lose your freshness.
Will you drift into the net willingly,
Or shall I drag you down
Into my exotic composure.[2]

July 17th

17

The hill of sea and sky is carried
High on the sounding wave,

To float, an island in its size,
And stem the waters of the sun
Which fall and fall.
Wind cannot spin the cloth
Of safety with such care,
Lacing the water and the air together;
Nor hail, nor season, weave
A hill like that.
Only the water loads its garden
With rich and airy soil,
Heaps on the paths the broken clouds,
And arches his long wave.
He is to plough the air,
Plough up and turn the sweet, blue fields,
And wrench the flowers by their roots;
He'll be at liberty
To plant what curious seeds he knows
When this is done.

July 20th

18

So I sink myself in the moment,
I let the fiery stream run.
How I vibrate, and the petunia too,
As, garden to your loving bird,
I'm all but cut by the scent's arc.
So in the sorrow after,
When you bird are flown away,
And the scent can please no more.
Your senses play the fool with me,
And, if you like, I ride

A knight upon a golden horse,
Or sit for you,
Or fly, or take the sea.

19

No, pigeon, I'm too wise;
No sky for me that carries
Its shining clouds for you;
Sky has not loved me much,
And if it did, who should I have
To wing my shoulders and my feet?
There's no way.
Ah, nightingale, my voice
Could never touch your spinning notes,
Nor be so clear.
I'm not secure enough
To tell what note I could reach if I tried,
But no high tree for me
With branches waiting for a singing bird,
And every nightingale a swan
Who sails on tides of leaves and sound.
I'm all for ground,
To touch what's to be touched,
To imitate myself mechanically,
Doing my little tricks of speech again
With all my usual care.
No bird for me:
He flys[1] too high.

Aug: 8th

20

The cavern shelters me from harm;
I know no fear until the cavern goes;
Without his dark walls I die,
Without his winged roof
I have no place to cover me.
His noises, too, swing out like bells,
But when they stop, why, other sounds
Go on, sadder and more remote.
Seraph, you should come down.
That's no cavern in the air
To shelter round and round,
That's no river, either, to purify,
And each slight wave to bless the foot.
Cavern, my Jordan,
His silence is a silver charm,
[Fine, bright stone.]
Seraph, I wear my river round my neck,
My cavern's this and that,
But still it keeps me from the wind,
And does me good.

Aug 11th.

21
Woman on Tapestry.

Her woven hands beckoned me,
And her eyes pierced their intense love into me,
And I drew closer to her
Until I felt the rhythm of her body

Like a living cloak over me.
I saw the cold, green trees,
Their silken branches unmoving,
Their delicate, silken leaves folded,
And the deep sky over them
With immeasurable sadness.

Her love for me is fierce and continual,
Strong, fresh, and overpowering.
My love for her is like the moving of a cloud
Serene and unbroken,
Or the motion of a flower
Stirring its pole stem in delight,
Or the graceful sound of laughter.
In the victory of her gladness
And the triumph of her pitiless gaiety
She became like a dancer or a pretty animal
Sauve[1] in her movements,
On the balance of her dark foot,
Stepping down.

[Let me beleive[2] in the clean faith of the body,
The sweet, glowing vigour
And the gestures of unageing love.]
She shall make for me
A sensitive confusion in the blood,
A rhythm I cannot break
Stroking the air and holding light.

And the roots of the trees climbed through the air
Touching the [silver] clouds,
Trailing their fingers on the hard edges
Pacing in kind praise.

[I have made an image of her

With the power of my hands
And the cruelty of my subtle eyes,
So that she appears entertaining
Like the arms of a clean woman
Or the branches of a green tree.]

[Death comes to the beautiful.]
[He]³ is a friend with fresh breath
And small, [feminine] shoulders,
And white, symmetrical lips
Drawing the energy from the love,
And the glitter from the fine teeth.

So the hills
Coiled into their bodies like snakes,
And the trees
⁴Away from the bright place.

[Let me beleive² in the clean faith of the body,
The sweet, glowing vigour,
And the gestures of unageing love.]

                                   28, 29 April 1929.

        Continuation of Woman on Tapestry.

You shall comfort me
With your symmetrical devotion
And the web of your straight senses.
Your bitterness is masked with smiles,
And your sharp pity is unchangeable.
I can detect a tolerance,
A compassion springing from the deep body,

Which goes around me easily
[Like the body of a girl.]
So the ilex and the cypress
Mix their wild blood
With yours,
And thrill and breathe and move
Unhealthily with dry veins.

Woman on Tapestry.
(Continued)

There will be a new bitterness
Binding me with pain,
And a clean surge of love moving.
In the fold of her arms
And the contact with her breasts
There will be a new life
Growing like a powerful root inside me.
The gestures of my love
Involve me in a gaiety,
Recall my old desire
Like a sweet, sensitive plant
In the barbed earth,
Holding a voluptuous clarity
Under the tent of its wings.

22

Pillar breaks, and mast is cleft
Now that the temple's trumpeter
Has stopped, (angel, you're proud),

And gallantly (water, you're strong—
You batter back my fleet),
Boat cannot go.

The raven's fallen and the magpie's still.
Silly to cage and then set free,
You loose, delicious will
That teaches me to wait,
Whose minute kindles more than the wise hour.
Temple should never have been filled
With ravens beating on the roof:
One day they had to fly,
And, there, what wings they had,
Poor, broken webs to strike the sky!
It was the magpie, after,
Bird on the mast, (he contemplated),
Who flew himself because the boat remained
Unmoving in a [showering]¹ sea,
Flew for a time in vain, to drop at last
And catch the uprising wave.

Pity is not enough:
Temple's broken and poor raven's dead;
Build from the ashes!
Boat's broken, too, and magpie's still;
Build, build again!

23

It's light that makes the intervals
Between the pyramids so large,
And shows them fair against the dark,
Light who compels

The yellow bird to show his colour.
Light, not so to me;
Let me change to blue,
Or throw a violet shadow when I will.
To-day, if all my senses act,
I'll make your shape my own,
Grow into your delicate skin,
Feel your woman's breasts rise up like flowers
And pulse to open.
Your wide smile for me.
Challenge my metamorphosis,
And I will break your spacing light.
Mock me,
And see your colour snap,
Glass to my hands endowed with double strength.
But if you break I suffer,
There'll be my bone to go:
Oh, let me destroy for once,
Rend the bright flesh away,
And twine the limbs around my hands.
I never break but feel the sudden pain,
The ache return.
I'll have to break in thought again,
Crush your sharp light,
And chip, in silence and in tears,
Your rock of sound.

24

Let me escape,
Be free, (wind for my tree and water for my flower),
Live self for self,
¹and drown the gods in me,

Or crush their viper heads beneath my foot.
No space, no space, you say,
But you'll not keep me in
[1]although your cage is strong.
My strength shall sap your own;
I'll cut through your dark cloud
To see the sun myself,
Pale and decayed, an ugly growth.

25

Oh, dear, angelic time—go on.
I'll try to imitate your going,
And turn my wheel round, too,
As sure and swift as yours.
Between each revolution,
(Wise time—go on,
My voice shall speed you
[1]though you need no strength
To make you turn, I know),
There's all my laughter smoke,
My grief a little empty sound,
And all my love a cloud
Who sails away from me.
[I can't be happy.
  Try to-day, try this time (sweet time),
  To-morrow's never.]

[30]

[The rod can lift its twining head
  To maim or sting my arm,

But if it stings my body dead
I'll know I'm out of harm,
For death is friendly to the man
Who lets his own rod be
The saviour off the cross who can
Compel eternity.
I'd rather have the worm to feed
Upon my flesh and skin,
Than sit here wasting, [while I bleed,]
My aptitude for sin.]

26

And the ghost rose up to interrogate:
["]When did you make the leopard yours,
Who was an animal but could not follow
The intricacies of another's path?
He follows now, smells you, and thinks,
A dolphin at a fountain's foot,
A sea-horse allegorically spouting
Water through his trembling nose.["]
I hear the peacock shouting: ["]Stop!
My high voice will never make you hear.
I stir my feathers to detract[1] you;
The sound is louder than the sea's,
Steely and sharp and rich,
But still you move as steadily.
Oh, stay and let me speak,
For though my tears are bright
And my long tail is just the same,
I am a different bird, too sad
To make my colours cut.
My plumes, scythes for the night,

Who saved the earth alone
From drooping to the dark,
Are blunt. You do not understand.
March as you do,
Mechanically, with deliberate steps,
And there's an end to me.
I'll go, taking the rainbow with me.
The parrot and the daliah'll[2] take my hand.
Gillyflower, Gillyflower, you will come with me.
This is our way,
The bright and hundred-coloured stairs.[3]
The wheels revolve, wheel within wheel,
Shining and multiplex machines;
Their voice obliterates the bird's,
Weaker and wiser, touching the highest air.
Peacock's gone.
Run smoothly, run carefully,
Run smoothly, run carefully.
Keep rhythm, keep rhythm,
You shall break the herb and the tree
Under your glistening heel.
I reproach the hollow perfection,
And the rootless power.
I praise the grotesque,
The peacock and the gillyflower,
The [peacock][4] and the mustard-bird.
[And] the[5] wheels go round and round.

27

When I allow myself to fly,
There is no sense of being free;
Only the other loosening me

Can send that voluminous delight,
And make the wind that hurries by
Keener to invigorate.
As you travel
My head shall follow your course,
Inclining as you incline.
No flower follows the ardent sun
More faithfully in every movement
Than I do at your garment's hem.
Unchain me, and I fly so high
I rest myself upon a cloud at will,
Sing with such pitiless technique
My tree bows down beneath the lyric weight,
The leaves drop down, a note on each.
You cannot shine for ever,
And when your lustre vanishes,
I follow your uncertain ghost.
But can he set me free?
Could his hand break the chain?
His light could never make me see,
Trembling, white rod which goes
Around me.
And is an echoe[1] worth my constancy?

28
Admit the Sun.

Admit the sun into your high nest
Where the eagle is a strong bird
And where the light comes cautiously
To find and then to strike;
Let the frost harden
And the shining rain

Drop onto your wings,
Bruising the tired feathers.

I build a fortress from a heap of flowers;
Wisdom is stored with the clove
And the head of the bright poppy.
I bury, I travel to find pride
In the age of Lady Franckinsense[1]
Lifting her smell over the city buildings.
Where is there greater love
For the muscular and the victorious
Than in the gull and the fierce eagle
Who do not break.[2]

Take heed of strength!
It is a weapon that can turn back
From the well-made hand
Out of the air it strikes

29
A Section of a Poem called
"Hassan's Journey into the World."

We sailed across the Arabian sea,
Restless to interrupt the season
And for our castles and unshaken trees
Take the bright minaret.
The world was tired, tide on tide
Falling below our boat
With slow deliberation,
And bearing its tiny water-lass
As if she were as big as we.
"If we are outcasts" Hassan said,

"Then what is she?"
Pointing to her who rode so easily.
The second clown began to laugh.
"Heigh-ho" he said, "anchor my joy
At seeing everything so upside-down
Or it will turn and strike against
Whatever grief you hide." His face
Was webbed in smiles; a foot
Of laughter spread upon the cheeks
That, cherry-red and touched with blue,
Quivered if any jest would spring
Out of the tall wave's murmuring.
But with the night none came
To close the door and step inside.
The second clown began to dream.
"Heigh ho" he thought, "she comes to me;
Button my collar; is my monkey trim?
Have I my best bucolic bells
To tinkle in her tiny ears
And make her laugh?"
So, softly, like a lady
Stept off the sounding moon,
She walked across to sit beside
The poor old fool who lay asleep.
"Boy!" [she sang] But his eyes
Were closed to catch the fullest light
That made the dream-world sweet,
Careless and light as water
Running down the chiming rocks,
Vapid as the rising night
Who comes but does not sncopate[1]
With other birds and animals.
["]I am the turtle,["] said the turtle,
["]My shell contains a thousand things,

My little eyes can see a lot.["]
"Boy!" The clown's goodnight
Was very hard to penentrate;[2]
The turtle laid a velvet foot
Upon the old fool's mouth.
"Imitate; not syncopate;"
Who heard the turtle's voice?
"Your kiss is soft, my lady-moon,
Your velvet lips delight mine own,
Send the gay moisture of your breath
[Scented with the clouds'   ,]
Into my lungs, and down and down.
You kiss my heart, and I am glad."
But, no, the turtle is awake
To every spark that kindles love
With such a free activity,
Pure and incorpereal,[3] a shell away
To leave the body pink and nice,
Untouched, unfalsified, a silver god
Who knows the wise flesh's wants.
The lady sang. Hassan said "Lady", but she did not look
Where he stood smiling at the cabin door.[4]
"One could not tarnish our love
By giving pain,
Or taking me away from you
And putting you to ridicule;
You are too worthy of my love
For anything or one to change it;
Beleive[5] in the wisdom of our love,
And we shall grow to hope for love
That gives and does not ask for anything."
But Hassan had waited too long;
The lady was melting, was melting,
Her poor little feet and her hands

Turning quite slowly to water.
Love, like a stone, struck the jester.
His old face was firm and young,
His voice was clear:
"Goodbye, my Aegis, but remember,
This is not your last visit.
You shall bring your love again
For me to hide behind,
Secrete my shame,⁶ my [silly] vanities,⁷
[And loose my great grief."]
He seized her snowy hand to kiss.

30

I know this vicious minute's hour;
It is a sour motion in the blood,
That, like a tree, has roots in you,
And buds in you.
Each silver moment chimes
in steps of sound,
And I, caught in mid-air perhaps,
Hear and am still the little bird.
You have offended, periodic heart;
You I shall drown unreasonably,
Leave you in me to be found
Darker than ever,
Too full with blood to let my love flow in.
Stop is unreal;
I want reality to hold
within my palm,
Not, as a symbol, stone
speaking or no,
But it, reality, whose voice I know

FIRST POEM
IN D. JONES'
SELECTION
AND
CHRONOLOGICAL
SEQUENCING
FOR
NEW DIRECTIONS
THE POEMS OF
DYLAN THOMAS,
REVISED ED.
2003.

To be the circle not the stair of sound.
Go is my wish;
Then shall I go,
But in the light of going
Minutes are mine
I could devote to other things.
Stop has no minutes,
but I go or die.

November 3rd   28 Nov 12

31
[Claudetta, You, and Me.]

Her voice is a clear line of light
Coming from the end of her world
Into the uneasy centre of mine,
And her hair is a forest whose trees
I have planted, in thought,
Time upon time.
Thus is the contact made,
The both flames rising come together,
And the tips of the fiery waves
Met lightly.
So shall we be comrades,
So shall we be lovers,
You in your clear serenity
I in my trembling obscurity,
And the rose shall grow to be a tall flower,
And the rain of seasons change my colour,
Before the love I bear you break.
Elucidate what binds us now;
Follow the path of every curious thought
We think between us,

And then, lady for lord, the shy gazelle
Has eyes to pierce beneath your mind,
And velvet skin to feel.
You have looked for a goddess
and found a lorette;
You would have been her god,
but now you are only her leman,
While Claudetta and I pass over the golden fields,
And still the gazelle has eyes for you
                                        November 4ᵗʰ

32

Come, black-tressed Claudetta, home
To me, who, when you go,
Fall into melancholy.
You said "The shepherd by the brook,
Singing to soothe his cares,
Befriended me, and told me how
The swallow was the bird he loved.
I love the quail."
Living within her eyes, I saw with them
The swallow darting up,
And he, the shepherd,
Seeing it fly so [splendidly] [queenly],¹
Telling his cares his secret love for it.
I felt her eyes
Gazing at where the quail would be,
And knew I never could possess
Her love so truly.
She was the quail's.
Its wings would break if she would touch,
So that she loved it more

If that could be.
Claudetta, when your quail is near,
You rise yourself on wings.
Come, black-tressed Claudetta, home;
The shepherd loves;
You are the queen
I could not bear to see be his—
His swallow flies too high.
Quail, then, be mine.

November 5th 1930

33

Cool, oh no cool,
Sharp, oh no sharp,
The hillock of the thoughts you think
With that half-moulded mind I said was yours,
But cooler when I take it back,
And sharper if I break asunder
The icicle of each deliberate fancy.
For when I bought you for a thought, (you cost no more)
How could I smoothe that skin
Knowing a dream could darken it,
And, the string pulled, some mental doll
Ravage and break,
How kiss, when doll could say
Master, her mouth is sawdust
and her tongue, look, ash,
   Part from her,
   Part from her,
Sweet, automatic me knows best.[1]
But you shall not go from me, creation;

Oh no, my mind is your panopticon;
You shall not go unless I will it
And my thoughts flow so uneasily
There is no measured sea for them,
No place in which, wave perched on wave,
Such energy may gain
The sense it has to have.
You wish to stay my prisoner
Closed in your cell of secret thoughts,
And I, your captor, have my love to keep
From which you may not fly.

34

They brought you mandolins
On which you might make song,
And, plucking each string lightly,
Send what you dreamt into the sky.
I'll make your thoughts for you,
Catch them in bird-like notes,
On fountains of the brightest sound
Rising, oh rising, above your own fair head.

The dreamer asks my pity.
"My fancies are fallen" she whispers,
Her finger to her lips,
"Secretly fallen like snow come at night
Or the sweet, invisible rain
You told me of.
I planted my dreams with the myrtle tree,
For, when it would grow,
I wished my flowers, too,

Like myrtle foliage to which you sing
'Myrtle, good myrtle, velvet tree, wither;
The turtle is come for his revenge;
He will not have you slight him so'.
I was a vain creature,
And a too proud lady."
And wishing for patience
So that you might not wait so anxiously,
You stood at the gates
But I would not let you in.
Your face was a dark shadow
I could not penetrate,
And your voice was cool and low
Telling me what I[1] knew.
I was aware of the garden
Only by the curious smell of the lemon-flower
Coming into my room,
Not by sight or by touch.[2]
"I should have chosen a common tree
To seed with my common dreams,
Feathery animals loving me much,
But no feather or[3] affectionate
Than the other's dear fancies
I laughed at, not guessing
Beauty was beauty to that one.
I should have made
An armour to cover my dreams,
To fasten it then, sweeten it then,
And to liberate at last.[4]

Now is my rare voice bidden
to hymn the lady I love;
I think she is fairer than any;
I know I am glad when she comes.

35

The air you breathe encroaches
The throat is mine I know the neck
Wind is my enemy your hair shant stir
Under his strong impulsive kiss
The rainbow's foot is not more apt
To have the centaur lover
So steal her not O goat-legged wind
But leave but still adore
For if the gods would love
Theyd see with eyes like mine
But should not touch like I
Your sweet inducive thighs
And raven hair.

36

When all your tunes have caused
The pianolas[1] roll to break,
And, no longer young but careful,
There are no words by which you might express
The thoughts you seem to let go by,
You might consider me.
I want no words to show
How many clever thoughts I have accumulated
With all the squirrel's shy avidity,
(Best thoughts keep closest to the breast
And never see their concrete shapes;
Your bosom's sun has no equivalent;)
You can express me
In wind, or snow, or wave, or sand.

37
Written in a classroom.

Am I to understand
You say what I should comprehend,
And make the words I knew
By sight and hearing
Words to the whirling head?
Your voice recedes,
Goes up to circle and comes down to earth,
But leaves no tail
Of reason for my penetrated mind
To clutch and use
For doing what you might have asked.
Shaft of winter morning light
Is realler than your faces, boys,
And I preoccupy myself.
Am I to understand
That those high sounds you speak,
Hope, hope against anger, hope against hope,
Pity for, despair, or [love]¹ of, me
Who hopes not anger,
Should strike my brain to answer yes,
Or smile the comprehending smile?
Your voice recedes. It drowns my thoughts.
It touches them I see unreal
Beside the river of the flowing sun,
And then is drowned itself
Within the bird's outcry.
[I loved her once,
 Lived for her smile and died too many times,
 Cried like a child

The more I knew
Love was a channel of delight
Clogged up with symbols of the tongue.]
[Love was a tiny boy.]²
[Love was a light on you
Speaking your sounds,
And, after that, regret,
Sad night to hope,
Dark, dark despair she fathomed for me.
You speak, and I can hear
Her saying in your words,
"No. No. No. You mean]
A voice, a smile to me.
How can I love a smile, my dear?"
Poor boy, she said,
And I preoccupy myself
Along with you.
Am I to understand
You say what I should comprehend?
Am I to understand, dear girl, dear girl?
[This thought and that.
Face upon voice and voice on face.
Speak your bewildering sounds.]

38

Hand in hand Orpheus
and Artemis go walking
into the void of sense
you stopped the eagle in its flight
you took Endymion to your place
now you go walking into sense
now you go walking into sense

and I am left to love your lies
and drown my thoughts
before I die of drowning.
so I place my hand upon my heart
the laugh clown laugh is all I have
roses and wine before I die
or cough my stomach up
the sweet sweet lie goes walking into sense
you sweet sweet trull
with drifting hair
and rotten breath gone
down the drain of sense
into the calculated sea
[so I am getting drunk
sense she has wings
and   is just as sane.]

39

I, poor romantic, held her heel
Upon the island of my palm,
And saw towards her tiny face
Going her glittering[1] calves that minute.
There was a purpose in her pointed foot;
Her thighs and underclothes were sweet,
And drew my spiral breath
To circumambulate for decency
Their golden and their other colour.
The band was playing on the balcony.
One lady's hand was lifted,
But she did not cry, "I see;
I see the man is mad with love."
Her fan burst in a million lights

As that my[2] heel was lifted,
Gone from my palm to leave it marked
With quite a kind of heart.
She is on dancing toes again,
Sparkling a twelve-legged body
And many arms to rise[3]
Over her heel and me.
I, poor romantic, contemplate
The insect on this painted tree.
Which is the metal wing
And which the real?

22[d] November. 1930.

40

Oh! the children run towards the door,
Opening a thousand times before they blink,
And there are fifty Xmas trees
Showing the snow on every thirtieth branch
Outside the house, but not too far.
Clap hands! Clap hands! Father has cherries
And mother a violin;
There's food and there's music for all of them now,
And the Xmas trees for the picking.
The salamanders sit them down
And eye the children all the while,
As if to stop
Them thinking they would miss
The table and the penny candles.
The nymphs, however, cannot look
Into the room behind the blinds,
And those that live
In channels underneath the earth

Pierce all in vain
Their walls to clamber through.
Each glass its note,
A corner's sound,
Full for their throats,
And for their ears,
The cherry and the violin
That eat and play in one.
Drink, you've ten fingers;
Eat, there's your mouth;
Bed for you, children,
But not before the violin
Has made the wine-glass fall
Upon the unpierced earth in shame.
Darkness is best;
The mouse knows that;
So do the salamanders,
And they awake to draw the blinds
The nymphs are barrierd[1] by;
So, air and fire, amused from them
Forget the mole
Snouting his dark hole all the time.

41

Tether the first thought if you will,
And take the second to yourself
Close for companion, and dissect it, too,
It stays for me[1]
With your no toil.
With fingers moving you will see it stir,
And then the stolen third—
Now you have turned the nervous tap—

Flow into place.
  Why does the foremost wave await
  Until its follower arrives
  Before it pulses and begins
  To weave, swallow, careful leap?
But you must see my images
From exultation to despair,
Or formed from speech
That's formed by smoke in sleep,
Or moving in the thoughts you steal.
Hope is for you and love,
But what remains of them when I have done with them—
I lift to look, to see,
Ah, it is fair I more than glance at,
And, clever wish, I long to kill,
Or kill—
Is not for your regard.
Have I to show myself to you
In every way I am,
Classic, erotic, and obscene,
Dead and alive,
In sleep and out of sleep,
Tracking my sensibilities,
Gratyfying[2] my sensualities,
Taking my thoughts piece from piece?
Look down.
[Look down.]

42

    How shall the animal
    Whose way I trace
    Into the dark recesses,

G

Be durable
Under such weight as bows me down,
The bitter certainty of waste,
The knowing that I hatch a thought
To see it crushed
Beneath your foot, my bantering Philistine.[1]

I build a tower and I pull it down;[2]
The flying bird's a feather,
Has no flesh or bone,
Carried by any wind to anywhere.

My senses see.
Speak then, o body, shout aloud,
And break my only mind from chains
To go where ploughing's ended.
The dancing women all lie down;
Their turning wheels are still as death;
No hope can make them glad,
Lifting their cheery bodies as before
In many shapes and signs,
A cross of legs
[Poor][3] Christ was never nailed upon,
A sea of breasts,
A thousand sailing thighs.

How shall the animal,
Dancer with sharpest foot;[4]
High bird
Who goes
Straight in a wingèd[5] line
Beyond the air;
Horse in the meadow
With the plough for toiling,

A boy to call,
And all the shining ground to tread,
Woman and sloe,
Still dance, fly, labour, be,
When sense says stop[. . .]⁶
Purpose is gone;
I try to hold, but can't,
Compress, inflate, grow old,
With all the tackle of my certain magic
Stone hard to lift

                        December 9ᵗʰ 1930

I

This love—perhaps I over-rate it,
And make my god an any woman
With lovely hair and teeth,
Praising an empty gesture as a world of meaning,
Thinking a smile meant faith,
And a word so lightly uttered
Immortality.
I am too gay perhaps,
Too solemn, insincere,
Drowned in too many thoughts,
Starved of a love I know
True and too beautiful.
But too much love, I know,
Will make me weak,
I spend my great strength so
In every motion
To your hand, or lip, or head.

Dec 1930

II

To-day, this hour I breathe
In symbols, be they so light, of tongue and air,
The now I have space
And time that is already half
More than that I tell you in,
I have divided
Sense into sight and trust.

The certain is a fable.
Oh, iron bird, you are not credited
But fly, against joy, for that is not
If sea is rare
That does not imitate
Boy with the voice, or tympani,
The same, you likeable machine.
As well, creature has no flesh
And does not try the sun with seeing,
But measures his own length on a wall,
And leaves his shell
A butterfly before the chrysalis,
A flying egg of inhibition.
My she loves me is easy pray[1]
For moving down another shaft,
Up to the hilt in going-backs,
And here, upon a hand,
A hundred years are by me cut.

Dec 18 1930

III //

Sometimes the sky's too bright,
Or has too many clouds or birds,
And far away's too [sharp][1] a sun
To nourish thinking of him.
Why is my hand too blunt
To cut in front of me
My horrid images for me,
Of over-fruitful smiles,
The weightless touching of the lip
I wish to know

I cannot lift, but can,
The creature with the angel's face
Who tells me hurt,
And sees my body go
Down into misery.[2]
No stopping. Put the smile
Where tears have come to dry.
The angel's hurt is left;
His telling burns.
Sometimes a woman's heart has salt,
Or too much blood;
I tear her breast,
And see the blood is mine,
Flowing from her but mine,
And then I think
Perhaps the sky's too bright;
And watch my hand,
But do not follow it,
And feel the pain it gives,
But do not ache.

Dec 19 1930

IV

Here is the bright green sea,
And, underneath, a thousand fishes
Moving their scaly bodies soundlessly
Among a bright green world of weeds.
These thousand pebbles are a thousand eyes
Each sharper than the sun;
These waves are dancers[1] [on an emerald floor;]
Upon a thousand, pointed toes

They step the sea,
Lightly, as in a pantomime.

Dec 28th. 1930

V

My golden bird the sun
Has spread his wings and flown away
Out of the swinging cage
You call the sky,
And, like his tired shadow
White with love,
My silver bird the moon
Flies up again
Onto her perch of stars.

December 30th 1930

VI

Live in my living;
When I am sad, be sad;
Take from our chaos
Few of your own wise smiles,
For I have merriment enough for both,
Too much for one to bear,
And, if we make it cruel laughter,
We shall have time,
A space of lies,
To show we can be kind.
Here is your breast,
And here is mine;
This is your foot,
And this is mine;

But live,   ,[1]
In all I offer for a little thing
So small you can but give it.

VII

Rain cuts the place we tread,
A sparkling fountain for us
With no fountain boy but me
To balance on my palms
The water from a street of clouds.
We sail a boat upon the path,
Paddle with leaves
Down an extatic[1] line of light,
Watching, not too aware
To make our senses take too much,
The unrolled waves
So starred with gravel,
The living vessels of the garden
Drifting in easy time;
And, as we watch, the rainbow's foot
Stamps on the ground,
A legendary horse with hoof and feather,
Impatient to be off.
He goes across the sky,
But, when he's out of sight,
The mark his flying tail has left
Branches a million shades,
A gay parabola
Above a boat of leaves and weeds.
We try to steer;
The stream's fantastically hard,
Too stiff to churn with leaves,

A sedge of broken stalks and shells.
This is a drain of iron plants,
For when we touch a flower with our oar
We strike but do[2] stir it.
Our boat is made to rise
By waves which grow again
Their own melodious height,
Into the rainbow's shy embrace.
We shiver uncomplainingly,
And taste upon our lips, this minute,
The emerald [kiss],[3]
And breath on breath of indigoe[4]

Jan 2 1931

VIII

The morning, space for Leda
To stir the water with a buoyant foot,
And interlude for violins
To catch her sailing down the stream—
The phrases on the wood aren't hers;
A fishing bird has notes of ivory
Alive within his craning throat—
Sees the moon still up,
Bright, well-held head,
And, for a pivot,
The shadows from the glassy sea
To wet the sky with tears,
And daub the unrisen sun with longing.
The swan makes strings of water in her wake;
Between the moon and sun
There's time to pluck a tune upon the harp,
Moisten the mouth of sleep

To kiss awake
My hand with honey that had closed upon a flower.
Between the rising and the falling
Spring may be green—
Under her cloth of trees no sorrow,
Under her grassy dress no limbs—
And winter follow like an echo
The summer voice so warm from fruit
That clustered round her shoulders,
And hid her uncovered breast.
The morning, too, is time for love,
When Leda, on a toe of down,
Dances invisibly, a swan to see
Who holds her clasped inside his strong, white wings;
And darkness, hand in hand with light,
Is blind with tears too frail to taste.

Jan 20th. 1931

IX

The spire cranes; its statue
Is an aviary,
And from the nest
Of stone not straw
He does not let the nightingales
Blunt their tawny necks on rock,
Or pierce the sky with diving—
So wing in weed
And foot an inch in froth.
The bell's chimes cheat the sun,
And drop in time,
Induced to fall
Like discs upon the water,

Tune for the swimmer's hands
And silver music for his bubbling mouth.
But let him keep his faculties.
The spire's hook drops birds and notes,
Each featherless and stony hearted;
The upward birds are choice for you,
And notes that breast the vertical,
Or run the corridor on ladder,
Not tread the cloudy steps like prodigals.

27ᵗʰ Jan.

X

Cool may she find the day,
And the night full of singing;
No snow may fall
But she shall feel it so,
Cool for her sinking wrist,
Melodious for her ear.
A pleasant fall, the robin says,
White as your neck.
But if she grieves—
Though tears shan't blunt her joy—
Let sorrow come down with the snow,
"For you," the robin's voice.

XI

Yesterday, the cherry sun
Hung in its space until the steel string snapped,
The voice lost edge,
And the guitar was put away,
Dropping from the window

Into the paper sea,
A silver dog, a gypsy's hoop.
The handle's turned this time;
The sun again, you pretty fruit,
I almost touch it, press you, vein for vein,
But other tunes meet mine,
Turned by the handles,
Sauve[1] on their chiming stilts.
Your serenade upon machines,
The fifty discs that soar to you
In notes like stone-made circles
Growing larger, tick by tick,
Should make you glad;
Your face is pale,
And when I catch your rays
Upon the garden fork,
The beds aren't bathed with light,
And the crocus does not cry for shade.
The handle and the clockwork turn,
But the nightingale
Does not please the emperor;
I pluck again
The sweet, steel strings
To bring the sun to life,
Laugh at the echo made,
The steel bird put away,
Guitar in hand

22ᵈ February 1931

XII //

Time enough to rot;
Toss overhead

Your golden ball of blood;
Breathe against air,
Puffing the light's flame to and fro,
Not drawing in your suction's kiss.
Your mouth's[1] fine dust
Will find such love against the grain.
And break through dark;
It's acrid in the streets;
A paper witch upon her sulphured broom
Flies from the gutter.
The still go hard,
The moving fructify;
The walker's apple's black as sin;
The waters of his mind draw in.
    Then swim your head,
    For you've a sea to lie.

Feb 24th

XIII

Conceive these images in air,
Wrap them in flame, they're mine;
Set against granite,
Let the two dull stones be grey,
Or, formed of sand,
Trickle away through thought.
In water or in metal,
Flowing and melting under lime.
Cut them in rock,
So, not to be defaced,
They harden and take shape again

As signs I've not brought down
To any lighter state
By love-tip or my hand's red heat.
March 20th

XIV

You be my hermaphrodite in logic,
My avocado temptress out of magic—
For who can keep illusions up
Before such honest chemistry
As turns love like a ring
From tip to cavity—
And when, in tune with me,
You're lost to sense,
With what coincidence
I'll wrip[1] your kiss from me,
And force you to a different sex.
The change will do my conscience good,
Before it blunts my tongue
And hurts whatever knows the joy
Of such cerebral sodomy.
There's truth in every word, there's gaiety,
To germinate in each chaotic move
Beyond the region of the mouth,
There's truth for the voluptuary
Inside satiety, or out of hate.
How is the cynic cancerized.
He cannot laugh with me at me;
He laughs from him at me;
We laugh at him with words and blood
Or paint and wood,

Safe in our wise orgasm,
Mind after body to endeavour.

24th March.

XV

Until the light is less,
And pity's shoulder-high
And full of sugar—
But does the waist entice,
Sweet smile sweet
Longer than time to meet the lips?—
Each gap for love lies heavily.
And you disturb the paradox,
That asks for water when it's wet.
Love's to the brim;
More love shan't spoil the balance,
But rather thin the [spreading][1] waves
Into their shade
Upon the careless lines.
No wrong in pity through the eyes,
Or even from the tongue
Wet with such speech
As turns the flaccid heart the wrong way up,
When your old look makes moisture,
Scalds, harms, and buries
Within an intake's age.
So pat my hand,
And many times
In temprament[2] with me,
Kiss on the ulcer
Till it learns to ache.

We're side by side,
Inches from home and yards from heaven,
You with an ageing glance,
And I, in pain and utter friendliness,
With little words to make forget,
Knowledge, no knowledge.

March 28ᵗʰ

XVI

The neophyte, baptized in smiles,
Is laughing boy beneath his oath,
Breathing no poison from the oval mouth,
Or evil from the cankered heart.
Where love is there's a crust of joy
To hide what drags its belly from the egg,
And, on the ground, gyrates as easily
As though the sun were spinning up through it.
Boy sucks no sweetness from the willing mouth,
Nothing but poison from the breath,
And, in the grief of certainty,
Knows his love rots.
Outdo your prude's genetic faculty
That grew for good
Out of the bitter conscience and the nerves,
Not from the senses' dualizing tip
Of water, flame, or air.
Wetten your tongue and lip,
Moisten your care to carelessness,[1]
For she who sprinkled on your brow
[Soft][2] shining symbols of her peace with you,[3]
Was old when you were young,

Old in illusions turned to acritudes,
And thoughts, be they so kind,[4]
Touched, by a finger's nail, to dust.

April 6ᵗʰ '31

XVII

To be encompassed by the brilliant earth
Breathing on all sides pungently
Into her vegetation's lapping mouths
Must feel like such encroachment
As edges off your nerves to mine,
The hemming contact that's so trammeled
By love or look,
In death or out of death,
Glancing from the yellow nut,
Eyeing from the wax's tower,
Or, white as milk, out of the seeping dark,
The drooping as you close me in
A world of webs
I touch and break,
I touch and break.

10ᵗʰ April 1931

XVIII

Who is to mar
My lying long,
Or blow away its grains,
Across my lover's sandy bed,
Sick at the coming close,
Yet iron-white and loth to part,

Ascetic, letting the hand loll
Upon my sybarite's strong calf?
Who is to stop,
Or mend the growth
Of such unreason in a time of magic
Whose order calls the fairy out
To stem and step the light
Before the little day is dark as sense?
Who's the logician
Sucking my gay disgust
Through love to shape,
Wit wise and heady no man knows,
Of numbers beyond me,
Of numbers beyond you,
Who's to infer the tragedy?
When the sand's away
By wind to leave the metal,
Then shall the epicene take pride of place.
Now drown and let drown,
Yellow like honey seed
Falling below the water;
Now shall the graph be stained with salt;
And the crying gone,
The crying aloud that never can
In age or motion,
Or the time of the thin blood.

May 18th '31

XIX

The natural day and night
Are full enough to drown my melancholy
Of sound and sight,

Vigour and harmony in light to none,
One hour spend my time for me
In tuning impulses to calls;
Kinder;
So phrase;
Don't hurt the chic anatomy
Of ladies' needles worn to breaking point
Sewing a lie to a credulity,
With zest culled from their ladylike heat,
Hedgerow, laboratory, and even glasshouse,
But the sun cracks it
But the stones crack it
Out of my hand in stopping up my mouth,
My ears, my nose, my eyes,
And all my thin perogative[1] of taste.
But while day is there's night to it,
And night to it.
The black shadow comes down,
And the beautiful noise is quelled,
For my merry words,
So rare—
Who taught me trouble?
I, said the bettle,[2] out of my thin black womb,
Out of my thin black lips,
Trouble enough for the world
Out of my filthy eyes
And my incorruptible[3] knowledge—
They are the words for weeping.
Crying aloud in pain,
Thick to the skull,
Oh gaiety!
Oh gaiety!
Penumbra derry,

Do the right thing to do the right;
Do, down a derry.

March 30th '31.

XX

Although through my bewildered way
Of crying off this unshaped evil,
Death to the magical when all is done,
Age come to you—you're bright and useless,
Soon to my care, my love,
But soon to die
In time, like all, through my unreason
In a gay moment's falsity—
There is no need of hope for hope,
You'll bring the place to me
Where all is well,
Noble among a crowd of lights.
Then shall your senses, out of joy,
Tingle on mine;
You're the perverse to lie across,
Out of the heart for me,
Sick, pale, and plain,
So that the process calls for laughs,
The silly binding
Snapped in a rain of pieces falling
On head and running foot,
For, if I could, I'd fly away,
For, if I could, I'd fly away
Before the last light is blown
Into the void again of this bewilderment and that insanity

June 1st. '31

XXI

High on a hill,
Straddle and soak,
Out of the way of the eyes of men,
Out of the way,
Straddle her wrinkled knees
Until the day's broken—
Christ, let me write from the heart,
War on the heart—
Puff till the adder is,
Breathe till the snake is home,
Inch on the old thigh
Till the bird has burst his shell,
And the carnal stem that stood
Blowing with the blood's ebb,
Is fallen down
To the ground.

June 1ˢᵗ '31

XXII

Refract the lady, drown the profiteer
Inside the angles of his sanguine cup[1]
If he is jew then rend his gaberdine,
If Christian cut him navel up.
Refract the lady, her visage bouncing
From cup to jew,
That vision dancing with tidy-knickered girl
For higher thrills than seeing limbs
And giving ices.

If he is jew, make him a christian swine,
If christian, ask him did christ mean
The christian jews to be unclean.

1931

XXIII

Into be home from home
And split the searching for the truth
Into a part for causuistry[1]
And then a part for ghost or jew,
Of Islam's poeple[2]
Paring the pennyweight of their accustomed love
For ghost or jew in the mythology,
A hundred times
And then a hundred times,
But Peter was a libertine.
The words are scattered down the canal
This time to rake hell
Until be nut-brown fiend—phonetic water
Washes to a wisp;
And I am all there is this second,
Genius for the chosen poeple[2]
From the cross and hundred men,
And thief I am at His side.
I'll put away the clock,
Scorn, intone again, the pride there is
Of hanging up the blue grape[,]
[Etching the mossy castle we lived in]
When there was grass on Calvary,
And the children's pond
Fit for my sails or for my wings.
The truth is only half

The sour minute drawing mine,
Floating through pitch
A long way to the prophet,
(He is a man of letters
Who hates me for a proselyte
From no faith to fanatic),
Sidling to the wits' trapezium,
But when I call on the sweet substance
Mind what I do,
For Jesus was a social poem
For Jesus though his death's a logogram.

June 10th

XXIV

if the lady from the casino
will stop the flacillating roof
de paris and many women from my thinking
over the running bannisters
who can tell I may be strong enough
to push the floor away with a great gesture
but for the navels and the chandelebra
mending my coloned head in hands
And are you parallel in thinking good with me
Of us beneath the shepherd's crook
Driving the wolves away
And walking the metallic fields
An inch's time away with every step
Who has no hope
I know him for he lives in me
lady gap
they're there I see them

on railings and on pots of ferns
seeking a sex in me
beneath the nose . . . .
Iif its no beginning in our love
wise woman true for heat.
it's no end to us
or even interlude between the abstract
and the side or shell
hindering my knuckles or my knife
our modern formula
of death to sense and dissolution
where there is love there's agony
Ttheres sex where our mad hands rest
. . . .
Of ever watching your light
Come to a point with mine
Your pity left me high and dry
For appetites aren't fed with
can they for ever
stop their navels with their finger tops
or
. . . . . Bbranch off straight to nonsense narrow . . . . .
Hope ah I know it
one naked hand upon the bracket
out of the pages
would I blind in puberty the phrases
grow and here's a castle
Hope I knew him out of Rreason
Faith messiah for what death
though they do not speak like that in France;
But while I'm deft and aphrodisiac
To her who her the nought for my loud nerves
Not to the incubator or the brain

A mass of words above the window
Chiming for room
One brings you allonal
Which bells grotesque parade
Of leg on breast
And vomit on a shining cheek
Of masks *two* can't take off
But in its true light devil naturally
And let there be an end to
evil
I have an explanation
And what is more an egg
So with my mind's catastrophe
And white and yellow anna
Three has no message in his sin
And *four* a skull for tympani
Choked up with wit
The *rest* shall wait for not engendering
And I along the skin
Think of my passionate alloy
I cool who's chastity
now nothing yes loud purity
With
bawdy
Eyes and with the nerves' unrest
shatter the french
to let the Old Seduced crowd on
over the hurdle of the belly de
through mercy to paris
I'll in a moment but my version's sane
space is too small
hover along the saxophone
and tread the mandoline a navel's length
the women on the ground are dead

who her dont care for clothes
and I no longer itch at every trouble

16th June. '31

XXV

Through sober to the truth when
All hold out their aequeous hands,
Touching me low
By any frond of smiles,
And that's transition worth my toil.
I have a friend in death,
Daywise, the grave's inertia
Mending my head that needs its hour's pain
Under the arc-lamp,
Or between my skull and me.
Through truth again, and there's sobriety
Touching me low
By any smile shaped
From the solid hand, good death,
To regularity,
Making the paradox
This glass's spring
Veracity, (I know your frond by smell).
The moment is so small,
The beam that wakes the highing urge
A way off from its so true state
Can't hope to have
The molten sand's deep autumn
Blown by this wind to death.
I have a friend who sends
Irregular reprisal
To laughing, in a shape,

And love, all beams,
Upon a thistle,
Who is my friend in truth.
Sober, he heaps his shadows on my aching mind,
But, with the water on your hands,
He plays his sun a time too loud,
Deafens, and with his blood
Drowns all the actions have I lied

July 3ʳᵈ '31

XXVI

It is the wrong, the hurt, the mineral,
That makes its stroke
Through wisdom, for my age,
And sin, for my two-headed joy—
The particle's[1] aren't more than dust,
And whose affections aren't corrupt?—
Listen and lie;
The head's vacuity can breed no truth
Out of its sensible tedium,
But if chastity's a hybrid freak
From the shy evil
And the reeking courage known to all
Who spend their love, my paradox,
Within the places of the mind,
Sink head and heart
In feelings that shan't last a day,
For I shall turn the strongest stomach up
With filth I gather
From the thousand minds, all lust and wind,
Like a beachcomber in the time of light.
You are untouched, unhurt,

Corroded by an acid heart
That eats and lets eat
Till the loin is dumb
That spoke the woman's passion musically.
She is the evil in the good,
Out of reason to the shuddering care,
Breath, limb, and blood
Over what time I'll set upon
A bridge of being,
And you're the logical who knows the hurt,
The wrong, the wound, the mineral,
And you're the chemically chaste.

July 28ᵗʰ '31

XXVII

Even the voice will not last[,]
Master can but vanish
Like a shaft no deader self it has
Refracting till the colour snaps
Time place and like a bell the chiming strength.
Even the patient eye and gesture
Meaning in the lightest touch
Upon the heart or flesh
And sense usurping use in this [gesture][1]
Of innocence that's built on ignorance
Will not see this instant's sun and moon out[,]
[Can't][2] but vanish[,] too[,]
And leave such chaos
As will confuse the hush-voice left[,]
As will confuse.
I look Sir at my adumbrastic[3] navel
Though what I see won't help progress

But rather pen me in a pleasant insularity
Unbalancing devoid of humour
And the wise thoughts wait until the sea is calmer;
Then can they scud as sailessly[4]
Reach breathe and multiply
Within the chaos that my dying voice has helped
Has struck its note unknowing
And will again before it joins its gesture.
A footprint makes me homesick
For Glaucus or a scabrous hearth
For Pan and pot a novel death
Out of the names the cankered greeks.
[These words come too easily]

Aug 2ᵈ '31

XXVIII

True love's inflated; from a truthful shape
Hope blew it to a cylinder
Of faithfulness where there is none
However true we are in falsities,
Of ease where there can never be
But pain,
Made big the busy lines,
The easy contours daft with symmetry.
But lest the metal prove too strong
And break resistance down—
A minute only,
Weak not too weak—
I'll draw invective for a truthful sake
From what has gone of wisdom in a touch.
But thank pollution if the cylinder
O Love, becomes its shape again,

For what I do lies in your vainest heart
Which thrives on hope of more than I can offer,
Or anyone, or anyone
While there is time for time to age,
Make all sweet sour,
And there's time to die.

Aug: 8th '31

XXIX

Since, on a quiet night, I heard them talk
Who have no voices but the winds'
Of all the mystery there is in life
And all the mastery there is in death,
I have not lain an hour asleep
But troubled by their curious speech
Stealing so softly into the ears.
One says: There was a woman with no friend,
And, standing over the sea, she'd cry
Her lonliness[1] across the empty waves
Time after time.
And every voice:
Oblivion is as loverless;
Oblivion is as loverless.
And then again: There was a child
Upon the earth who knew no joy,
For there was no light in his eyes,
And there was no light in his soul.
Oblivion is as blind,
Oblivion is as blind,
I hear them say out of the darkness
Who have no talk but that of death.

Aug: 12th '31

I

XXX //

They are the only dead who did not love,
Lipless and tongueless in the sour earth
Staring at others, poor unlovers.
They are the only living who did love,
So are we full with strength,
Ready to rise, easy to sleep.
Who has completeness that can cut
A comic hour to an end through want of woman
And the warmth she gives,
And yet be human,
Feel the same soft blood flow thoroughly,
Have food and drink, unloving?
None, and his deadly welcome
At the hour's end
Shall prove unworthy for his doing,
Which was good at word,
But came from out the mouth unknowing
Of such great goodness as is ours.
There is no dead but is not loved
Awhile, a little,
Out of the fulness of another's heart
Having so much to spare.
That, then, is fortunate,
But, by your habit unreturned,
And by your habit unreturnable.
So is there missed a certain godliness
That's not without its woe,
And not without divinity,
For it can quicken or it can kill.

Look, there's the dead who did not love,
And there's the living who did love,
Around our little selves
Touching our seperate[1] love with badinage

Aug 16th

XXXI

Have old[1] on my heart utterly,
Or let it go; pierce through and through
Or leave unpierced,
For I am faithless as the rest,
And would, if you not love
Strong this day unto its finish
When comes its age and loss, relinquish
All, and take what thing I offer
As blithely to another lover,
Confessing, though it woundeth much,
Our love as such that passes at a glance,
A moving, or an itch.
[2]Not till the ripest fruit is fallen
Of what our meeting was,
And joy has given way to woe,
Not till there'll be a manner of regret
Springing out of the lithe morning
With every time of new caressing,
Oh, do not fear that I shall lessen
All that is old;
I warned you, lover, of a woeful host,
Of weariness at best and last;
Before death you should count the cost.

XXXII

The caterpillar is with child;
The leopard stirs his loin,
And there is temper in his cry,
And there is cunning in his stride,
A hard, sleek cataract of fear
Running through his yellow eyes,
Awareness of the insect's love,
A fibrous contact hard to touch
With paw, or side, or tongue.

Unless the sparrow's mating with the twig,
Their hands inlaced,
Here is your time that asks for reason;
The poor reply is lost in smiles,
The armadillo shaking his leather sides,
And Pierrot with a stolen Toby
Showing his teeth to Punch.
La la! Parisian lady,
You've a way with men,
And I've a way with words there's no denying,
But now I snap my fingers.
Do, do, a pet for bed;
Sleep with his fur upon your skin;
His tongue's for kissing.
When you were young . . .
        Too many songs,
        Too little tears,
Inflection in the rising voice
Means now it's over, and the sun's gone down.

Play on my mouth,
Or blow along a bird's feather.

January 1931

XXXIII //

Foot, head, or traces
Are on sandy soil their spirit level;
Their level is the length
Of foot or head we'll be the time
In tracing
For a purpose (head to foot is head and foot,
             No wit, is one),
That'll make, it's brittle, diaphram
For use of sense, (no hurt no sense).
Foot head compressed,
It's easy tracing what each gives the other
By toe or foot to common good,
             (Good for can run
             And know why run),
Though, after's done, I
See the reason for undoubling doubling not,
Unless for poetry, which, if it asks me
For a spirit, can
Run and know why
And know why know, no wit,
Can ever further,
Though no ask brings it
For a lazy sake that won't create
But plumb such depths as you,
Original, derive.

18ᵗʰ August '31

XXXIV

[When you have ground such beauty down to dust
As flies before your breath,
And, at the touch, trembles with lover's fever,
Or sundered it to look the closer,
Magnified and made immense
At one side's loss,
Turn inside out, and see at glance
Wisdom is folly, love is not,
Sense can but maim it, wisdom mar it,
Folly purify and make it true.
For folly was
When wisdom lay not in the soul,
But in the body of the trees and stones,
Was when sense found a way to them
Growing on hills or shining under water.
Come wise in foolishness,
Go silly and be Christ's good brother,
He whose lovers were both wise and sensible
When folly stirred, warm in the foolish heart.]

XXXV

Or be my paramour or die,
Lie or be lost to love,
Give up your gravity
Holding a too-heavy heart,
And take a gaiety without regret.
For let love go by a time
It goes for ever,

Each lighest[1] kiss the last
From one or any lover,
Each single motion of the hand,
The head, the breast, is unrepeated,
And the body, not to last, has not kith nor ghost.

XXXVI

The womb and the woman's grave
Lie near, the thumb and thread
Are gone—no labour'll thrive
Which asketh not from God
Some strength no labour has.
Womb was for life she gave,
And woman was;
Grave was for death she hath.
She takes and she returns
From God and then to God,
Gives what her body had
And takes a little death from Him
Not one man can.

XXXVII

Let Sheba bear a love for Solomon
Out of her woman's heart and her content
That bridges time and like the morning sun
Lays its bright rod on all contempt,
For she was young in years and rich in fare,
Woman as you are woman but love dies—
The song of Solomon upon the ways of men,
Love dies, dies as the rose or fruit,

Leaf, hand, or animal,
Is and is not,
The words that bridge content and time,
Is and is not.

XXXVIII

There was one world and there is another,
For in our life we're dead as wood,
No bones or blood,
Out of a wooden mother,
And in our death learning such truth
As thought and told
That wood shall rot, but wood shan't rot.
The heavy night we breathe's unlit
When the heart stops,
Unstarred when the veins [be][1] chill,
And, night or night, the same remorse
Heavy on head and heart,
Oblivion or oblivion, the same heartbreak
Under and over the earth.

XXXIX

For us there cannot be welcome
For sleep at the day's end or the night's end
For many a time of tiredness,
For welcoming sleep we welcome death,
And death's an end to sleep,
And sleep to death, an end to love,
Ending and sleeping,
Love sleeps and ends for it cannot last.

And if we love we sleep,
Love, sleep, and end, for
Love is sleep, and ends and sleeps;
All can be compassed thus therin,[1]
Love, sleep, and death the only plan.

Sept 11th

XL

An end to substance in decay's a sequence
Showing here and there a sign of wear,
Used as it is by man and beast,
Turned by the artist to an alchemy,
So we have tired of dying,
Tired like Lot of the flesh
But turning it not to salt but to romance,
And with one gesture
Drowning the hare-lipped gods
For one unstained to rise up from the depths.
Mother who bore me loved unchemically,
Mixing her acids with a mans[1]
For other than a physic urge,
And I borne[2] from her pain
Have, too, coarsened another's blood.
So are we tired of reality;
My rubber hands upon your flesh
Owe nothing to it,
Wise, spiritual hands; our reek is scent;
Our sweat is wine,
And all our dropping blood's symbolic.
Let's prick the young man he can't bleed,
But a stream of thin water will flow from him,
Let's kill the young man he don't care

For without any blood he don't wish to live,
And who took his blood and who took his blood
And you took his blood, and I took his blood,
Wanting to die for we got no blood,
No guts or no bones to catch on the stones.
Take an emetic, some strong emotion,
Suck it down deep with no reaction,
Do not be steady for that was the ruin of me.
I think I am steady for a time
Not savage any more but steady
I who am steady was once savage
I was savage but now I am steady.

Sept 11th

XLI

Why is the blood red and the grass green
Shant[1] be answered till the voice is still
That dryeth[2] the veins with its moan
Of man and his meaning, for the voice is cruel
That dryeth[2] the veins from the vines
And the blood from the high hills.
It shall be Job's voice or Israel's voice,
Or the voice from the wilderness,
That cryeth[3] for reason till the night is won
Or the still night begun,
And man has no meaning, for the blood says,
And who taught it red, and the grass which is green.
He has no meaning but the blood's.
Shall it be wise then to make a mystery of nothing
Until the mysterious blood is questioned.[4]
He has no meaning but the blood's;
He has no knowing, be he wiser than his veins,

Of love and the passing of time,
A breath, step and gesture; he lifteth his hand
But he is not seen.

Sept: 12th

XLII

Have cheated constancy
Of mood and love,
Have worn stuff thin
That made air fit to breathe
And the dark brain cool
When lover lay for man to touch
Untouched by any other,
Have cheated mood, have not been chaste[1]
Shall we then suffer
For the cauldron of the brain's not cool
Through lover leaving man for other kisses
Soft as they were soft upon the cavernous lips?
Have cheated constancy,
Am knave stealing all to give nothing,
Lover untouched by any but all,
And the dark brain's cool again
Under a second constancy
Of lover, lover, and the soft-lipped lover.

21st September '31

XLIII

There's plenty in the world that doth not die,
And much that lives to perish,
That rises and then falls, buds but to wither;

The season's sun, though he should know his setting
Up to the second of the dark coming,
Death sights and sees with no misgiving
A rib of cancer on the fluid sky.
But we, shut in the houses of the brain,
Brood on each hothouse plant
Spewing its sapless leaves around,
And watch the hand of time unceasingly
Ticking the world away,
Shut in the madhouse call for cool air to breathe.
There's plenty that doth die;
Time can not heal nor resurrect;
And yet, mad with young blood or stained with age,
We still are loth to part with what remains,
Feeling the wind about our heads that does not cool,
And on our lips the dry mouth of the rain.
Plenty that dieth like to man and his;
Death take us all and close the tired lids.

September 24th '31

XLIV

This time took has much
In breath[1] and width with that
Old other known as pressure,
For it's love one word or not,
Though call it god and hurt me,
Heat and offend the widow,
Each to his seperate[2] lesson
To mould, alone, masonic reason.
And baby-do is baby-come,
Out of the infant's mouth
Learn what is infant truth,

See what the boy writes on the wall,
The facts of being in a doggerel.
This time took
Holds the same lie as any girl's,
Love's a descension of the drawers
An earlier time and now;
Pressure may change,
The widow's word confess to age,
And mine be burnt with vinegar,
Shall not disturb or alter,
Breath³ with the girl's or regular.

Sept:ʼ 30ᵗʰ ʼ31

XLV

Which of you put out his rising,
And turned his flame into a blind wick,
Of you pale-minded virgins which shook down your tress
Onto his lifted face, who is so pitiless,
Can wipe away the thought of passion like a crumb,
Hates him for loving, hates him,
Who, narrow-necked, broke all his heart,
Left it among the cigarette-ends and the glasses?
Would for a moment she conceal all else,
And open out to him her grassy arms
With, "Undisturbed, loin undisturbed
On lap for pillow, of the moving breast,
Peace on thy resting head."
O women, lead him by the hand;
O women, lead me by the hand;
Take this my hand;
Take this his hand.

October 15ᵗʰ.

XLVI //
WRITTEN FOR A PERSONAL EPITAPH.

Feeding the worm
Who do I blame
Because laid down
At last by time,
Here under the earth with girl and thief,
Who do I blame?
Mother I blame
Whose loving crime
Moulded my form
Within her womb,
Who gave me life and then the grave,
Mother I blame.
Here is her labour's end,
Dead limb and mind,
All love and sweat
Gone now to rot.
I am man's reply to every question,
His aim and destination.

17th Oct '31

XLVII

When you have ground such beauty down to dust
As flies before the breath
And, at the touch, trembles with lover's fever,
Or sundered it to look the closer,
Magnified and made immense
At one side's loss,

Turn inside out, and see at glance
Wisdom is folly, love is not,
Sense can but maim it, wisdom mar it,
Folly purify and make it true.
For folly was
When wisdom lay not in the soul
But in the body of the trees and stones,
Was when sense found a way to them
Growing on hills or shining under water.
Come wise in foolishness,
Go silly and be Christ's good brother,
He whose lovers were both wise and sensible
When folly stirred, warm in the foolish heart.

Oct: 10th '31

XLVIII

Sever from what I trust
The things, this time, I love,
Death and the shy entanglement of sense
Crying for age to bless its sad sobriety;
It's blind and out of tune,
Moving symmetrically in chaos
Day through till we're all older,
Wise to the seasons' touch on us
Of hope, and time, and sun.
Death out of sense,
Then what I love I trust,
And, careless child again,
Am, from your look and smile,
Same head-in-air.

July '31

XLVIX //

Never to reach the oblivious dark
And not to know
Any man's troubles nor your own—
Negatives impress negation,
Empty of light and find the darkness lit—
Never is nightmare,
Never flows out from the wound of sleep
Staining the broken brain
With knowledge that no use and nothing worth
Still's vain to argue after death;
No use to run your head against the wall
To find a sweet blankness in the blood and shell,
This puss[1] runs deep.
There's poison in your red wine, drinker,
Which spreads down to the dregs
Leaving a corrupted vein of colour,
Sawdust beneath the skirts;
On every hand the evil's positive
For dead or live,
Froth or a moment's movement
All hold the sum, nothing to nothing,
Even the words are nothing
While the sun's turned to salt,
Can be but vanity, such an old cry,
Nothing never, nothing older
Though we're consumed by loves and doubts.
I love and doubt, it's vain, it's vain,
Loving and doubting like one who is to die
Planning what's good, though it's but winter,

When spring is come,
The jonquil and the trumpet.

*Oct 26*th

L
Introductory Poem.

So that his philosophy be proven
Let the philosopher go to the oven,
And the wise man from the fools
Escape under the motor-wheels.
[Thus [we]¹ defy all poetry
By staying in this aviary.]

October

LI

Take up this seed, it is most beautiful,
Within its husk opening in fire and air
Into a flower's stem and a flower's mouth,
To lean upon the wall of summer
And touch the lips of the dark wind.
Lift up this seed; life from its circle
Spins towards light,
Full-voiced from many seasons' sounds
And, in a fruit's fall or a bird's fall,
Is one with all plants in the earth's well,
Such is its miracle.
Touch these broad leaves, all fiery-veined,
Touch these green leaves and this fair stalk;
Fair as they are the seed is fairer,

K

Budding to light out of it's¹ own darkness;
What once was hot beneath the earth's as cool as rain,
As sweet as rain, as falling soft as snow;
What lay unknowing in the soil
Of any weariness at all
Now droops and sleeps at the day's end,
And at its hour's end lets death be friend and comforter.
What once was beautiful is dead,
Was sweet is sour.

LII

There in her tears were laughter and tears again,
O so unstable, never to love for long
While the body's full of the heart's pain
And the heart breaks down
A mechanism oiled with lily's sap
And weighed with age,
O so unstable, no time is actual

I know this minute counts in the blood
Rising to the nerves' rim to fall again
But in the heart no easy pyramid,
O so unstable, in the blood and brain
But in the heart no more than water
Than tears which flow with laughter,
O so unstable, which will run with tears.

November 3ʳᵈ '31

LIII

How can the knotted root
Be trapped in a snare of syllables,

The tendril or, what's stranger, the high flower
Caught, like a ferret though a thought it is,
Inside a web of words,
Taken for good, each moving feature.[1]
Get your gardener in some notes,
But not his thoughts
Creaking on barrow-wheels along the gravel,
They won't be stopped or snared;
Spoon them about with honey,
His or mine, they're easier stuck than barred in;
Easier to have a ferret than a bird in,
So lay on sweet words,
Lay on neat words,
The only way[2] the world knows;
I have you in my dung as inescapably
As you in your hive, and quite as capably.

5ᵗʰ & 6ᵗʰ Nov '31

LIV

Children of darkness got no wings,
This we know we got no wings,
Stay, dramatic figures, tethered down
By weight of cloth and fact,
Crystal or funeral, got no hope
For us that knows misventure
Only as wrong; but shan't the genius fail,
Gliding, rope-dancing, is his fancy,
Better nor us can't gainsay walking,
Who'll break our necks upon the pavement
Easier than he upon the ice.
For we are ordinary men,
Sleep, wake, and sleep, eat, love, and laugh,

With wide, dry mouths and eyes,
Poor, petty vermin,
Stink of cigarettes and armpits,
Cut our figures, and retreat at night
Into a double or a single bed,
The same thoughts in our head.
We are ordinary men,
Bred in the dark behind the skirting-board,
Crying with hungry voices in our nest.

Children of darkness got no wings,
This we know, we got no wings,
Stay, in a circle chalked upon the floor,
Waiting all vainly this we know.

October.

LV

It's not in misery but in oblivion,
Not vertically in a mood of joy
Screaming the spring
Over the ancient winter,
He'll lie down, and our breath
Will chill the roundness of his cheeks,
And make his wide mouth home.
For we must whisper down the funnel
The love we had and glory in his blood
Coursing along the channels
Until the spout dried up
That flowed out of the soil
All seasons with the same meticulous power,
But the veins must fail.
He's not awake to the grave

Though we cry down the funnel,
Splitting a thought into such hideous moments
As drown, over and over, this fever.
He's dead, home, has no lover,
But our speaking does not thrive
In the bosom, or the empty channels.
Our evil, when we breathe it,
Of dissolution and the empty fall,
Won't harm the tent around him,
Uneaten and not to be pierced
By us in sin or us in gaiety.
And who shall tell the amorist
Oblivion is so loverless.

                              March. '31

LVI

What lunatic's whored after shadow,
Followed the full-voiced stream
To stoop and taste it vinegar,
Can find the body anything but shade,
That, too, wet with his tears,
And anything but acid the clear water?
He shall be fed with dreams till there's no other food
But sickens or sits wearily,
Shall look for woman,
And shall lie with cloud.
Then has the written word
To give the love he haggard lacked from her,
The lifted note and the carven stone
Be his mate, and his kiss, and his company.

Mad, mad, praising the sweep from neck to breasts,

This woman's celluloid; drip your contagious thoughts
Into the basin;
Mad, mad with other's lunacy
That pares the substance off the rind,
Hot with their written heat,
And when the page is turned, oh stone, cold stone!
None know why the heart is vexed,
And the lax brain,
When loving means nothing, housed in the bosom
Man feels no safety in his heart,
And goes away, and goes away.
Lunatic, was she not mate, and kiss, and company?
She was all that to me.

November '31

LVII

Here is a fact for my teeth
That I've snapped off the bone,
Robs death of its comforter,
That bites good and deep,
There's much sense in sleep.
I own negation, we are the lie-a-bed,
Lie-a-lap, wind-in-our-heads,
Knowing all's nothing,
Worth nothing, ends nothing,
We own negation.
Head in the oven, no nearer heaven,
Full-veined, we may be empty,
The good we get
In [slowly] for an empty end
Senselessly lifting food to mouth, and food to mouth,
To keep the senseless being going.

LVIII

Any matter move it to conclusion
Begs for a refuge with the bone
So any talk carefree as words can
Down in the sweet-smelling earth
Takes start and end into the warmth
All argument speaker not a nickel's worth

And[1] handymaid shall split the apple
For Eve and her soft-bellied both
And ladling or half-leaved
Both fit for bull and man
Bull not complaining and man shall not envy
Eve's and her evil not for a moment's thought.

Any matter start it with levity[,]
Brevity[,] poetry[,]
Brimmed with sure fire spit it up
Out and the air's as fresh as cider-cheek
Breast fit for sipping and chin to chuck.

January '32

LVIV

Too long, skeleton, death's risen
Out of the soil and seed into the drive,
Chalk cooled by leaves in the hot season,
Too long, skeleton, death's all alive
From nape to toe, a sanatorium[1] piece
Clean as a whistle, rid of fleas.

Take now content, no longer posturing
As raped and reaped, the final emblem.
Thy place is filled, bones bid for auction,
The prism of the eye now void by suction,
New man best whose breast hangs low,
Rather than charnel-house as symbol
Of the moment and the dead hour.

Jan 20 '32

LVV

No man knows lovliness[1] at all,
Though he be beauty blessed,
Who has not known the lovliness[1] of May,
The blossoms and the throated trees
Lifting their branches lit with singing birds
Into the laden air;
Neither can woman, though she be peacock-fair,
And, like the peacock, proudly dressed,
Know all of love who has not known this lovers' season.

What can I make out of it all,
Flowers, trees, birds, and so much singing?
No man, I said, knows lovliness[1] at all,
Nor woman love.
But this is true, and the high words
Flutter to the ground beside this truth.

April '32

LVVI

Do thou heed me, cinnamon smelling,
Crying my blind love across the brain,

With every tingling nerve
Bidding thee bend who will not kiss and mate.
Vein calls to vein but the heart says vanity,
Colder she is than the water's face;
Cinnamon-smelling,
Print my kiss on thy left breast and thy right.
(Fragment. April '32.)

LVVII

They said, tired of trafficking,
The sea moves and man moves blind,
While the sea moved calm
And man, obsessed,
Moved like a mole within his fleshy prison,
Taking how gladly the lips' poison,
And, as they told, obsessed
With drink and work, the tame machines,
Money, graft, lust and incest.
All this to drive him mad, they said,
Too blind, mad, too, themselves,
Men in disease and women mad in hospitals.
The world is growing up,
And what fits father'll fit the world,
Will hurt they said, but will be worn,
Is growing up to be a man,
Though man, their logic, is both daft and drunk,
And cannot close his [[riddled] eaten] lids.
May 5 1932.

LVVIII

Be silent let who will
Speak ill of age

Who does not advocate
The oven or the old adage
Drink and be merry
Tom Dick and Harry
For tomorrow if not dead
One's old or mad.

May '32

LVVIV

Being but men, we walked into the trees
Afraid, letting our syllables be soft
For fear of waking the rooks,
For fear of coming
Noislessly[1] into a world of wings and cries.

If we were children we might climb,
Catch the rooks sleeping, and break no twig,
And, after the soft ascent,
Thrust out our heads above the branches
To wonder at the unfailing stars.

Out of confusion, as the way is,
And the wonder that man knows,
Out of the chaos would come bliss.

That, then, is lovliness[2] we said,
Children in wonder watching the stars,
Is the aim and the end.

Being but men we walked into the trees.

May 7th '32

LVVV

The hunchback in the park,
A solitary mister
Propped between trees and water,
Going daft for fifty seven years,
Is [getting]¹ dafter,
A cripple children call at,
Half-laughing, by no other name than mister,
They shout hey mister
Running when he has heard them clearly
Past lake and rockery
On out of sight.

There is a thing he makes when quiet comes
To the young nurses with the children
And the three veteran swans,
Makes a thing inside the hanging head,
[A]² figure without fault
And sees it on the gravel paths
Or walking on the water.

The figure's frozen all the winter
Until the summer melts it down
To make a figure without fault.
[It is a poem and it is a woman figure.]

Mister, the children call, hey mister,
And the hunchback in the park
Sees the³ figure on the water,
Misty, now mistier,
⁴Hears it's⁵ woman's voice;

Mister, it calls, hey mister,[6]
[And the hunchback smiles.]

May 9th '32

LVVVI

Out of the sighs a little comes,
But not of grief for I have vanquished that
Before the agony. The spirit grows,
Forgets, and cries.
A little comes, is tasted and found good;
All could not dissapoint;[1]
There must, be praised, some certainty,
If not of loving well, then not,[2]
[And that is true after perpetual defeat.]

After such fighting as the weakest know
There's more than dying;
[Can][3] lose the pain or stuff the wound,
But ache too long through no regret
Of leaving woman waiting, saving, lying,
For her warrior stained with split[4] words
That spill such acrid blood.

June 7

Here is a beauty on a bough I can't translate
Through words or love,
So high it is, a bird unto his mate
Singing to prove
That in each note she lives for him again

A fledgling in the fall of winter rain.
Him would I be if to your mind
I could but sing for proof
That, though to you my crying soul's assigned,
I hold aloof,
Seeing a thousand times your bright smile glance
Across to me, without your love, and all by chance.

At last, in hail and rain,
The family failings lose the gain
Made by these ten years' [reading][1]:—
Enterprise, [machine],[2] and devildom
All [windward][3] of the [cleft][4] skies.

[Rain][5] blew the man down
Who could not stand such strain,
For [work][6] to live is [work][7] to die,
And labour's lost in venom.

The [collier lad][8] has [found][9] his master;[10]
[He is a rake on holiday,
But master goes prancing from a family malady
To words or melody,
Smiling with cigarette and stick,
Going no place, no place at all.]
                                        [*May.*]

Upon your held-out hand
Count the endless days until they end,

Feel, as the pulse grows tired,
The angels' wings beating about your head
Unsounding, they beat so soft.
Why count so sadly?
Learn to be merry with the merriest,
Or (change the key!) give vent to utterances
As meaningless as the bells (oh change the life!),
The sideboard fruit, the ferns, the picture houses
And the pack of cards.

When I was seven I counted four and forty trees
That stood before my window,
Which may or not be relevant
And symbolise[1] the maddening factors
That madden both watchers and actors.
I've said my piece: count or go mad.
The new asylum on the hill
Leers down the valley like a fool
Waiting and watching for your fingers to fail
To keep count of the stiles
The thousand sheep
Leap over to my criss-cross rhythms
I've said my piece.

June 25 '32

Nearly summer, and the devil
Still comes visiting his poor relations,
If not in person sends his unending evil
By messangers,[1] the flight of birds
Spelling across the sky his devil's news,
The seasons[2] cries, full of his intimations.

He has the whole field now, the gods departed
Who cannot count the seeds he sows,
The law allows,
His wild carouses, and his lips
Pursed at the ready ear
To whisper, when he wants, the senses' war
Or lay the senses' rumour.
The welcome devil comes as guest,
Steals what is best—the body's splendour—
Rapes, leaves for lost (the amorist!),
Counts on his fist
All he has reaped in wonder.

The welcome devil comes invited,
Suspicious but that soon passes.
They cry to be taken, and the devil breaks
All that is not already broken,
Leaves it among the cigarette ends and the glasses
                                              April '32

Pome

How the birds had become talkative,
No longer criss-cross on the sky
Or flying—lo there razor foot—
Near to water—lo there foam foe[1]
Brusing[2] the long waves with thy wing,
On branches over his metal shoulder
Crouching and talking,
But for his cold intelligence
Breaking the sky with song.
To him they trilled, running their golden ladders up and down;
He heard no syllables,

And so missed what divinity
Their messages could hold for man unmaidened
And with helmet multiplying sun on sun
Till all the metal was parhelion.

June '32

Were that enough, enough to ease the pain,
Feeling regret when this is wasted
That made me happy in the sun
And, sleeping, made me dream
How much was happy while it lasted,
Were vaguenesses enough, and the sweet lies plenty,
Then hollow words could bear all suffering,
And cure me of ills.
Were this enough—bone, blood, and sinew,
The twisted brain, the fair formed loin,[1]
Groping for matter under the dog's plate—
Man should be cured of distemper.
For all there is to give I offer:
Crumbs, barn, and halter.

July 1

Poems.

This Book Started February 1, 1933.

One.

Sweet as [a dog's][1] kiss night sealed
New faith, and dark the new friend fell,
With an ease and a smoothness I knew of old,
Irregular cries in the wind
Meaning no more than before, but with peace,
Peace of the grave, grave images,
Lending what wounded when light,[2]
Hurt the nerves and the heavy heart,
New light, grave light.

With night's coming was going,
Night's faces stared out the day's,
Smiles and white teeth giving place
To coldstone gazing through the ice,
Unchanging, unmoving, coldfrost.
Night's voices drowned the day's.

Companionship with night has turned
Each ugly corpse into a friend,
And there are more friends if you wish[—][3]
The maggots feasting on dead flesh,
The vulture with appraising beak,
The redcheeked vampire at the neck,
There is the skeleton and the naked ghost.
Friend of the night, you are friend of the night's friends.

Night's music crept through the tunnels

Of sleep, sleep of the grave, cracked passages,
Sounded fever of sounds soon dying,
Dark messages, terrors before waking,
Of the terrors of men, of men broken,
Maimed men and men killed by smiles,
By the lifting of Leah's hand
And the patient drooping of Rachel's head.

The fever passed, hot palms
Were cool again, touched by the night.
What were dreams between friends
Ran through sleep to dead ends,
[Unwholesome thoughts struck sanitary checks,
Taut thoughts were lax,]
Kind as a dog, the night,
Night of the grave, grave night,
Made its friends yours—the skeleton,
The eaten corpse, the black moth,
Symbols of peace and death—
For you are the night's friend,
Friend of the grave, grave friend.

February 1 1933.

Two.

It is death though I have died
Many deaths, and have risen again
With an unhealed wound and a cracked heart,
It is death to sink again
My breath and blood into another
Who, too, has been wounded, has shown fight,
Has been killed, raised with a cracked heart
And is ready for the hundredth dying,

Ready to perish again and be hurt, is mad.
It is death to sink or to refuse,
Death either way.
Let me love then and let my old corpse lie
Among my other skeletons
Staring into the cracked sky.

February 2 '33.

Three.

Had she not loved me at the beginning
There would have been no beginning,
Life in my mouth would not have tasted surely,
I would not have gone up to the places of the angels,
[Seen heaven, known hell,]¹ known life [turn]² in my mouth
From vinegar to sugar and then to vinegar again.
There would have been no beginning,
End would have come before the wind of heaven
[Stirred],³ like a [lizard],⁴ [in]⁵ my hair.
My hands would not have changed to snakes.

[I planted a rose in her head.
 I parted the serpents on her brow,
 And drew the maggots from her breast.]

Four.

Before the gas fades with a harsh last bubble,
And the hunt in the hatstand discovers no coppers,
Before the last fag and the shirt sleeves and slippers,
The century's trap will have snapped round your middle,
Before the allotment is weeded and sown,

And the oakum is picked, and the spring trees have grown
   green,
[And the state falls to bits,
  And is fed to the cats,]
  Before civilization rises or rots,
  (It's a matter of guts,
  Graft, poison, and bluff,
  Sobstuff, mock reason,
  The chameleon coats of the big bugs and shots,)
  The jaws will have shut, and life be switched out.
  Before the arrival of angel or devil,
  Before evil or good, light or dark,
  Before white or black, the right or left sock,
  Before good or bad luck.

Man's manmade sparetime lasts the four seasons,
Is empty in springtime, and no other time lessens
The bitter, the wicked, the longlying leisure,
Sleep punctured by waking, dreams
Broken by choking,
The hunger of living, the oven and gun
That turned on and lifted in anger
Make the hunger for living
When the purse is empty
And the belly is empty,
The harder to bear and the stronger.
The century's trap will have closed for good
About you, flesh will perish, and blood
Run down the world's gutters,
Before the world steadies, stops rocking, is steady,
Or rocks, swings and rocks, before the world totters.

Caught in the trap's machinery, lights out,
With sightless eyes and hearts that do not beat,

You will not see the steadying or falling,
Under the heavy layers of the night
Not black or white or left or right.

Feb 6, 33.

Five.

Hold on whatever slips beyond the edge
To hope, a firefly in the veins, to trust
Of loving, to keeping close, lest
Words set septic, the loving thinking, [grudge
Not others' trust, to trample not to dust
The others' closekept loves with merciless hooves,]¹
To what's unharmed by truths and lies, stays
Fixed fair in the brain, its closet shut
From wind and speech and this and that.

Was there a time when any fiddles,
Moaning in unison, could stop day troubles,
Start some new loving, cure ten aches?
There was a time I could cry over books.
But time has [set]² its maggots on my track.

This laststraw hope, secure from blight[,]
And trust of loving what the seconds' germs
Have left unfouled, must never see the light.
Under the arc of the sky they are unsafe;
What's never known is safest in this life;
Under the skysigns you who have no arms
Have cleanest hands; out of the grave the ghost
[Is least unhurt],³ having no heart; you with no ears
Shall not be killed by words. And the blind man sees best.

Feb. 8. '33.

Six.

After the funeral[1] mule praises, brays,
Shaking of mule heads, betoken
Grief at the going to the earth of man
Or woman,[2] at yet another long woe broken,[2]
Another theme to play on[1] and surprise
Fresh faults and till then hidden flaws[1]
Faded beyond ears and eyes,[2]
At [he or she],[3] loved or else hated well,
So far from love or hate[,] in a deep hole.

The mourners in their Sabbath black[4]
Drop[5] tears unheeded or choke back a sob,
Join[6] in the hymns, and mark with dry bright looks
The other heads,[7] [bent],[8] spying,[9] on black books.

Death has rewarded him or her for living,
With generous hands has slain with little pain,
[Wounded with a sharp sword,]
And let the ancient face die with a [smile].[10]

Another gossips' toy has lost its use,
Broken lies buried amid broken toys,
Of flesh and bone lies hungry for the flies,
Waits for the natron and the mummy paint[,]
With dead lips pursed and dry bright eyes,
Another well of rumours and cold lies
Has dried[, and one more [joke][11] has lost its point.][12]

Feb 10. '33.

Seven.

"We who [are]¹ young are old. It is the oldest cry.
Age sours before youth's tasted in the mouth
And any sweetness that it [hath]²
Is sucked away."

We who are still young are old. It is a dead cry,
The squeal of the damned out of the old pit.
We have grown weak before we could grow strong,
For us there is no shooting and no riding,
The Western man has lost one lung
And cannot mount a clotheshorse without bleeding.

Until the whisper of the last trump louden
We shall play Chopin in our summer garden,
With half-averted heads, as if to listen,
Play Patience in the parlour after dark.
For us there is no riding and no shooting,
No frosty gallops through the winter park.
We who are young sit holding yellow hands
[Before the fire, and [hearken]³ to the wind.]⁴

Feb 16 '33

Eight.

To take to give is all, return what given
Is [throwing]¹ manna back to heaven,²
[Receive, not asking, and examine
Is looking gift god in the mouth.]

To take to leave is pleasing death;[3]
Unpleasant death will take at last[,]
All currencies[4] of the marked breath.
Surrender at the very first
Is paying twice the final cost.

Nine.//
(Conclusion of Poem Seven)

No faith to fix the teeth on carries
Men old before their time into dark valleys
Where death lies dead asleep, one bright eye open,
No faith to sharpen the old wits leaves us
Lost in the shades, no course, no use
To fight through the invisible weeds,
No faith to follow is the world's curse
That falls on chaos.

There is but one message for the earth,
Young men with fallen chests and old men's breath,
Women with cancer at their sides
And cancerous speaking dripping from their mouths,
And lovers turning on the gas,
Exsoldiers with horrors for a face,
A pig's snout for a nose,
The lost in doubt, the nearly mad, the young
Who, undeserving, have suffered the earth's wrong,
The living dead left over from the war,
The living after, the filled with fear,
The caught in the cage, the broken winged,
The flying loose, albino eyed, wing singed,
The white, the black, the yellow and mulatto
From Harlem, Bedlam, Babel, and the Ghetto,

The Picadilly[1] men, the back street drunks,
The grafters of cats' heads on chickens'[2] trunks,
The whole, the crippled, the weak and strong,
The Western man with one lung gone—
Faith fixed beyond the spinning stars,
Fixed faith, believing and worshipping together
In god or gods, christ or his father,
Mary, virgin, or any other.
Faith. Faith. Firm faith in many or one,
Faith fixed like a star beyond the stars,
And the skysigns and the night lights,
And the shores of the last sun.

We who are young are old, and unbelieving,
Sit at our hearths from morning until evening,
Warming dry hands and [hearkening][3] to the [wind].[4]
We have no faith to set between our teeth.
Believe, believe and be saved, we cry, who have no faith.
                                        Feb 17 '33.

                    Ten.

Out of a war of wits, when folly of words
Was the world's to me, and syllables
Fell hard as whips on an old wound,
My brain came crying into the fresh light,
Called for confessor but there was none
To purge after the wits' fight,
And I was struck dumb by the sun.
Praise that my body be whole, I've limbs[1]
Not stumps[1] after the hour of battle,
For the body's brittle and the skin's white.
Praise that only the wits are hurt after the wits' fight.

[The sun shines strong, dispells
  Where men are men men's smells.]
  Overwhelmed by the sun, with a torn brain
  I stand beneath the clouds' confessional,
  But the hot beams rob me of speech,
  After the perils of [fools']² talk
  Reach asking arms up to the milky sky,
  After a volley of questions and replies
  Lift wit-hurt head [up] for sun to sympathise,³
  And the sun heals, closing sore eyes.
  It is good that the sun shine,
  And, after it has sunk, the sane moon,
  For out of a house of matchboard and stone
  Where men would argue till the stars be green,
  It is good to step onto the earth¹ alone¹
  And be struck dumb, if only for a time.

February 22 '33

Eleven.

In wasting one drop from the heart's honey cells,
One precious drop that, for the moment, quells
Desire's pain, eases love's itch and ills,
There's less remains, for only once love fills,
When love's mouth knows its greatest thirst.
That great love, in its passion, demands all
The honey that man had at first
Before, unthinkingly, he shared its gold
With one and all, being love's child.
In those far days he was not very old
In love, knew little of love's wrong.
Wrong love took much, and when love's¹ mouth called,

In earnest from a woman's face,
Little there was to moisten of the honey hoard.

Feb 23 '33.

Twelve.

With all the fever of the August months,
The winter convalesence,[1]
In this damned world there's little to moan over
But the passing of the one and the coming of the other.
Lines of verse call out their echoes,
The lambs at teat with every rural note
Blown out of the tin-whistle,
Jerk infirm legs and patter little feet,
Goats describe a measure at the flute[2]
[Of every nature-writer from Fleet-street.]
Though sucked year in year out
There's life in the earth's teat still.
What life in the pit of the soul?
Dry as an adder, it's a dark hole.
(Squeeze with the top of a cracked quill
Farts out of a dead mule).

A crazy man, who might pass minutes
Of a bad day, when his thoughts slunk
Up all the [dead][3] ends, blind drunk,
In laughing fits at cul-de-sacs and sanities,
Might, in the dark, under the sheets' warmth,
Find some few things to cherish on the earth,
Under the layers of a mad mind
Perceive the gropings after love, and blind
As a mole, know not that what is cherished perishes.

With flowers to smell and fruits to eat,
He knows the horrible desires.
With winter passing and near heat
Of summer, knows the killings and cures,
(Kill to stop what will be stopped,
And cure to delay).
With rags on the ragged bones and a bent hat
A crazy man might make some good
Out of a bad day.
The seasons are
Nothing more
Than [numerical][4] markings from one to four,
With little for a sane man to deplore
But the passing[5] of one and the coming[6] of one more.

End of Feb. '33

Thirteen. //

Their faces shone under some radiance
Of mingled moonlight and lamplight
That turned the empty kisses into meaning,
The island of such penny love
Into a costly country, the graves
That neighboured them to wells of warmth,
(And skeletons had sap). One minute
Their faces shone; the midnight rain
Hung pointed in the wind,
Before the moon shifted and the sap ran out,
She, in her [cheap][1] frock, saying some [cheap] thing,
And he replying,
Not knowing radiance came and passed.
The suicides parade again, now ripe for dying.

Fourteen.

I have longed to move away
From the hissing of the spent lie;
And the old terrors' continual cry
Growing more terrible as the day
Goes over the hill into the deep sea,
Night, careful of topography,
Climbs over the coal-tips where children play;
And the repetition of salutes
For ladies, the stale acts of the mutes;
And the thunder far off but not far enough
Of friendships turned to ghosts' hates
By telephone calls or notes,
For there are ghosts in the air
And ghostly echoes on paper;
I have longed to move but am afraid.

Some life, yet unspent, might explode
Out of the lie hissing on the ground
Like some sulphurous reminder of November,
And, cracking into the air, leave me half blind.
This must be avoided at all costs.
I would not care to die at the hands of ghosts,
Or lose my eyes through the last sparks of half lies.
Neither by night's ancient fear,
The parting of hat from hair,
Pursed lips at the receiver,
Shall I fall to death's feather.
The terror of night is a half terror,
Day no sharer of the black horror,
Out of the hours' span, half

Alone allowing the last thief
To breathe, stopping breath;
Salutation is a half convention
Regaining impoliteness when the hat's in position,
Half decorum kills what's left
Of the sane half no need to lift;
Then there is the sweet smile
And the snake's head grinning in the soul;
These are the smiles of night and day;
What I see is a half smile,
Half convention and half lie;
By these I would not care to die.

March 1 '33

Sixteen.

The waking in a single bed when light
Fell on the upturned oval of her face
And morning's sun shone vast in the sky,
(Her last nights' lover), is gone forever,
Her [legal honour]¹ sold to one man for good
Who will disturb the [rhythms]² of her blood.
Where there was one are two, and nothing's shared
Of love and light in all this spinning world
Save the love-light of half love smeared
Over the countenance of the [two-backed]³ beast
[Which nothing knows of rest but lust]
And [lust],⁴ love knows, soon perishes the [breast],⁵
Reducing the [rose],⁶ for want of a [lovlier]⁷
Image on the ghost of paper,
Of single love to dust.

No longer with its touch kind as a mother's

Will the vibrations of [day][8] settle on
The pillow in [pale][9] lights where once she [lay][10] alone,
Heart [hardly beating][11] under its [frame][12] of ribs,
Lips catching the honey of the golden
[Sun][13] small as a farthing
[Hiding][14] behind a cloud, for where
She lies another lies at her side,
And through his circling arm she feels
The secret coursing of his[15] blood
[Filling her fingers with a hundred pins
Each sharper than the last.
And the [moon][16] -ghost no longer
Will come as a [stranger] in the night
[Filling][17] her head with [moon's][18] light.]

[Two lay where one lay lover for the sun.
Death, [last lover],[19] is the lover to come.
Who, warm-veined, can love another
Mortal thing as an immortal lover?
No moon or sun, two taking one's couch,
Will shine the same, love each
As once he loved her who hd[20] one name.]

It can be called a sacrifice. It can
With equal truth under the [vast][21] sun
Be calling[22] the turning of sun'[23] love to man,
And now in the cold[24] night
There can be no warming by sun['s] light.

March 22 '33.

Seventeen. /

See, on gravel paths under the harpstrung [leaves][1]
He steps so near the water that a [swan's][2] wing

M

Might play upon his lank locks with its wind,
The [pond's][3] voice and the rolling of mock waves
Make discord with the voice [beneath][4] his ribs
That thunders as heart thunders, slows as heart slows.
Is not his heart imprisoned by the summer
Snaring the whistles of the birds
And fastening in its cage the [rose's][5] colour?
No, he's a stranger[6] outside the season's humour,
Moves, among men caught by the sun,
With heart unlocked upon the gigantic earth.
He alone is free, and, free, moans to the sky.
He, too, could touch the season's lips and smile,
Under the hanging branches hear the wind's [flute].[7]
But he is left. Summer to him
[Is the ripening of apples,]
[8]The unbosoming of the sun,
[And a delicate confusion in the blood.]

So shall he step till summer loosens its hold
On the canvas sky, and all hot colours melt
Into the browns of autumn and the sharp whites of winter,
And so complain, in a vain voice, to the stars.

Even among his own kin is he lost,
Is love a shadow on the wall,
Among all living men is a sad ghost.
He is not man's nor woman's man,
Leper among a clean poeple[9]
Walks with the hills for company,
And has the mad trees' talk by heart.

[There is no place, no woman bares her breasts
For him to lay his head, weary with images, in the valley
Between the breasts, no silver girl

Offers her body to him as a lover
Offers her silver body; he is no lover,
And though he battle against the skies
And the stars is no warrior.]

An image of decay disturbs the crocus
Opening its iris mouth upon the sill
Where fifty flowers breed in a fruit box,
And washing water spilt upon their necks
Cools any ardour they may have
And he destroys, though flowers are his love,[10]
If love he can being no woman's man.
An image born out of the uproarious spring
Hastens the time of the geranium to breathe;
Life, till the change of mood, forks
From the unwatered leaves and the stiff stalks,
The old flowers' legs too taut to dance,
But he makes them dance, cut capers
Coreographed[11] on paper.
The image changes, and the flowers drop
Into their prison with a [sad][12] sound,
Fresh images surround the tremendous moon,
Or catch all death that's in the air—[13]
[Whether from passing smiles set on stale lips,
The deadly rain that strikes the slates,
The bloated dogs floating upon the river.]

O lonely among many, the gods' man,
Knowing exceeding grief and the gods' sorrow
That, like a razor, skims, cuts, and turns,
Aches till the metal meets the marrow,
You, too, know the exceeding joy
And the triumphant crow of laughter.
Out of a bird's wing writing on a cloud

You capture more than man or woman guesses;
Rarer delight shoots in the blood
At the deft movements of the irises
Growing in public places than man knows;
[There in the sunset and sunrise
Joy lifts its head, wonderful with surprise.
A rarer wonder is than man supposes.]

See, on gravel paths under the harpstrung trees,
Feeling the summer wind, hearing the swans,
Leaning from windows over a length of lawns,
On level hills admiring the sea
[Or the steeples of old towns
Stabbing the changing sky,] he[14] is alone,
Alone complains to the stars.
Who are his friends? The wind is his friend,
The gloworm[15] lights his darkness, and
The snail tells of coming rain.

Poem completed March 31 '33.

Eighteen.

Make me a mask to shut from razor glances
Of men's eyes and the stare of day,
Rape and rebellion on my face,
A countenance hewed out of river ice,
Glass image that with no glance compromises,
Or wooden with uncompromising lenses
To let my own edged eyes perceive
Others betraying the inner love or lie
By the curve of the mouth or the laugh up the sleeve.
Graft on me a perpetually untwinkling smile,

A slit from ear to ear on ice or glass
[Deceiving each each¹ pretty miss who passing
Smiles back confessing a treacherous heart,
Unlicensed promise under a cheap skirt,
Bee's sting under her mask of paint.]²

A snake, charmed by the sketching of two hands
In lunatic gestures on the market air
[Or rank breath in the booths of a bazaar,]
Hissed the little circle of its mouth,
Feeling some music rub against its senses,
And, to the pipe, wriggled the wet length of its tail,
Lifting two cold eyes to catch men's glances.
There is an old evil in the snake's dancing,
But where it lies passes men's guesses
Which cannot probe the evil of the dark
Slaying daylight and turning the wind sick.
There is an old evil in the snake's eyes,
Two black circles squeezed in a squat head.
Its eyes see nothing, are stone-cold and dead.
The mouth hissed, quick to kill. Men cannot tell
The evil [in]³ those two [stones]⁴ in the sun[,]
[Or glimpse]⁵ the [wickedness]⁶ [in that wet]⁷ mask.

Make *me* a mask to wall away
My face from the face of day
And the colloquial stare that tears in six
The inner love or lie, the eyes of snakes
Themselves envisored from men's looks,
The loop-holes of the spying houses
Picking from virtues a live nest of vices,
The sly vermine,⁸ and the grimaces
Of men whose smiles were stamped upon their faces
By furrows of the black plague or the pox.

Nineteen. //

To follow the fox at the hounds' tails
And at their baying move a tailor's inch
To follow, wild as the chicken stealer,
Scent through the clutches of the heather,
Leads to fool's paradise where the redcoated killer
Deserves no brush, but a fool's ambush,
[Broken flank or head-on crash.]
Following the nose down dell, up rise
Into the map-backed hills where paths
Cross all directions, bracken points to the skies,
Leads, too, to a lead pit, whinny and fall,
No fox, no good, fool's, not a fox's, hole,
And that is the reward of labour
Through heath and heather at the mind's will.
To follow the nose if the nose goes
Wisely at the dogs' tails, leads
Through easier heather to the foul lair
Over a road thick with the bones of words.
If hunting means anything more than the chase
On a mare's back of a mare's nest or a goose,
Then only over corpses shall the feet tread,
Crunching the already broken, [breaking
But-ends[1] lying at dead-ends forsaken,]
And this way leads to good and bed,
Where more than snails are friends,[2]
[There is a smell that carries glamour
Into the nostrils, man's blooded by Diana,
Or by a clean, not hare-lipped, god.]

March 28 '32

Twenty.

The ploughman's gone, the hansom driver,
Left in the records of living a not-to-be-broken picture,
In sun and rain working for good and gain,
Left only the voice in the old village choir
To remember, cast stricture on mechanics and man.
The windmills of the world still stand
With wooden arms revolving in the wind
Against the rusty sword and the old horse
Bony and spavined, rich with fleas.
But the horses are gone and the reins are green
As the hands that held them in my father's time.
The wireless snarls on the hearth.
[Beneath a balcony the pianola plays
  Black music to a Juliet in her stays
  Who lights a fag-end at the flame of love.]
No more toils over the fields
The rawboned horse to a man's voice
Telling it this, patting its black nose:
You shall go as the others have gone,
Lay your head on a hard bed of stone,
And have the raven for companion.
The ploughman's gone, the hansom driver,
With rain-beaten hands holding the whip,
Masters over unmastered nature,
Soil's stock,[1] of the moon lit, ill lit, field and [street],[2]
Lie cold, with their horses, for raven and kite.

Man toils now on an iron saddle, riding
In sun and rain over the dry shires,

Hearing the engines, and the wheat dying.
Sometimes at his ear the engine's voice
Revolves over and over again
The same [things]³ as in my father's time:
You shall go as the others have gone,
Lay your head on a hard bed of stone,
And have the raven for companion.
It is the engine and not the raven.
Man who once drove is driven in sun and rain.
It is the engine for companion.
It is the engine under the unaltered sun.

March 28 '33

Twenty One.

Light, I know, treads the ten million stars,
And blooms in the Hesperides. Light stirs
Out of the heavenly sea onto the moon's shores.
Such light shall not illuminate my fears
And catch a turnip ghost in every cranny.
I have been frightened of the dark for years.
When the sun falls and the moon stares,
My heart hurls [at]¹ my side and tears
Drip from my open eyes as honey
Drips from the humming darkness of the hive²
I am a timid child when light is dead.
Unless I learn the night I shall go mad.
It is night's terrors I must learn to love,
Or pray for day to some attentive god
Who on his cloud hears all my wishes,
Hears and refuses.
Light walks the sky, leaving no print,

And there is always day, the shining of some sun,
In those high globes I cannot count,
And some shine for a second and are gone,
Leaving no print.
But lunar light will not glow in my blackness,
Make bright its corners where a skeleton
Sits back and smiles, a tiny corpse
Turns to the roof a hideous grimace,
Or mice play with an ivory tooth.
Stars' light and sun's light will not shine
As clearly as the light of my own brain,
Will only dim life, and light death.
I must learn night's light or go mad.

[I am a timid child when day is sped,
And my god is a child's god.][8]

April 1 '33

Twenty Two.

My body knows its wants that, often high
As a high cloud attendant on the sun,
Or small as the small globes of the dew,
Defy the trying of a host of men
Who cannot satisfy, might satisfy the sky
As easily, or cut [the moon][1] in two.
Men want the stars to hang on cherry trees,
Drop, with a fruit's sound, at their shoes,
And the fantastic circle of the sun,
Will never rest, being mad men,
Until they dam and turn the lunar lake
Behind the railings of a private park,

And graft the mad plants of the moon
On to the green arbutus grown at home.
But, though they reach, they cannot touch and take
Sun, moon, and stars, to be their own.
These they cannot compass in their thoughts,
Nor can they spangle the miles of city streets
With the globes of the dew and the celestial lights.[2]

Finding new friends you breed new wants;
A friend is but an enemy on stilts[3]
Striding so high above the common earth
Where war moves not the planets in their course
An inch more than armistice, signed with a cross,
You cannot see his eyes or know his faults.
[[These][4] wants remain unsatisfied till death.
Then, when his soul is naked, is he one
With the man in the wind, and the west moon,
[And][5] the harmonious thunder of the sun.]

April 2. '33

Twenty Three.

And death shall have no dominion.
Man, with soul naked, shall be one
With the man in the wind and the west moon,
With the harmonious thunder of the sun;
When his bones are picked clean and the clean bones gone,
He shall have stars at elbow and foot;
Though he fall mad he shall be sane,
And though he drown he shall rise up again;
Though lovers be lost, love shall not;

[Though he lose he shall gain;][1]
And death shall have no dominion.

And death shall have no dominion.
Under green shiftings of the sea
Man shall [lie][2] long but shall not die,
And under the white darkness of the snow;
Twisting on racks when sinews give way,
Strapped to a wheel, yet he shall not break;
Faith[3] in his hands[3] shall snap in two,
And all the swords of evil run him through;
Split all ends up, he shan't crack;
And death shall have no dominion.

And death shall have no dominion.
No more may gulls cry at his ear,
Or waves break loud on the sea shore,
Telling some wonder to the salty air;
Where blew a flower may a flower no more
Lift its head to the blows of the rain;
Beauty may vanish at his stare,
And, when he shield his eyes, again be fair;
Beauty may blossom in pain;
And death shall have no dominion.

And death shall have no dominion.
Under the sea or snow at last
Man shall discover all he thought lost,
And hold his little soul within his fist;
Knowing that now can he never be dust,
He waits in the sun till the sun goes out;
Now he knows what he had but guessed
Of living and dying and all the rest;

He knows his soul. There is no doubt.
And death shall have no dominion.

April '33

Twenty Four.

Within his head revolved a little world
Where wheels, confusing music, confused doubts,
Rolled down all images into the pits
Where half dead vanities were sleeping curcled[1]
Like cats, and lusts lay half hot in the cold.

Within his head the engines made their hell,
The veins at either temple whipped him mad,
And, mad, he called his curses upon God,
Spied moon-mad beasts carousing on the hill,
Mad birds in trees, and mad fish in a pool.
Across the sun was spread a crazy smile.
The moon leered down the valley like a fool.

Now did the softest sound of foot or voice
Echo a hundred times, the flight of birds
Drum harshly on the air, the lighting[2] swords
Tear with a great sound through the skies,
And there was thunder in an opening rose.

All reason broke, and horror walked the roads.
A smile let loose a devil, a bell struck.
He could hear women breathing in the dark,
See women's faces under living snoods,
With serpents' mouths and scalecophidian voids
Where eyes should be, and nostrils full of toads.

Taxis and lilies to tinned music stept

A measure on the lawn where cupids blew
Water [from nose and arse],³ a Sanger's show
Paraded up the isles⁴ and in the crypt
Of churches made from abstract and concrete.
Pole-sitting girls descended for a meal,
Stopped non-stop dancing to let hot feet cool,
Or all-in wrestling for torn limbs to heal,
The moon leered down the valley like a fool.

Where, what's my God among this crazy rattling
Of knives on forks, he cried, of nerve on nerve,
Man's ribs on woman's, straight line on a curve,
And hand to buttock, man to engine, battling,
Bruising, where's God's my Shepherd, God is Love?
No loving shepherd in this upside life.

So crying, he was dragged into the sewer,
Voles at his armpits, down the sad canal
Where floated a dead dog who made him ill,
Plunged in black waters, under hail and fire,
Knee-deep in vomit. I saw him there,
And thus I saw him searching for his soul.

And swimming down the gutters he looks up
At cotton worlds revolving on a hip,
Riding on girders of the air, looks down
On garages and clinics in the town.

Where, what's my God among this taxi stepping,
This lily crawling round the local pubs?
It was November there were whizzbangs hopping,
But now there are the but-ends⁵ of spent squibs.

So crying, he was pushed into the Jordan.
He, too, has known the agony in the Garden,

And felt a skewer enter at his side.
He, too, has seen the world as bottom rotten,
Kicked, with a clatter, ash-bins marked verboten,
And heard the teeth of weazels drawing blood.

And thus I saw him. He was poised like this,
One hand at head, the other at a loss,
Between the street-lamps and the ill-lit sky,
And thus, between the seasons, heard him cry:

Where, what's my God? I have been mad, am mad,
Have searched for shells and signs on the sea shore,
Stuck straw and seven stars upon my hair,
And leant on styles[6] and on the golden bar,
I have ridden on gutter dung and cloud.
Under a hideous sea where coral men
Feed in the armpits of drowned girls, I've swum
And sunk; waved flags to every fife and drum;
Said all the usual things over and again;
Lain with parched things; loved dogs and women;
I have desired the circle of the sun.
Tested by fire, double thumb to nose,
I've [mocked] [gibed][7] the moving of the universe.
Where, what? There was commotion in the skies,
But no god rose. I have seen bad and worse,
[Mocked][8] the coitus of the stars. No god
Comes from my evil or my good. Mad, mad,
Feeling the pinpricks of the blood, I've said
The novel things. But it has been no good.

Crying such words, he left the crying crowds,
Unshackled the weights of words from tired limbs,
And took to feeding birds with broken crumbs

Of old divinities, split bits of names.
Very alone, he ploughed the only way.
And thus I saw him in a square of fields,
Knocking off turnip tops, with trees for friends,
And thus, some time later, I heard him say:

Out of the buildings of the day I've stept
To hermits' huts, and talked to ancient men.
Out of the noise into quiet I ran.
My God's a shepherd, God's the love I hoped.
The moon peers down the valley like a saint.
Taxis and lilies, noise and no noise,
Pair off, make harmonies, [a] harmonious chord,
For he has found his soul in lonliness,[9]
Now he is one with many, one with all,
Fire and Jordan and the sad canal.
Now he has heard and read the happy word.
Still, in his hut, he broods among his birds.
I see him in the crowds, not shut
From you or me or wind or rat
Or this or that.

Started April 16 '33
Completed April 20 '33

Twenty Five.

Not from this anger, anticlimax after
Refusal struck her face, a clap of laughter,
And smiles sucked out from[1] the humour from her offer,
Shall she receive a bellyful of stones,
Nor from surprise at what turned out
Wrong choice, later, in the hotkneed night,

Shall sin amuse her limbs, and hands
Leap over the barbed lands.
For she made no adjustment to how men
React to offers of a home for semen,
Refused to fit the voice of passion
Into men's laughs and smiles set in position,
So felt passion and reaction not at all
[But] lay,[2] [un]flowered, on a lily bed,
Lilies reposing in the cool
Of pit and limb, a lily for a lad.

Behind my head a square of sky sags over
The smile tossed from lover to lover,
And the golden ball shines in another.
Among the couples, I sit and mark
Love wet its arrow in the park,[3]
Combinations, operations, generations.
There's the same cry in friction and pistons,
In the voice of engines churning
Butter from milk, the same questions.
Love has only one turning.
Why, then, the lowroads and high roads,
By roads[4] to no roads? Shall it matter
If anger or laughter or letter
Leads from hauteur to offer? Take
What is offered before it break.

Not from this anger, anticlimax after
Refusal struck her face, shall I
Be one with many under the sagging sky,
With Harry and Gladys and Herbert and May,
And all the others who lie,
Cats in a basket, catching the moment's honey.
There should be no surprise, wrong choice;

Two are as good as one
Under the spinning circle of the sun;
A bad one's better than one,
Says the daisy's, the engine's, voice.

April 20 '33

Twenty Six.

The first ten years in school and park
Leapt like a ball from light [and]¹ dark,
Bogies scared from landing and from corner,
Leapt on the bed, but now I've sterner
Stuff inside, dole for no work's
No turnip ghost now I'm no minor.
Dead are the days of thumbstained primer,
Outpourings of old soaks in censored books;
Brother spare a dime sounds louder
Than the academicians' thunder; sooner
Be fed with food than dreams. Still,
There was sense in [Harrow on the Hill,
The playing fields of Eton,] matchboard huts
Where youths learnt more than cigarettes and sluts,
Or on the coal tips near the engines
Where children played at Indians, scalps
Littered the raven Alps. There was meaning in this.
The next five years from morn to even
Hung between hell and heaven,
Plumbed devil's depths, reached angel's heights;
Dreams would have tempted saints at nights;
Night after night I climbed to bed,
The same thoughts in my head.
The last five years passed at a loss,
Fitting, all vainly, hopes dead as mown grass,

N

Fire and water of my young nonsense,[2]
[Height and depth, into the modern synthesis.]
There were five years of trying
Mingling of living and dying.
So much of old and new, the old and new
Out of the war to make another,
Past and present, would not fit together,
And I, as you, was caught between
The field and the machine.
What was there to make of birds'
And factory's whistles but dischords?[3]
No music in the dynamo and harp.
Five years found no hope
Of harmony, no cure, till this year,
For bridging white and black,
The left and right sock, light and dark,
Pansy and piston, klaxon horn
And owl addressing moon.

Until you learn the keyboard, keys,
Struck down together, make harsh noise.
Follow this best of recipies.[4]

Tune in to a tin organ at Toulouse,
[Or in Appreciation Hour, run by the States,]
Let pinches of tinned Mozart please,
Never forget, when hearing Bach on flutes,
Or after-dinner symphonies, that lots
Of poeple[5] like that sound of noise,
Let cataracts of sound fall on your ears,
Listen in pain, till pain agrees.

That music understood, then there's another:
The music of turbine and lawn mower,

Hard, soft headed extasy,[6]
Of plough and Ford along the earth,
Blackbird and Blue Bird, moth and Moth.

So much of old and new, the old and new
Out of the war to make another,
Past and present, will fit together
When the keys are no mysteries.
Twenty years; and now this year
Has found a cure.
New music, from new and loud, sounds on the air.

April 22 '33

Twenty Seven.

Pass through twelve stages, reach the fifth
By retrograde moving from near death,
And puberty recoils at callow youth
Knowing such stuff as will confuse
That phantom in the blood, used to misuse,
Red rims, a little learning, and calf sense.
In carpet slippers, with a broken crutch,
Retrogress from pitch to pitch,
Leave the oncoming shadow at the door,
Leave it your odd shoes.
Let the scales fall from rheumy eyes,
And, stepping back through medium of abuse,
Excess or otherwise, regain your fire.
Graft a monkey gland, old man, at fools' advice.

Shall it be male or female? say the cells.
The womb deliberates, spits forth manchild
To break or to be broken by the world,

A body cursed already by heredity.
The hundred-tainted lies in the cold and cools.

A one legged man ascending steps
Looks down upon him with regrets
That whips and stools and cistern sex
Have yet to add to that that mother strips
Upon her knee and shields from metal whisper
Of wind along the cot,
Sees cool get cold and childmind darker
As time on time sea ribbon rounds
Parched shires in dry lands.

The hundred-tainted must pulse and grow,
Victim of sires' vices breed heirs
To herring smelling fevers,
By way of ditch and gap arrive full stop.

Old man, would you arrive at pain,
Although new pain, by back lane,
Not dodging ruts but stepping through them,
Soaking old legs and veins,
And reach your youth again by them.[1]

The child on lap is a nice child,
Has learnt, through cold, to love the heat,
On female knees takes a warm seat,
And this is all there is to it:
The victim of grandfather's
Unwise desires, or even earlier's,[2]
Has a hundred stigmas,
More chance to hand on
Unclean Round Robin,

And more to hear air engine,
May yet find wings as airman,
And parachute old scabs and branded spots.
                                    April 23 '33

Twenty Eight.

First there was the lamb on knocking knees,
The ousel and the maniac greens of spring;
I caught on yard of canvas inch of wing,
Kinfisher's,[1] gull's swooping feather and bone,
Goodnight and goodmorning of moon and sun;
First there was the lamb which grew a sheep.

There along the spring sky deep with milk
I chanced upon a vision in surprise;
I caught the self same vision treading trees,
A season's fancy flown into a figure;
First there was the spring lamb which grew bigger;
I saw the vision at the last moon's lip

Kiss and be answered: Spring fell spent on summer;
I heard the season's corpses in wind's walk
Talk with the voices of scissors through silk;
One sentence was spelt to me
By the typewriter ribbon of sea:
First there was the young man who grew old.

Summer spent spring's hoard, fell spent on winter;
Brown in the clouds rose autumn's rumour,
A season's fancy formed into a tumour;
The lamb grown sheep hd[2] lambs around its belly,

And teats like turnips for the lambs to bully;
First there was a body which grew cold.

First there was the boy, young man, and lover;
Love's face, he dared not think, would taint and tatter;
First love brought forth a fullvoiced litter,[3]
A knockneed[4] calf pulled at the navel string;
First love, calf love, is seldom wrong;
First there was the calf which grew a cow.

The seasons parturate; spring begets summer,
And summer autumn; autumn begets another,
The black sheep, shuffling of the fold, old winter;
And love's first litter begets more.
First there was innocence and then desire,
A maggot in the veins; there's nothing now.

There's nothing but the lamb on knocking knees,
The season's vision treading clouds and trees,
The ousel and the maniac greens of spring;
All this goes on for ever and too long;
I catch on a yard of canvas inch of wing.

May 13. '33

Twenty Nine.

We lying by seasand watching yellow
And the grave sea, mock who deride
Who follow the red rivers, hollow
Alcove of words out of cicada shade,
Navy blue bellies of the tribes,
For in this yellow grave twixt sea and sand
A calling for colour calls with the wind
That's grave and gray as grave and sea

Supine on either hand.
Bound by the yellow strip, we lie,
Watch yellow, wish for wind to blow away
The strata of the shore and leave red rock.
But wishes breed not, neither
Can we fend off the sandy smother,
Nor tear the spindwind from our breath,
The seaweed from our chests,
Lie, watching yellow, until the yellow mists
Proclaim the last smother of death.

May 16 '33.

Thirty.
BEFORE WE SINNED.

Incarnate devil in a talking snake,
When god incarnate walked the garden,
Some sunless time when we were half awake,
Proffered in wind and leaf forbidden fruits,
Spoke evil with its scales.
And god walked cool, the ghostly warden,
And proffered pardon in the ghostly notes
His robe plucked from the hills.

We touched our hands upon a blade of grass;
One evil edge stung deep and bitter,
While from the other stole the sweetest juice
That, falling on our wounds, soon made them better.

When storm noised in the trees, unrisen stars
And the half moon halfhiding in the clouds
Talked good and evil till a world of fears
Grew sick around us, and made foul our words.
And when the moon came out, it was

Half white as wool, half green as grass.
And when the stars crept breathing from their shrouds,
Half were sweet signs, and half were scars.

We in our eden knew the ghostly warden
In crystal waters that no frost could harden
Nor any heat turn tepid in the mouth,
In treeroots tunneling beneath the earth,
And knew that he and evil both
Spoke in the wind that tumbled from the north.

For unroused senses there were pepper trees;
Sharp lemons cured the twitching of the knees;
Knowing a cause and cure,
We knew the good and evil in desire.

Before we sinned we knew all evil,
Hearing in snow that turned to ice
The sibilant horror of the devil's voice,
And in the mutterings of the birds.
Before we sinned we heard god's words,
Condemning and then pardoning. Before we sinned.
Before we sinned was evil in the wind.

May 16 '33

Thirty One.

Now understand a state of being, heaven
A state of being unbound by traitor senses,
Transforming to a thought that shapes it,
Ready for him who hates or rapes it,
Cool as ice, hot as an oven;
Now understand the fallacy of fancies
That gave god whiskers to his navel,

A tail and two horns to the devil.

Now understand a state of being, nothing
A state of being; future, past, and present;
Now understand the heaven prayed for
By men heaven was not made for,
By deacons out of a church coffin,
Is true to every detail and most pleasant;
Angels are there, and harps to strum on;
All things are uppperclass, not common.

Now understand a state of being, future
A state of being, and present is soon past;
Each is a state in some set country
Explored by gangsters and the gentry,
Tinker, tailor, king, and preacher,
All who will find their paradise a frost,
And in eternal state of being
Wish for the nevergift of dying.

Now understand a state of being,
Reason for understanding these
Black words two eyes are seeing,
For being, reason, words and eyes.
Now understand a state of being.
                                        May 18 '33.

                    Thirty Two.

Interrogating smile has spoken death
To every day since I lay dumb
Upon a black lap in a swaddling cloth,
Pierced me with pain another knew
Who, once, a million [years]¹ ago,

Longed for the tomb, bled like a lamb,
And knew forsaken horror on the tree.

A lifted arm has sketched a world enough
To fill with life ten times by mortal time,
And there has been a kingdom in a laugh.
But arm and lifted laugh have spoken doom,
Said acid things that burnt an hour in half,
Or split a foul day into three.

A football has its moon and sun,
A single syllable its many words;
Within the first note of a nursery tune,
A lifted laugh out of the flute,
There sound a heavenly host of chords.
What need I hear more than a single note,
Of what more than a single fist of clouds
That threatens and that never strikes need write?

A drop of water is both kind and cruel.
These worlds of foot and hand, of laugh and smile,
Hold every joy. Smile pierces quick to kill,
Smile eases. Here in this deep water all
Pain and all ease lie wonderful.
Here in this hesitating foot
Lies more of all than all the years can tell.

May 20 '33

Thirty Three.

No man believes who, when a star falls shot,
Cries not aloud blind as a bat,
Cries not in terror when a bird is drawn
Into the quicksand feathers down,

Who does not make a wound in faith
When any light goes out, and life is death.

No man believes who cries not, god is not,
Who feels not coldness in the heat,
In the breasted summer longs not for spring,
No breasted girl, no man who, young
And green, sneers not at the old sky.
No man believes who does not wonder why.

Believe and be saved. No man believes
Who curses not what makes and saves,
No man upon this cyst of earth
Believes who does not lance his faith,
No man, no man, no man.

And this is true, no man can live
Who does not bury god in a deep grave
And then raise up the skeleton again,
No man who does not break and make,
Who in the bones finds not new faith,
Lends not flesh to ribs and neck,
Who does not break and make his final faith
                                    May 23 '33

Thirty Five.
Children's Song.

[When I lie in my bed and the moon lies in hers,
    And when neither of us can sleep
For the brotherly wind and the noise of the stars,
    And the motherless cries of the sheep,
I think of a night when the owl is still
    And the moon is hid and the stars are dim,

And that is the night that death will call,
And the night that I most fear him.
Let the owl hoot and the sheep complain;
Let the brotherly wind speak low;
Death shall not enter in west wind and rain,
Let the wind blow.]

July 1. '33. [For P.T.]

Thirty Six.

The tombstone tells how she died.
She [wed]¹ on [a wild March]² morning;
Before she lay on her wedding bed
She died, was death's bride.
The tomstone³ tells how she died.
She [wed]¹ on a [wild March]⁴ morning,
With March flowers over her head,
A farmer up valley who needed a [lass]⁵
To sleep with and talk with [and clean the pig]⁶ sheds.
She died in her white wedding dress,
With a garland of roses, a [Catholic]⁷ cross,
A cake, and a ring, and a [clean]⁸ inside.
The tombstone tells how she died.

[July '33]

Thirty Seven.

Why east wind chills and south wind cools
Shall not be known till windwell dries
And west's no longer drowned
In winds that bring the fruit and rind
Of many a hundred falls.
Why grass is sweet and thistles prick,

And nightime[1] rain and mother's milk
Both quench his hourly thirst,
The fool shall question till he drop;
And till the mother mare at last
Lies on her bed, the colt at her dry pap
Nosing and wondering at dead flesh,
She shall have no reply.
Manure the field, and manure the field;
Isinglas,[2] pelt, and ash;
And snow shall be fresh and dust be harsh,
And a whip cut weal and a spur draw blood.
What colour is glory? the children ask.
Shall they clasp a comet in their fists?
When cometh Jack Frost?

Not till, from high and low, their dust
Sprinkles in children's eyes a longlast sleep,
And dusk is crowded with the children's ghosts,
Shall there be answer and the world be lost
[Where once a vulture with a naked neck
Caught up a lamb who watered at the brink,
Felt sweetness round the hollow of its tongue
And talons on its back.]
Not till the moon falls from its place
Shall I know why the trees are dumb,
Or, in my innocence, know their mild voice;
Not till the worms feed at my face,
Shall there be answer, and the brain find silence.

What colour is glory? the children ask.
Shall they clasp a comet in their fists?
When cometh Jack Frost?

All things are known. The stars' advice
Calls some content to travel with the winds

Around the head where many questions meet.
Though what the stars say on their business
Of rounding time on time the shires of sky
Is heard but little till the stars go out.
I hear content, and,³ Be content,³
Ring through the country of the air,
And, Walk content, and walk content
Though famine strips [the valley big with war],⁴
And, Know no answer, and I know
No answer to the children's ghostly cry
Of glory's colour, and the man of frost,
And ghostly comets over the raised fists.

July 1. 33

Thirty Eight.

This is remembered when the hairs drop out:
Love, like a stone, that struck and hurt;
And promise in the night.
When rheum around the eyes blinds sight
This is remembered: the winy¹ wood
Where a wild pig sprang on its mate;
The smelling of roses; the first cigarette;
The first womb; the brain is heir to
The first attacking shot.
You'll remember appendix, a souvenir slit;
The preacher's buzz, communion blood;
A promise to a mother, if you care to;
A drunk, a head in the abbey;
There's a text and a photo, a garter, a drunk,
And a fair face you half forgot.
This is remembered when the veins are scrubby,
And the shellholed gums no longer pink.

What's not remembered is the way of walking;
Wood and no trees where wooden scorpion
Measured its scales' bisector;
Dreams' gall and nectar;
What's not remembered is half the mortal lecture.
(Who lectures but old God, a phantom rector,
A walking bible printed polyglot.[2]).

Half is forgotten since your mother's milking,
And half the span of threescore years and ten;
Wind and no noise, walk and no stepping,
Wood and no trees, round half the rim of man.
Remember sleep; half metaphrase the circus,
And catch death like a trickhorse at your whip;
On sleep's sector of your [sixty] span
Walk, with no stepping, and surprise the plan.
The purpose shines along your trembling lip
That trembles with a snore. In the beginning
Was the word, the word began
In sleep no clock or calendar could time.

Half is remembered since your halfhands' knocking,
And ten teredo fingers bored the womb.

                                    July 4 & 5. 33

                    Thirty Nine.

    In me ten paradoxes make one truth,
    Ten twining roots meet twining in the earth
    To make one root that never strangles light
    By thrusting a green shrub from underneath;
    And never shall the truth translate
    From epileptic whispering in the night,

And never shall the roots bear to bear fruit
Till life and death shall cancel out,
First and last paradox are cancelled out.

As I am man, this paradox insists:
I am the one man living [amid]¹ ghosts,
The one ghost [amid]¹ men; I am the chosen
One, the one neglected [amid]² mists.
In me man and woman's brazen,
Yet have I played the eunuch to all passion,
Having no sex and every feeling frozen.
Till life is death there'll be no reason,
Till life and death unite there'll be no reason.

July 33

Forty.   //
(After the performance of Sophocles'
Electra in a garden.
Written for a local paper)

A woman wails her dead among the trees,
Under the green roof grieves the living;
The living sun laments the dying skies,
Lamenting falls. Pity Electra's loving

Of all Orestes' continent of pride
Dust in the little country of an urn,
Of Agamemnon and his kingly blood
That cries along her veins. No sun or moon

Shall lamp the raven darkness of her face,
And no Aegean wind cool her cracked heart;

There are no seacaves deeper than her eyes;
Day treads the trees and she the cavernous night.

Among the trees the language of the dead
Sounds, rich with life, out of a painted mask;
The queen is slain; Orestes' hands drip blood;
And women talk of horror to the dusk.

There can be few tears left: Electra wept
A country's tears and voiced a world's despair
At flesh that perishes and blood that's spilt
And love that goes down like a flower.

Pity the living who are lost, alone;
The dead in Hades have their host of friends,
The dead queen walketh with Mycenae's king
Through Hades' groves and the Eternal Lands.

Pity Electra loveless, she whose grief
Drowns and is drowned, who utters to the stars
Her syllables, and to the gods her love;
Pity the poor unpitied who are strange with tears.

Among the garden trees a pigeon calls,
And knows no woe that these sad players mouth
Of evil oracles and funeral ills;
A pigeon calls and women talk of death.

July 7. 33

Forty One.

Praise to the architects;
Dramatic shadows in a tin box;

o

Nonstop; stoppress; vinegar from wisecracks;
Praise to the architects;
Radio's a building in the air;
The poster is today's text,
The message comes from negro mystics,
An old chatterbox, barenaveled at Nice,
[Who steps on the gas;]
Praise to the architects;
A pome's a building on a page;
Keatings is good for lice,
A pinch of Auden is the lion's feast;
Praise to the architects;
Empty, To Let, are signs on this new house;
To leave it empty's lion's or louse's choice;
Lion or louse? Take your own advice;
Praise to the architects.

July 7. '33

Forty Two.

Here in this spring, stars float along the void,[1]
[Tealeaves on curd;][2]
Here in this mothernaked winter
Down pelts the naked weather;
This summer buries a spring bird.

Symbols are selected from the years'
Slow rounding of four seasons' coasts,
In autumn teach three seasons' fire[3]
And four birds' notes.
[From symbols I know four in one,
The holy three from any fact or figure,

Christ from an ass's cross,
God from its bray, Ghost from its halter.]

I should know summer from the trees, the worms
Tell, if tell at all, the [season's]⁴ storms
Or the funeral of the sun;
I should tell spring by the cuckooing,
And the slug should [say]⁵ me destruction.
A worm tells summer better than the clock,
The slug's a living calendar of days?⁶
What shall it tell⁷ me if a [summer bug
Tell me]⁸ spring wears away?
This,⁹ that a symbol's spring and summer;
I have the seasons' germs about my blood
That itch to action when a season's rumour,
In man or midge, is got and understood.
More than a bloody heart beats at my side;
A stone, a water's drop, behind the ribs
Lie living close; I have a stable god
In stall, heart's fodder, and will's whip.

July 9 '33

Forty Three.

A praise of acid or a chemist's lotion
Waiting and willing on an elbow rest,
Resound and stick a needle of vibration
Through death's wax.¹
A hymn of ether and a surgeon's mask,
A fencer's edge dependent on the thumbs,
Follow the leaden echo of a coward's task,
Tap death's drum.¹

Praise and lament the chlorophorm[2] that eases,
The spewing rock and acid tusk,
Eases an easy way and empties glasses.
Than such an [easy][3] poison sooner trust
A full vessel
Spilt not on Onan's mat,
And than the doctor's morsel
Longer if not so sweet.

July 9 '33

Forty Four.

Too many times my same sick cry
Has [echoed][1] in a bag of words,
Too many times new notes I play
Have struck the same sick chords.
My thoughts may be a flock of birds
A shout can drive away,
A pack of cards a little breath blow down,
For though I utter all the day
My meaning in my little way,
You close your ears or call me clown.
Death and his sickle still alarm you,
Though very little can they harm you,
And god is still a deacon in the clouds;
Well, keep your fancies fat; time and again
I'll echo my old words.

July 9 '33

Forty Five.

We have the fairy tales by heart,
No longer tremble at a bishop's hat,

And the thunder's first note;
We have these little things off pat,
Avoid church as a rat;
We scorn the juggernaut,
And the great wheels' rut;
Half of the old gang's shot,
Thank God, but the enemy stays put.

We know our Mother Goose and [Eden],[1]
No longer fear the walker in the [garden],[2]
And the fibs for children;
The old spells are undone.
But still ghosts madden,
A cupboard skeleton
Raises the hairs of lad and maiden.

If dead men walked they, too, would holler
At sight of death, the last two fisted killer
Stained a blood colour;
A panic's pallor
Would turn the dead yellow.

We have by heart the children's stories,[3]
Have blown sky high the nursery of fairies;[3]
Still a world of furies
Burns in many mirrors.

Death and evil are twin spectres.
What shall destruction count if these are fixtures?
Why blot the pictures
Of elves and satyrs
If these two [gnomes][4] remain unmoved by strictures?

We have the stories backwards,

Torn out magic from the hearts of cowards
By nape and gizzards;
There are two laggards,
Death and evil, too slow in heeding words.

Tear by the roots these twin growths in your gut;
Shall we [learn]⁵ fairy tales off pat,
Not benefit from that?
Burn out the lasting rot,
Fear death as little as the thunder's shot,
The holy hat.

July 14 '33

Forty Six.

"Find meat on bones that soon have none
And drink in the two milked crags;
Eat till all's gone, drink to the dregs¹
Before the waxred breasts are hags²
And the limbs are worn.³
Disturb no winding sheets, my son,
But when the [fodder's]⁴ cold as stone
Then hang a ram rose over the rags.

Rebel against the binding moon
And the parliament of sky,
The kingcraft of the cunning⁵ sea,
Autocracy of night and day,
Dictatorship of sun;
Rebel against the flesh and bone,
The seed and blood,⁶ the jailing⁷ skin,
And the maggot no man can slay."

"The thirst is quenched, the hunger gone,

And my heart is cracked across;
My face is haggard in the glass,
My lips are withered with a kiss,
My breasts are thin.
A lovely[8] girl took me for man;
I laid her down, and told her sin,
And put beside her a ram rose.

The maggot that no man can kill
And the bird no bullet sting[9]
Rebel against the reason's wrong
That penetrates the drum and lung
And cataracts the soul.
I cannot murder, like a fool,
Season and sunlight, grace and girl,
Nor can I smother the soul's[10] waking.

The stars still minister the moon,
And the sky lays down the laws;
The sea speaks in a kingly voice;
Night and day are no enemies
But one companion.
'War on the spider and the wren!
War on the destiny of man!
Doom on the sun!'
Before death takes you, O take back this."

July 15 '33

Forty Seven.

Ears in the turrets hear
Hands grumble on the door,
Eyes in the gables see

The fingers at the locks.
Shall I unbolt or stay
Alone to the day I die,
Unseen by stranger-eyes,
In this white house?
Hands, hold you poison or grapes?

Beyond this island, bound
By a thin sea of flesh
And a bone coast,
The land lies out of sound,
And the hills out of mind.
No bird or flying fish
Disturbs this island's rest.

Ears in this island hear
The wind pass like a fire,
Eyes in this island see
Ships anchor off the bay.
Shall I run to the ships,
With the wind in my hair,
Or stay to the day I die,
And welcome no sailor?
[Hands],[1] hold you poison or grapes?

Hands grumble on the door,
Ships anchor off the bay,
Rain beats the sand and slates.
Shall I let in the stranger,
Shall I welcome the sailor,
Or stay to the day I die?

Hands of the stranger and holds of the ships,
Hold you poison or grapes?

July 17, '33.

Forty Eight.
(From A Play)

The Woman Speaks:
  No food suffices but the food of death;
  Sweet is the waxen blood, honey the falling flesh;
  There is no fountain springing from the earth
  Cool as the waxred fountains of the veins;
  No cradle's warmer than this perished breast,
  And hid behind the fortress of the ribs
  The heart lies ready for the raven's mouth,
  And lustreless within the ruined face
  The eyes remark the antics of the hawk.

  A sniper laid him low and strew[1] his brains;
  One would not think the greeness[2] of this valley
  Could in a day be sick with so much blood;
  What were young limbs are faggots on the land,
  And young guts dry beneath the sickened sun.
  Let me not think, O God of carnage,
  Of ravens at the hero's meat and nerves
  Pecking and nestling all the time of night.

  The grass he covers is a pretty green;
  He has the still moon and the hundred stars;
  He learns the carrion pickers of the sky,
  And on his shoulders fall their world of wings,
  And on his ears hosannas of the grave.

  His narrow house is walled with blades of grass,
  Roofed with the sky and patterned with blond bones;
  The birds make him his cerements of plumes,

Cerecloth of weed, and build an ordured bed.

Since the first flesh of man was riven
By scalpel lightning from the rifted sky,
Man's marrow barbed, and breast ripped with a steel,
All that was loved and loved made the fowls' food,
Grief, like an open wound, has cried to heaven.
No food suffices but the food of death;
Death's appetite is sharpened by the bullet's thumb;
Yet he is dead, and still by woman's womb
Hungers for quickening, and my lonely lips
Hunger for him who dungs the valley fields.

There shall be no mute mourning over his acre,
Sorrow shall have no words, no willow wearing;
Rain shall defile and cover, wind bear away
The saddest dust in all this hollow world.

Old men whose blood is hindered in their veins,
Whom cancer crops, whose drinking rusts, these die;
These die who shovel the last home of man;
The sniper dies; the fingers from the sky
Strangle the little children in their beds;
One day my woman's body will be cold.

So I have come to know, but knowledge aches;
I know that age is snow upon the hair,
Wind carven lines around the drooping mouth;
And raven youth will feast but where he will.

Since the first womb spat forth a baby's corpse,
The mother's cry has fumed about the winds;
O tidal winds, cast up her cry for me;

That I may drown, let loose her flood of tears.

It was a haggard night the first flesh died,
And shafted hawks came snarling down the sky;
A mouse, it was,[3] played with an ivory tooth,
And ravens fed confection to their young.

Palm of the earth, O sprinkle on my head
That dust you hold, O strew that little left;
Let what remains of that first miracle
Be sour in my hair. That I may learn
The mortal miracle, let that first dust
Tell me of him who feeds the raging birds.

July 33.

Fifty.

Let the brain bear the hammering,
And heart the stabbing of the forks;
The devil hammers hell out of the ribs,
His playmates fork the skull.
The ears shall stand the clamouring,
Domdaniel shall not snip my sex;
I hear the little voices dropping jibes
As pigs' mouths drop their swill.
For all the devil's scissors I am male.
Let not the hands garotte,
The bullet wing, the bayonet gut;
The labyrinthine body must keep whole.

Be strong before my poeple[1] fall,
The hair falls out, and tongues that foul
The dark dart at the ears of men.

The devil hammers hell out of the skull;
No bones shall break and no vein fail;
[His playmates play with heart and brain.][2]

August 33

Fifty One.

The minute is a prisoner in the hour,
[Lest brain keep watch][1] will break [its hours'][2] cell
And play the truant in the den of days;
But[3] [Argus][4]-eyed[3] my senses shall not lose,
Nor sentinel my heart set free the frail
First vision that set fire to the [air].[5]

A minute wound that wonderment about,
When on the stivy[6] wind a giant's voice
Told truth and rang the valley with its crying;
With falling wind down fell the giant's shout,
The meaning dropped and truth fled to the grass.
Deep in the valley's[7] herbs I hear it dying.

Some see a living vision of the truth,
And some hear truth upon the wind, once only.
Forget, it dies, and lose, it's never found.
I shall remember losing until death,
Keep in my memory the minute lonely
Of truth that told the deaf and showed the blind.

August '33

Fifty Two.

Shall gods be said to thump the clouds
When clouds are cursed by thunder,
Be said to weep when weather howls?
Shall rainbows be their tunics' colour?

When there is rain where are the gods?
Shall it be said they sprinkle water
From garden cans, or free the floods?

Shall it be said that, venuswise,
Some old god's dugs are pricked and pressed
When milky night is mother of the air?

Shall it be said that this moon's face
Is but the face reflected of some god
Admiring the acres of his brow?
Does gods' blood die[1] the sun?

It shall be said that gods are stone.
Shall a dropped stone thud on the ground,
Flung gravel chime? Let the stones speak
With tongues that talk all tongues.

The gods of stone our fathers worshipped
Are brass and wood[2] if gods weep rain.
If gods thump thunder, then the clouds
Are gods and water, and the bark is brass.
All things are god if gods are thunder.

August.

Fifty Three.

Matthias spat upon the lord
And gained an everlasting curse;
The Reverend Crap, a pious fraud,
Defiles his maker with a word
Dropped from those educated jaws.
Which is the most to be abhorred—
Jew's gob or gentile's praise?

The Reverend Crap, a holy pimp,
Reads the bible and loves children,
Loves to pat a choirboy's rump,
And, following the band of hope,
To stroke the girls behind the organ.
Who shall be cursed—the virgin Crap
Or the poxy whoreman?

August 16.

AUGUST

1933

NOTEBOOK

To others caught
Between [Twixt] black and white
This Book Started. 23rd August 1933.

One.

To A.E.T.

The hand that signed the paper felled a city;
Five sovereign[1] fingers taxed the breath,
Doubled the globe of dead and halved a country;
These five kings did a king to death.

The mighty hand leads to a sloping shoulder,
The finger joints are cramped with chalk;
A goose's quill has put an end to murder
That put an end to talk.

The hand that signed the treaty bred a fever,
And famine grew, and locusts came;
Great is the hand that holds dominion over
Man by a scribbled name.

The fingers count the dead but do not soften
The crusted wounds nor pat the brow;
The hand rules pity as a hand rules heaven;
Hands have no tears to flow.

[These five blind kings have quills for sceptres;
Each has a parchment for his shield,
Debates with vizier words what time he shatters
The four walls of the world.]

August 17 '33.

[225]

Two.

To T.H.

Let for one moment a faith statement
Rule the blank sheet of sleep,
The virgin lines be mated with a circle.
A circle spins. Let each revolving spoke
Turn and churn nightseed till it curdle.

Let for one moment a faith statement
Strip the dreams' livery,
And gods be changed as often as the shift.
God is the same though he be praised as many,
Remains though gods be felled till none are left.

Let for one moment a faith statement
See the first living light,
And your maieutic slumber drag it forth.
The child tells, when the trembling cord is cut,
God shall be gods and many deaths be death.

August 20, 33.
Rayner's Lane.

Three.

You are the ruler of this realm of flesh,
And this hill of bone and hair
Moves to the Mahomet of your hand.
But all this land gives off a charnel stench,

The wind smacks of the poor
Dumb dead the crannies house and hide.

You rule the thudding heart that bites the side;
The heart steps to death's finger,
The brain acts to the legal dead.
Why should I think on death when you are ruler?

You are my flesh's ruler whom I treason,
Housing death in your kingdom,
Paying heed to the thirsty voice.
Condemn me to an everlasting facing
Of the dead eyes of children
And their rivers of blood turned to ice.

August 22 '33.

Four.

That the sum sanity might add to nought
And matrons ring the harebells on their lips,
Girls woo the weather through the Sabbath night
And rock twin floods upon their starry laps,
I would enforce the black aparelled[1] flocks,
And raise a hallelujah to the Lamb,
Trace on my breast a covert crucifix;
I would be woven at the Sabbath loom.[2]

I would be woven a religious shape;
That earth might reel upon its block of reason
I would resound the heavens with my homage,
I would make genuflexion with the sheep[3]

That men might holla, when the dawn has risen,
At day burnt bright by one fanatic image.

August 24 '33.

Five.

Grief, thief of time, crawls off
With wasted years and half
The loaded span of days.
Marauding pain steals off
With half the load of faith
That weighed thee to thy knees.

The old forget their cries,
Lean times on evil seas,
And times the wind blew rough,
Remember the sea-boys
Riding sea-bear and horse
Over the salty path.

The old forget the grief,
And the hack of the cough,
And the friends fed to crows,
Remember the sea-youth,
And plucking wild radish,
And seed that was promise.

Grief is the price of peace,
And age forgets the cries,
The thief of time steals death.
Forget the prince's price,
Remember all thy days
Thy thieven load of faith.

August 26, '33.

Six.

Shiloh's seed shall not be sewn[1]
In the garden of the womb
By a salty dropsy sipping,*
No Redeemer shall be born
In the belly of a lamb
Dumbly and divinely leaping
Over the godbearing green.

From the meadow where lambs frolic
Rises every blade the Lamb,
From the heavens falls a dove.
Now is sun and summer phallic,
Promise is its fiery limb,
And a baby god its thief,
Thieving bone and flesh's tunic.

Through the floodgates of the sky
Grains of seed shall be dropped loose,
Manna for the hungry globe,
Quickening for the land and sea.
Settling in a virgin sluice,
It shall hammer at the rib,
Wall of wood or side of hay.

Prince's seed shall find a harbour,
[2]Hundred wombs shall say him nay,
A hundred virgins hide him.
May a humble village labor,[3]

* Southcott?

And a continent deny?
A hemisphere may scold him,
And a green plot be his bearer.

The wren may warm him in her nest,
A water catch and cover
One falling grain, it knows not why,
And diggers find him in the dust.
A saviour with the break of day[4]
Falls and is found, falls and is lost.

If veins are flowing with their juice,
It matters not if wood or brass,
Or man or woman, chances
Upon a fallen grain.
If veins are dry, the fortune changes;
If flesh hangs ragged on the bone,
The miracle shall change its face.

Life must stir before the seed,
And before the twilight sleep.
Brass must shudder, water swirl,
Sap must rustle in the wood.
And the dove shall fill its crop
Before the brazen Dove is whole
And the wooden Lamb is God.

Shiloh's seed shall not be sewn[1]
In the pastures of the worm;
Not in the fanatic womb
Shall the jelly mix and form
That shall be the three in One,
God and Ghost, Annointed[1] Son.

August 29 33.

Seven.

Before I knocked and flesh let enter,
With liquid hands tapped on the womb,
I who was shapeless as the water
That shaped the Jordan near my home,
Was the brother to Mnetha's daughter
And sister to the fathering worm.

I who was deaf to spring and summer,
Who knew not sun or moon by name,
Felt thud beneath my flesh's armour
As yet was in a molten form,
The leaden stars, the rainy hammer
Swung by my father from his dome.

I knew the message of the winter,
The darted hail, the childish snow,
And the wind was my sister suitor;
Wind in me leaped, the hellborn dew;
My veins flowed with the valley weather;
Ungotten I knew night and day.

As yet ungotten, I did suffer;
The rack of dreams my lily bones
Did twist into a living cipher,
And flesh was snipped to cross the lines
Of gallow crosses on the liver
And brambles in the wringing brains.

My milk was curdled by the thunder;
The lightning forked into the jaw,

The lilac gums, that kissed me murder;
Deep in my bowels jumped the fire,
The false lips cursed me like an adder
Who bares his sting to wound the air.

My throat knew thirst before the structure
Of skin and vein around the well
Where words and water make a mixture
Unfailing till the blood runs foul;
My heart knew love, my belly hunger,
I smelt the maggot in my stool.

And time cast forth my mortal creature
To drift or drown upon the seas
Acquainted with the salt adventure
Of tides that never touch the shores.
I who was rich was made the richer
By sipping at the vine of days.

I, born of flesh and ghost, was neither
A ghost or man, but mortal ghost.
And I was struck down by death's feather.
I was mortal to the last
Long breath that carried to my father
The message of his dying Christ.

A virgin was my sad-faced dam,
My sire was of wind and water.
Get thee behind me, my blood's tempter,
I cried out when the blood was dumb.

You who bow down at cross and altar,

Remember me and pity him
Who took my flesh and bone for armbour,[1]
And double-crossed his mother's womb.

September 6

Eight.

We see rise the secret wind behind the brain,
The sphinx of light sit on the eyes,
The code of stars translate in heaven.
A secret night descends between
The skull, the cells, the cabinned ears
Holding for ever the dead moon.

A shout went up to heaven like a rocket,
Woe from the rabble of the blind
Adorners of the city's forehead,
Gilders of streets, the rabble hand
Saluting the busy brotherhood
Of rod and wheel that wake the dead.

A city godhead, turbine moved, steel sculptured,
Glitters in the electric streets;
A city saviour, in the orchard
Of lamp-posts and high-volted fruits,
Speaks a steel gospel to the wretched
Wheel-winders and fixers of bolts.

We hear rise the secret wind behind t[1] brain,
The secret voice cry in our ears,
The city gospel shout to heaven.

Over the electric godhead grows
One God, more mighty than the sun.
The cities have not robbed our eyes.

September 8.

Nine.

Take the needles and the knives,
Put an iron at the eyes,
Let a maggot at the ear
Toil away till music dies.

Let me in the devil's groves
Cut my fingers on a rose,
Let the maggot of despair
Drain the spring where promise goes.

Take the scissors and the pan,
Let the tiny armies lap,
And the heralds of decay,
At the labyrinthine pap.

Choke the bladder with a stone,
Fill the veins the fevers broke,
All the cabinned[1] faiths deny
And the feeble house of hope.

And a child might be my slayer,
And a mother in her labour
Murder with a cry of pain;

Half a smile might be her sabre.

Let it be a sword of fire,
Lightning or the darting viper,
Thunder's rod or man's machine;
God and I will pay the sniper.

Flesh is suffered, is laid low,
Mixes, ripens, in the loam;
Spirit suffers but is still
In its labyrinthine home.

In the wilderness they go,
Flesh and spirit, babe and dam,
Walking in the evening's cool
With the leper and the lamb.

In the darkness dam and babe
Tremble at the starry stain,
And the ruin of the sky;
Darkness is the dam of pain.

Take the scissors to this globe,
Firmament of flesh and bone
Lawed and ordered from on high
By a godhead of my own.

Mother root that shot me forth,
Like a green tree through the [sward],[2]
Mothers me until I [die],[3]
[And my father was the lord.][4]

When I yield the tree to death,

In the country of the dead
Dam and sire, living, lo,
Will be breathing by my bed.

Take the needles to this tree
Bowing on its mossy knees,
Stitch the stem on to the leaf,
Let the sap leak in the breeze.

Thread and torture all the day;
You but wound the lord of days;
Slay me, slay the god of love;
God is slain in many ways.

Question: Shall the root be true
And the green tree trust the root?
Answer: Shall a mother lie
In the face of seed and fruit?

Question: When shall root-dam die?
Answer: When her babe denies her.
Question: When shall root-dam grow?
Answer: When the green leaves prize her.

September 12.

Ten.

To B.C.

Not forever shall the lord of the red hail
Hold in his velvet hand the can of blood;
He shall be wise and let his brimstone spill,
Free from their burning nests the arrows' brood.
And sweet shall fall contagion from his side,

And loud his anger [morse][1] upon the hill.

As fire falls, two hemispheres divide,
The fields yet undivined behind the skull
Are made divine by every lightning rod,
And perish as the level lands of steel.
Both mind and matter at the golden word
Shall fall away, and leave [a][2] singing shell.

A hole in space shall keep the shape of thought,
The lines of earth, the curving of the heart,
And from this darkness spin the golden soul.
Intangible my world shall come to nought,
The solid world shall wither in the heat,
How soon, how soon, o lord of the red hail!

September 15. '33
Llangain Carms.

Eleven.

Before we mothernaked fall
Upon the land of gold or oil
Between the raid and the response
    Of flesh and bones
Our claim is staked for once and all
Near to the quarry or the well
Before the promises fulfill
    And joys are pains.

Then take the gusher or the field
Where all the hidden stones are gold
We have no choice our choice was made
    Before our blood

And I will [plumb][1] my liquid world
And you, before the breath is cold
And doom is turned and veins are spilled,
   Your solid land.

Choose the field of brick and bone
Or the dark well of the brain
Take one away let one remain.
   [All is foreknown.]

September 16. 33.
Llangain

Twelve.

[Our][1] sun burns the morning, a bush in the brain;
 Moon walks the river and raises the dead;
 Here in my wilderness wanders the blood;
 And the sweat on the brow makes a sign,[2]
 And the wailing heart's nailed to the side.

 Here is a[n] universe bred in the bone,
 Here is a saviour who sings like a bird;[3]
 Here the night shelters and here the stars shine;[3]
 Here a mild baby speaks his first word
 In the [Bethlehem][4] under the skin.

 Under the ribs sail the moon and the sun;
 A cross is tatooed on the breast of the child,
 And sewn on his skull a scarlet thorn;
[For the price of Christ is paid in pain,[5]
 And a labouring mother pays twofold.]

September 16.
Llangain.

Thirteen.

My hero bares his nerves along my wrist
That rules from wrist to shoulder
Unpacks the head that like a sleepy ghost
Leans on my mortal ruler
The proud spine spurning turn and twist.

And these poor nerves so wired to the skull
Ache on the lovelorn paper
I hug to love with my unruly scrawl
That utters all love-hunger
And tells the page the empty ill.

My hero bares my side and sees his heart
Tread like a naked Venus
The beach of flesh and wind her bloodred plait;
Stripping my loin of promise
He promises a secret heat.

He holds the wire from this box of nerves
　　[Turning]¹ the mortal error
Of birth and death the two sad knaves of thieves
　　And the hunger's emperor;
He pulls the chain the cistern moves.

[Jack my father let the knaves steal off
　Their little swag, the gems of life and death,
　The lightest bubbles that we breathe
　　Out of the living grave

And let my hero show his double strength
And all his laughter hidden up my sleeve.]

September 17 '33.
Llangain

Fifteen.

In the beginning was the three-pointed star,
One smile of light across the empty face;
One rib of flesh across the frame of air,
The substance spread that moulded t¹ first sun;
And heaven was, a cloudy hole, and hell
A burning stick across the bum of space.²

In the beginning was the dim signature
Spelt with the three syllables of light,
And after came the imprints of the water,
Stamp of the minted face upon the moon;
The blood that touched the brim of Joseph's grail
Touched the first sky and left a living clot.

In the beginning was the three-eyed prick,
The red eyed genitor of mind and matter,
Set on the stone of space, the ageing rock
As empty as a skeleton's ear;
And roots exploded in the powdered land,
And there were trees and there was water.

In the beginning was the word, the word
That was all words and one, the word of time,
The word of darkness and the spinning void;
[The star translated into all-tongued light

The word of peace, of time, one word and all,
The three-eyed word spelling a single name.]³

In the beginning was a secret thought,
Before the word was lodged in the clouds' mouth
And the first star changed all the sounds to light;
In the beginning was the house of air
Ruled by the thought to be the word and hand,
The prayer and deed, the body and the breath.

September 18 '33
Llangain.

Sixteen.

Love me, not as the dreamy¹ nurses
My falling lungs, nor as the cypress
In his age the [maiden's] lass's clay.
Love me and lift your mask.

Love me, not as the girls of heaven
Their airy lovers, nor the mermaiden
Her salt lovers in the sea.
Love me and lift your mask.

Love me, not as the ruffling pigeon
The tops of trees, nor as the legion
Of the gulls the lip of waves.
Love me and lift your mask.

Love me, as loves the mole his darkness
And [as] the timid deer the tigress:

Ω

Hate and fear be your twin[2] lover.
Love me and lift your mask.

September 18. '33.

In Three Parts
Seventeen.
(Part One).

For loss of blood I fell where stony hills
Had milk and honey flowing from their cracks,
And where the footed dew was on the pools
I knelt to drink the water dry as sticks.
Where was no water ran the honeyed milks,
And where was water was the drybacked sand.

I met the ghost of water on the paths,
And knelt before the ghostly man of milk;
Where was no honey were the humming wraiths
Descending on the flowers' cup and stalk.
Where was no water there the image rides,
And where was water was the stony hand.

For [leak][1] of faith I fell upon the desert
Where eagles tenanted the single palm;
Where was no god I heard his windy visit,
And saw the spider weave him on her loom.
And where god was his holy house was sculptured,
A monster lie upon the middened land.

I fell upon the ugly vales and wept;
The ravens crowed to spy my drooping eyes,

And with their crowing was my wet grief stopped,
A feather said a blessing from the trees;
And² pretty here² a malediction stirs,
Upon these slopes is burnt a killer's brand.

For lack of love I fell where love was not,
The plains by the still sea, and there love sat,
My child did knock within her happy heart.
And where love was sat fever on her throne,
My child did scream and burn within her womb
And where love lay was laid her hot-veined³ brat.

At last I came to a remembered cave,
There made my lodge, and sucked the fallen figs,
Where no thief walked leapt through my neighbour's grove,
My skin not waxen old upon my dugs.
Where no thief was there came the padded knave
To set his famined hands upon my fat.

The thief of light did sew upon my lids
His checquered⁴ shades, and at my open ear
The thief of sound poured down his fluids,
The thief of speech was busy at the jaw.
When all was peace there came these palming lads
To nick my senses but to leave the breath.

And all was dim, and stilly went the wind,
Under my granite roof I lay and healed,
And peace was with me as a pleasant sound.
When all was peace there came the thieving king,
Sat at my feet and told this summing song:
When all is lost is paid the sum of death.

September 25 33.

Eighteen.
(Part Two).

Jack my father, let the knaves
Fill with a swag of bubbles their sad sacks,
No fingers press their fingers on the wax
Red as the axe, blue as a hanging man.

Jack my father, let the thieves
Share their fool spoil with their sad brood of sneaks,
No silver whistles chase them down the weeks'
Daybouldered peaks into the iron van.

Let them run off with laden sleeves,
These stolen bubbles have the bites of snakes,
These sacked wines raise a thirst no liquor slakes,
No vitual[1] breaks this hunger son of pain.

Lust and love both be your loves,
Wean the well-loved on one symmetric breast,
Please the one-minded hand, and suck to rest
The body pressed upon one flesh and bone.

One dies all die, all live one lives,
And slopes and vales are blessed as they are cursed;
Both sweet and bitter were the last and first
Truths to be nursed with their same mother's groan.

Where is no god there man believes,
And where god is his homage turns to dust;
God who is all tells in his desert gust

That one man must be all and all be one.

When the knave of death arrives,
Yield the lost flesh to him and give your ghost;
All shall remain, and on the cloudy coast
Walk the blithe host
Of god and ghost with you, their newborn son.

September 26. '33.

Nineteen.

(Part Three)

The girl, unlacing, trusts her breast,
Doubts not its tint nor how it leans;
Faith in her flesh maintains its shape
From toe to head.
Their maiden cloths the stars unslip,
And from her shift the worn moon turns
One bosom to her lover's bed
Red in the east.

Should the girl doubt, a sallow ring
Would rim her eyes and sphere her breast;
And should the stars blush as they strip,
Ashamed of light,
Their manypointed light would drop;
If the moon doubts, her dew is dust;
If day lacks faith, it turns to night,
And light is done.

It shall happen that time's venom
Darts to your cheek and leaves its scars;

Burning like age upon your mouth,
The old-veined wind
Shall bear away the kiss of youth;
And it shall happen that the stars,
[Lorn] of their naked welcome,
Shoot as they fade.

Trust, in the first, the desert hills,
And milk will [flow][1] along their udders;[2]
Let the hilly milk sit sweet
Upon the tongue,
And honey quiet every gut;
Trust the lips the honey colours:
Lips shall be smiling, always young,
Though the flesh falls.

The girl, unlacing, trusts her breast:
Forever shall the breast give milk;
The naked star stands unashamed:
It shall forever.
You who believe the stony hand,
And, groaning, trust the [needles' stroke],[3]
Shall be star-fathered on the air
And [Jack][4] of Christ.

End.

September 29 '33.

Twenty.

Through these lashed rings set [in][1] their hollows
I eye the ring of earth, the airy circle,
My Maker's[2] flesh that garments my clayfellows.
And through these trembling rings set in their valley
Wheron[3] the hooded hair casts down its girdle,

A holy voice acquaints me with His glory.

Through these two rounded lips I pray to heaven,
Unending sea around my measured isle
The water spirit moves as it is bidden;
⁴And, With not one fear-beggared syllable,
Praise God who springs and fills the tidal well;
Through [my]⁵ heartpit I know his⁶ miracle.

And through these eyes God marks myself revolving,
And [on]⁷ these [musiced]⁸ senses [plays]⁹ his tune;
Inside this mouth I feel his message moving
Acquainting me with my divinity;
And through these ears he harks my fire burn
His [ghostly]¹⁰ heart into some symmetry.

September 30. '33.

                    Twenty One.

            Ape and ass both spit me forth,
            I am spawn of leech and frog;
            Crawling from the serpent's egg
            I am born to breed and breathe.

            Couch I in the weasel's bag,
            Suck I at the monkey's thumb;
            From the shell I show a leg
            Thin as a crow's womb.

            Got together sow and pig,
            I was franked in the sow's side;
            I am son of fish and bird,
            Daughter of the ferret's hug.

Twenty Two.

The eye of sleep turned on me like a moon,
Let fall the tear of time; the hand of sleep
Let fall the snail of time and wound his horn.
So, featherheeled, I journeyed through a dream,
And had the lip of darkness on my lip.

I fled the earth, and, naked, climbed the weather,
Reaching a second ground, far from the stars;
And there we wept, I and a ghostly other,
My mother-eyed, upon the tops of trees;
I fled the ground, as lightly as a feather.

I climbed a cloud, and poised above the earth,
Ghost at my arm, and dawn about my head;
And soon the mouth of darkness at my mouth
Kissed and was answered as the kiss of death;
For dark I spoke and the black ghost replied.

"My father's globe knocks on its nave, and sings."
"This that we tread was, too, thy father's land."
"But this we tread bears the angelic gangs,
Sweet are their fathered faces in their wings."
"These are but dreaming men: breathe, and they fade.¹

I breathed aloud, and with the fading men
Faded my elbow-ghost, the mother-eyed.
And on the airy steps I climbed again,
Over the prick of earth, towards a plane
Set near the stars and by the weak moon-side.

There all the matter of the living air

Raised its harmonious voice; the pulse of God
Hammered within the circling roads of fire;
There was the song of God the singing core
Under the graveclothes of the cloudy dead.

Around me shone the faces of the spheres,
And hung the comets' hair, the meteor ropes
Whereby I swarmed up to the starry spires.
Beneath me leapt the salamandrine [furies][2]
Out of the half moon where a mad man sleeps.

And stripped I stood upon a columned cloud,
Fear at my heart of all the laws of heaven
And the mysterious order of the Lord.
And, like a bloodred-ribbon where I stood
There grew the hours' ladder[3] to the sun.

Oct 5 '33.

Twenty Three.

To E.P.

[The force that through the green fuse drives the flower
Drives my green age; that blasts the roots of trees
Is my destroyer.
And I am dumb to tell the eaten rose
How at my sheet goes the same crookèd worm,
And dumb to holla thunder to the skies
How at my cloths flies the same central [storm].]

The force that through the green fuse drives the flower
Drives my green age, that blasts the roots of trees
Is my destroyer.
And I am dumb to tell the crookèd rose

My youth is bent by the same wintry fever.

The force that drives the water through the rocks
Drives my red blood; that dries the mouthing streams
Turns mine to wax.
And I am dumb to mouth unto my veins
How at the mountain spring the same mouth sucks.

The hand that whirls the water in the pool
Stirs the quicksand; that ropes the blowing wind
Hauls my shroud sail.
And I am dumb to tell the hanging man
How of my clay is made the hangman's lime.

The lips of time leech to the fountain head;
Love drips and gathers, but the fallen blood
Shall make her well;
And I am dumb to tell the timeless sun
[How time is all.][1]

And I am dumb to tell the lover's tomb
How at my sheet goes the same crookèd worm.

October 12. '33

Twenty Four.

From love's first fever to her plague, from the soft second
And to the hollow minute of the womb,
From the unfolding to the scissored caul,
The time for breast and the green apron age
When no mouth stirred about the hanging famine,
All world was one, one windy nothing,

My world was christened in a stream of milk.
And earth and sky were as one airy hill,
The sun and moon shed one white light.

From the first print of the unshodden foot, the lifting
Hand, the hatching of the hair,
And to the miracle of the first rounded word,
From the first secret of the heart, the warning ghost,
And to the first dumb wonder at the flesh,
The sun was red, the moon was gray,
The earth and sky were as two mountains meeting.[1]

The body prospered, teeth in the marrowed gums,
The growing bones, the rumour of manseed
Within the hallowed gland, blood blessed the heart,
And the four winds, that hd[2] long blown as one,
Shone in my ears the light of sound,
Called in my eyes the sound of light,
And where one globe had spun a host did circle
The nave of heaven, each with its note.
And yellow was the multiplying sand,
Each golden grain spat life into its fellow,
Green was the singing house.

The plum my mother picked matured slowly,
The boy she dropped from darkness at her side
Into the sided lap of light, grew strong,
Was muscled, matted, wise to the crying thigh
And to the voice that, like a voice of hunger,
Itched in the noise of wind and sun.

                    (Incomplete)

                                        October 14 '33

Twenty Five.

The almanac of time hangs in the brain;
The seasons numbered by the inward sun,
The winter years, move in the pit of man;
His graph is measured as the page of pain
Shifts to the redwombed pen.

The calendar of age hangs in the heart,
A lover's thought tears down the dated sheet,
The inch of time's protracted to a foot
By youth and age, the mortal state and thought
Ageing both day and night.

The word of time lies on the chaptered bone,
The seed of time is sheltered in the loin:
The grains of life must seethe beneath the sun,
[The syllables be said and said again:]
Time shall belong to man.

October 16. 33

Twenty Six.
(Continuation of Twenty Four)

And from the first declension of the flesh
I learnt man's tongue, to twist the shapes of thoughts
Into the stony idiom of the brain,
To shade and knit anew the patch of words
Left by the dead who, in their moonless acre,
Need no word's warmth.
The root of tongues ends in a spentout cancer,
That but a name, where maggots have their X.

I learnt the verbs of will, and hd[1] my secret;
The code of night tapped on my tongue;
What hd[1] been one was many sounding minded.

One womb, one mind, spewed out the matter,
One breast gave suck, the fever's issue;
From the divorcing sky I learnt the double,[2]
The two-framed globe that spun into a score;
A million minds gave suck to such a bud
As forked my eye.
Youth did condense: the tears of spring
Dissolved in summer and the hundred seasons;
One sun, one manna, warmed and fed.

Now that drugged youth is waking from its stupor,
The nervous hand rehearsing on the thigh
Acts with a woman, one sum remains in cipher:
Five senses and the frozen brain
Are one with wind, and itching in the sun.
Stone is my mate? who shall brass be?[3]
What seed to me?
[The soldered world debates.]

How are they seeded, all that move,
With all that move not to the eye?
What seed, what seed to me?

                                        October 17 '33

                    Twenty Seven.

    All that I owe the fellows of the grave
    And all the dead bequeathe[1] from pale estates
    Lies in the fortuned bone, the flask of blood,

Like senna stirs along the ravaged roots.
O all I owe is all the flesh inherits,
My fathers' loves that pull upon my nerves,
My sisters' tears that sing upon my head,
My brothers' blood that salts my open wounds.

Heir to the scalding veins that hold love's drop,
My fallen filled, that had the hint of death,
Heir to the telling senses that alone
Acquaint the flesh with an[2] remembered itch,
I round this heritage as rounds the sun
His winy sky, and, as the candle's moon,
Cast light upon my weather. I am heir
To women who have twisted their last smile,
To children who were suckled on a plague,
To young adorers dying on a kiss.
All such disease I doctor in my blood,
And all such love's a shrub sown in the breath.

Then look, my eyes[3] upon this bonebound fortune
And browse upon the postures of the dead;
All night and day I eye the ragged globe
Through periscopes rightsighted from the grave[3]
All night and day I wander in these same
Wax clothes that wax upon the ageing ribs;
All night my fortune slumbers in its sheet.
Then look, my heart, upon the scarlet trove,
And look, my grain, upon the falling wheat;
All night my fortune slumbers in its sheet.

Twenty Eight.

Here lie[s] the [worm][1] of man and here I feast,
The dead man said,

And silently I milk the devil's breast.
Here spring the silent venoms of his blood,
Here clings the meat to sever from his side.
Hell's in the dust.

Here lies the [worm]² of man and here his [rose],³
The dead man said,
And silently I milk the buried flowers.
Here drips a silent honey in my shroud,
Here [goes]⁴ the ghost who made of my pale bed
The heaven's house.

October 25 33.
Llangain.

Twenty Nine.

When once the twilight locks no longer
Locked in the long worm of my finger
Nor damned the sea that sped about my fist,
The mouth of time sucked, like a sponge,
The milky acid on each hinge,
And swallowed dry the waters of the breast.

When the galactic sea was sucked
And all the dry sea bed unlocked,
Rose the dry ghost of night to suck the day;
No hyleg but the Sleeper's star
Shone on this globe of bone and hair,
No star but sleep's was nodding in the sky.

Some dead upon a slab of wind
Where middle darkness spins around
Undid their lungs and leaked their midnight seed;

Along the wind the dead men drove
The redhaired cancer at their stuff,
And drove the midge that fluttered in their blood.

The horrors took the shapes of thoughts,
The wings of flies, the tails of rats,
And, cancervoiced, did crow upon my heap;
The midge that put a fever in
The bag of blood that swelled a vein
Hopped in my eyes and drew the straws of sleep.

The issue armoured, of the grave
Of violet fungus still alive
And winking eyes that catch the eye of death;
The seed of dreams that showed a bud
Through dust and sleep nods in my side;
Sleep is the winding lover in my cloth.

Sleep navigates the tides of time;
The dry Sargossa[1] of the tomb
Gives up its dead to the divining hours;
And sleep drags up the kicking heart,
The driving brains, the brain of night
That day put down as age knocks down the flowers.

Crow on my heap, O living deaths;
There is no horror death bequeathes[2]
I cannot number on this sleepy hand;
The golden emerods of the sun,[3]
The dung that cometh out of man,
Spread in my sleep that makes the stars go round.

A sweet shrub rises from the wrecks

And sprouts between the coffins[4] crack;
The dead are singing in the cypress[5] yard;
My sleep is scented by the shrub
That scents the dead man in his robe,
My sins fly through the window like a bird.

There is no sweetness in the dead
I feel not in my sleeping blood;
Then sleep and dream, sleeps dreams and dies;[6]
When once the twilight locks no longer
Locked in the long worm of my finger
I did unlock the Sleeper's eyes.

                        November 11. 33.

Thirty.

Light breaks where no sun shines;
Where no sea runs, the waters of the heart
Push in their tides;
And, broken ghosts with gloworms[1] in their heads,
The things of light
File through the flesh where no flesh decks the bones.

A candle in the thighs
Warms youth and seed[2] and burns the seeds of age;
Where no seed stirs
The fruit of man unwrinkles in the stars,
Bright as a fig;
Where no wax is the candle shows its hairs.

Dawn breaks behind the eyes;
From pole of skull and toe the windy blood

Slides like a sea;
Nor fenced, nor staked, the gushers of the sky
Spout to the rod
Divining in a smile the oil of tears.

Night in the sockets rounds,
Like some pitch moon, the limit of the globes:
[Day lights the bone;][3]
Where no cold is the skinning gales unpin
The winter's robes;
The film of spring is hanging from the lids.

Light breaks on secret lots,
On tips of thought[2] where thoughts smell in the rain;
When logics die
The secret of the soil grows through the eye,
And blood jumps in the sun;
Above the waste allotments the dawn halts.

November 20 33.

Thirty One.

I fellowed sleep who kissed between the brains;
Her spinning kiss through my lean sheets
Stopped in the bones.
I fathered dreams as races from the loins
And sleep, pit-wombed, who kissed the pits.

Sleep shifts along the latches of the night;
The shifting night inched in as she
Drew back the bolt;

My fellow sleep who kissed me in the heart
With her salt hairs unlocked the sky.

I fellowed sleep who drained me with a kiss;
Where went but one grave-gabbing shade
Now go the stars;
Now stirs a ruined moon about my bed;
And worlds hang on the trees.
November 27th 33.

Thirty Two.

See, says the lime, my wicked milks
I put round ribs that packed their heart,
And elbowed veins that, nudging blood,
Roused it to fire;
Once in this clay fenced by the sticks
That starry fence the clay of light
The howling spirit shaped a god
Of death's undoer.

On these blue lips, the lime remarks,
The wind of kisses sealed a pact
That leaping veins threw to the wind
And brains turned sour;
The blood got up as red as wax
As kisses froze the waxing thought,
The spirit racked its muscles and
The loins cried murder.

The strings of fire choked his sex
And tied an iris in his throat

To burst into a hanging land
Where flesh's fever
Itched on the hangman's silks;
The brains of death undid the knot
Before the blood and flame were twined
In love's last collar.

See, says the lime, around these wrecks
Of growing bones the muscles slid;
I chalked upon the breastbone's slate
And ran a river
Up through the fingers' cracks;
The milk of death, I filled the hand
That drove my stuff through skin and gut;
Death's death's undoer.

December 13 '33

Thirty Three.

This bread I break was once the oat,
This wine upon a foreign tree
Plunged in its fruit;
Man in the day or wind at night
Laid the crops low, broke the grape's joy.

Once in this wine the summer blood
Knocked in the flesh that decked the vine,
Once in this bread
The oat was merry in the wind;
Man broke the sun, pulled the wind down.

This flesh you break, this blood you let
Make desolation in the vein,
Were oat and grape,

Born of the same sweet soil and sap.
My wine you drink, my break[1] you break.

Dec: 24 '33

Thirty Four.

Your pain shall be a music in your string
And fill the mouths of heaven with your tongue
Your pain shall be
O my unborn
A vein of mine
Made fast by me.

Your string shall stretch a gully twixt the thumbs
Whose flaming blood shall rub it at the rims
Your pain shall be
O my unsown
A ragged vein
[Twixt] you and me.

Your pain shall be a meaning in your lips
As milk shall be a music in the paps
Your pain shall be
O my unknown
A stream of mine
Not milked by me.

Your pain shall not unmilk you of the food
That drops to make a music in your blood
Your pain shall be
O my undone
[Flesh blood and bone][1]
Surrounding me.

January 12. '34.

Thirty Five.

A process in the weather of the heart
Turns damp to dry; the golden shot
Storms in the freezing grave.
A weather in the quarter of the veins
Turns night to day; blood in their suns
Lights up the living worm.

A process in the eye forewarns
The bones of blindness; and the womb[1]
Drives in a death as life leaks out.

A darkness in the weather of the eye
Is half its light; the fathomed sea
Breaks on unangled land.
The seed that makes a forest of the loin
Forks half its fruit; and half drops down,
Slow in a sleeping wind.

A weather in the flesh and bone
Is damp and dry; the quick and dead
Move like two ghosts before the eye.

A process in the weather of the world
Turns ghost to ghost; each mothered child
Sits in their double shade.
A process blows the moon into the sun,
Pulls down the shabby curtains of the skin;
And the heart gives up its dead.

February 2. '34

Thirty Six.

Foster the light, nor veil the bushy sun,
Nor sister moons that go not in the bone,
But strip and bless the marrow in the spheres;
Master the night, nor spite thy starry spine,
Nor muster worlds that spin not through t^1 skin,
But know the clays that burrow round the stars.

Murmur of spring, nor crush the roaring eggs,
Nor hammer back the season in the figs,
But wind the summer-bearer in thy get;
Farmer the wilds, nor fill the corny bogs,
Nor harm a weed that wars not in thy legs,
But set and grow a meadow in thy heart.

And father all, nor fail with barren winds;
The weather moves like acid in thy glands;
The ass shall find a thistle in thy seed.
O gather all, nor leave the seas and sands
To cut and smother in a tide of wounds
One inch of flesh that glories in its blood.

But move unmarrowed in thy ragged shifts,
O sea and sky, nor sorrow as this flesh
Goes from another with a nitric smile;
Nor as my bones are bridled on her shafts,
Or when my locks are shooting in the turf,
Shalt thou fetch down the comets with a howl.

God gave the clouds their colours and their shapes;

He gave me clay, and dyed the crowded sea
With the green wings of fish and fairy men;
Set thou thy clouds and daylights on my lips,
Give me thy tempers and thy tides as I
Have given flesh unto the sea and moon.

February 23. '34.

Thirty Seven.

I

The shades of girls all flavoured from their shrouds,
The bones of men, the broken in their beds,
Even the dancing ash,
When sunlight goes go dainty in the yards;
And even we, ascending through the lids,
Dance in our drowsy flesh.

The skeletons return when cocks go mad,
And dust and girl blow backward to their trash,
Night of the flesh is shaken of its blood,
Night of the brain stripped of its burning bush.

Our eunuch dreams, all seedless in the light,
Of light and love, the tempers of the heart,
Whack their boys' limbs,
And, winding-footed in their shawl and sheet,
[Go groom the brides and kiss t salt shades sweet
As the bees' creams.]¹

The brides return, freed from the[ir] starry knot,
The midnight pulleys that unhoused the tomb;
No children break, all flavoured into light[,]
[When, sad of gut, love sacks her dream.]²

II

In this our age the gunman and his moll,
Two one-dimensioned ghosts, love on a reel,
Strange to my moony eye,
And speak their midnight nothings as they swell;
When cameras shut they hurry to their holes
Down in the yard of day.

They dance between their arclamps and my skull,
Impose their shots, throwing the nights away;
I watch the show of shadows kiss or kill,
Flavoured of celluloid give love the lie.

III

Which is the world? Of my two sleepings, which
Shall fall awake when cures and their itch
Raise up this red-eyed earth?
Pack off the shapes of daylight and their starch,
[The sunny gents who piddle in the porch,]³
Or drive the night-geared forth.

[Which is the dream, and which the photograph?
And which is life, is death?
This is the world which whispers in our breath:
Tis is the world. Have faith.]⁴

[*March '34.*]

The photograph is married to the eye,
Grafts on its bride one-sided skins of truth;
The dream has sucked the sleeper of his faith

That shrouded men might marrow as they fly.

This is the world: the lying likeness of
Our strips of stuff that tatter as we move
Loving [and being loth];[5]
The dream that kicks the buried from their sack
And lets their trash be honoured as the quick.
[This is the world. Have faith.][6]

For we shall be a shouter like the cock,
Blowing the old dead back; our shots shall smack
The image from the plates.
And we shall be fit fellows for a life,
And who remain shall flower as they love,
Praise to our faring hearts.

March '34.

Thirty Eight.

Where once the waters of your face
Spun to my screws, your dry ghost blows,
The dead turns up its eye;
Where once the mermen through your ice
Pushed up their hair, the dry wind steers
Through salt and root and roe.

Where once your green knots sank their splice
Into the tided cord, there goes
The green unraveller,
His scissors oiled, his knife hung loose
To cut the channels at their course[1]
And lay the salt fruits low.

Invisible, your clocking tides

Break on the love-beds of the weeds;
The weed of love's left dry;
There round about your stones the shades
Of children go who from their voids
Cry to the dolphined sea.

Dry as a tomb, your coloured lids
Shall not be latched while magic glides
Sage on the earth and sky;
There shall be corals in your beds,
There shall be serpents in your tides,
Till all our sea-faiths die.

March 18. '34.

Thirty Nine.

I

I see the boys of summer in their ruin
Lay the gold tithings barren,
Setting no store by harvest freeze the soils;
There in their heat the winter floods
Of frozen loves they fetch their girls,
And drown the cargoed apples in their tides.

These boys of light are curdlers in their folly,
Sour the boiling honey,
The jacks of frost they finger in the hives;
There in the sun the frigid threads
Of doubt and dark they feed their nerves,
The signal moon is zero in their voids.

I see the summer children in their mothers
Split up the brawned womb's weathers,
Divide the night and day with fairy thumbs;
There in the deep with quartered shades

Of sun and moon they paint their dams
As sunlight paints the shelling of their heads.

I see that from these boys shall men of nothing
Stature by seedy shifting
Or lame the air with leaping from its heats;
There from their hearts the dogdayed pulse
Of love and light bursts in their throats.[1]
Oh see the pulse of summer in the ice.

II

But seasons must be challenged or they totter
Into a chiming quarter
Where, punctual as death, we ring the stars;
There in his night the black-tongued bells
The sleepy man of winter pulls,
Nor blows back moon-and-midnight as she blows.

We are the dark deniers, let us summon
Death from a summer woman,
A muscling life from lovers in their cramp,
From the fair dead who flush the sea
The bright-eyed worm on Davy's lamp,
And from the planted womb the man of straw.

We summer boys in this four-winded spinning,
Green of the seaweeds' iron,
Hold up the noisy sea and drop her birds,
Pick the world's ball of wave and froth
To choke the deserts with her tides,
And comb the county gardens for a wreath.

In spring we cross our foreheads with the holly,

Heigh ho the blood and berry,
And nail the merry squires to the trees;
Here love's damp muscle dries and dies,
Here break a kiss in no love's quarry.
Oh see the poles of promise in the boys.

III

I see you boys of summer in your ruin.
Man in his maggot's barren.
And boys are full and foreign in the pouch.
I am the man your father was.
We are the sons of flint and pitch.
Oh see the poles are kissing as they cross.[2]

April '34.

Forty.

In the beginning was the three-pointed star,
One smile of light across the empty face;
One bough of bone across the rooting air,
The substance [spread][1] that marrowed the first sun;
And, burning ciphers on the round of space,
Heaven and hell mixed as they spun.

In the beginning was the pale signature,
Three-syllabled and starry as the smile;
And after came the imprints on the water,
Stamp of the minted face upon the moon;
The blood that touched the crosstree and the grail
Touched the first cloud and left a sign.

In the beginning was the mounting fire

That set alight the weathers from a spark,
A three-eyed, red-eyed spark blunt as a flower;
Life rose and spouted from the rolling seas,
Burst in the roots, pumped from the earth and rock
The secret oils that drive the grass.

In the beginning was the word, the word
That from the solid bases of the light
Abstracted all the letters of the void;
And from the cloudy bases of the breath
The word flowed up, translating to the heart
First characters of birth and death.

In the beginning was the secret brain;
The brain was celled and soldered in the thought
Before the pitch was forking to a sun;
Before the veins were shaking in their sieve,
And blood was scattered to the winds of light,
A secret heart rehearsed its love.

                              [*March*] *April. '34.*

Forty One.

If I was¹ tickled by the rub of love,
A rooking girl who stole me for her side,
Broke through her straws, breaking my bandaged string,
If the red tickle as the cattle calve
Still set to scratch a laughter from my lung,
I would not fear the apple nor its flood
Nor the bad blood of spring.

Shall it be male or female? says the cells,
And drop the plum like fire from the flesh.

If I was tickled by the hatching hair,
The winging bone that sprouted in the heels,
The itch of man upon the baby's thigh,
I would not fear the gallows nor the axe
Nor the crossed sticks of war.

[If from the first some mother of the wind
  Gave suck to such a bud as forks my eye,
  I would not fear the howling round the cots
  As time on time the lean searibbons round
  Parched shires in dry lands, and the rat's lot,
  Nor all the herring smelling of the sea
  Nor the death in the light.]

Shall it be male or female? say the fingers
Chalking the [jakes]² with green [things of]³ the [brain].⁴
I would not fear the muscling-in of love
If I was tickled by the urchin hungers
Rehearsing heat upon a raw-edged nerve.
I would not fear the devil in the loin
Nor the outspoken grave.

If I was tickled by the lover's rub
That wipes away not crow's-foot nor the lock
Of sick old [age]⁵ [up]on the falling jaws:
Time and the crabs and the sweethearting crib
Would leave me cold as butter for the flies:
[The biting days would soften as I struck
  Bells on the dead fools']⁶ toes.

This world is half the devil's and my own,
Daft with the drug that's smoking in a girl
And curling round the bud that forks her eye.
An old man's shank one-marrowed with my bone,

And all the herrings smelling in the sea,
I sit and watch the worm beneath my nail
Wearing the quick away.

And that's the rub, the only rub that tickles.
The knobbly ape that swings along his sex
From damp love-darkness and the nurse's twist
Can never raise the midnight of a chuckle,
Nor when he finds a beauty in the breast
Of lover, mother, lovers or his six
Feet in the rubbing dust.

And what's the rub? Death's feather on the nerve?
Your mouth, my love, the thistle in a kiss?
My Jack of Christ born thorny on the tree?
The words of death are dryer than his stiff,
My wordy wounds are printed with your hair.
I would be tickled by the rub that is:
Man be my metaphor.

April 30, '34.

NOTES TO
THE INTRODUCTION

[1] The four poetry exercise books in the Lockwood Library of the State University of New York at Buffalo have been named by the library as follows: (I) "1930 Notebook" (II) "1930–1932 Notebook" (III) "February 1933 Notebook" (IV) "August 1933 Notebook." All are approximately 6" by 8"—though of differing bulkiness. Covers are lacking, but traces in the staple of the August 1933 Notebook indicate a red cover like the Red Prose Notebook also in the Lockwood Library, which, in keeping with Thomas' description in "The Fight," has "Danger Don'ts" on the back—see *Portrait of the Artist as a Young Dog* (Dent edition, p. 77; New Directions Paperbook No. 51, p. 52). The Prose Notebook contains mainly published stories.

[2] During the final stages of editing these Notebooks I was fortunate to have access to a copy of the typescript of the early letters to be included in the selection of letters by Dylan Thomas edited by Constantine FitzGibbon, from which this quotation is taken. Mr. FitzGibbon also kindly made available to me a galley proof of his official biography of Dylan Thomas, which naturally covers some of the same ground as this Introduction. I indicate in these notes wherever I am specifically indebted to these two sources.

[3] Dylan Thomas' letters to Henry Treece are in the Lockwood Library of the State University of New York at Buffalo, along with his letters to Trevor Hughes and Pamela Hansford Johnson, from which I quote below.

[4] In April 1941, penniless and uncomfortable in borrowed quarters, Thomas balanced future possible use of the Notebooks against immediate financial gain, and decided to sell them. An undated House of Books sale catalog paraphrases a letter by Thomas of 8 April 1941 ("name of recipient obliterated"):

> Very interested in selling his poems, but that most of his poems are in exercise books which also contain utter failures that he will never print. Will send the books along and hopes there will be a market for the work in bulk as he is in need of money.

The value of such manuscripts had been suggested to Thomas by an inquiry from Charles D. Abbott of the Lockwood Library at Buffalo (Mr.

Abbott's comment to the editor), and it was to Buffalo that the manu-scripts were offered. "I cannot imagine," wrote Bertram Rota, the book-seller, on 1 September 1941, "any collection of manuscripts which illus-trates better the genesis and development of poetic ideas, which I under-stand to be the aspect which appeals to you particularly." "According to all rules and regulations I cannot buy them," replied Charles Abbott on 24 September. "But I want them so badly that I have . . . persuaded a private friend to buy them for us. It is a transaction which is most unlikely to occur again." From Thomas B. Lockwood, the library's chief benefactor, came the $140 which completed a sale the like of which, considering today's prices, will certainly not occur again. The four poetry Notebooks were priced at £6, £7.10, £6.10, and £5 respectively. The rest of the lot comprised the *Ballad of the Long-legged Bait* worksheets £10, the Red Prose Notebook £5, and the manuscript of a short story £1.10. On the library's self-imposed rule of nonpayment for worksheets of living poets, see Charles D. Abbott's introduction to *Poets at Work* (New York: Harcourt, Brace and Co., 1948), pp. 33–35. In chapter 10 of *The Life of Dylan Thomas* Constantine FitzGibbon makes an inter-esting connection between Thomas' selling of the Notebooks at the age of twenty-six and Keats' death at the same age.

⁵ I tabulated the information that the Notebooks reveal about Thomas' revisions in the article "Dylan Thomas' *Collected Poems*: Chronology of Composition," *Publications of the Modern Language Association,* LXXVI (June 1961), 292–297; and provided further dis-cussion on the point in Appendix I to my *Entrances to Dylan Thomas' Poetry* (Pittsburgh: University of Pittsburgh Press; Lowestoft: Scorpion Press, 1963).

⁶ There were undoubtedly many more similar exercise books. When Thomas began submitting poems to publishers he could boast to Geoffrey Grigson of his "innumerable exercise books full of poems" (letter in Lockwood Library, Buffalo, of about August 1933). Writing to Henry Treece as late as May 1938, he mentions "about 10 exercise books full of poems." In the story "The Fight" the young poet sits in his bedroom "by the boiler" and reads through his "exercise-books full of poems" (*Portrait of the Artist as a Young Dog:* Dent edition, p. 77; New Direc-tions Paperback No. 51, p. 52), and some of these must have still been around when he compiled the quotations from his early poems that appear in that story, written in 1939.

⁷ Quoted by Rota in his letter to Abbott dated 1 September 1941.

⁸ P. E. S[mart]., " 'Under Milk Wood'—and Reminiscence of School Days," *The Spread Eagle,* XXIX (April 1954), 134. The school teacher in "Return Journey" remembers that young Thomas "was thirty-third in trigonometry"; see *Quite Early One Morning* (Dent edition, p. 84; New Directions Paperback No. 90, p. 81).

[9] *South Wales Daily Post* (19 June 1929), and *Swansea Grammar School Magazine*, XXVI (July 1929), 54.

[10] J.D.H., review in *South Wales Daily Post* (21 February 1930). For a full account of Thomas' early acting career, see Ethel Ross, "Dylan Thomas and the Amateur Theatre," *The Swan*, No. 2, Third Series, (March 1958), 15–21.

[11] P. E. S[mart]., *The Spread Eagle*, p. 134. Smart adds: "We may not at the time have realised that Dylan was already instinctively excluding from his life everything that might distract him from his fixed path." Daniel Jones confirms this in his memoir in *Encounter*, II (January 1954), 10; included in E. W. Tedlock, ed., *Dylan Thomas: The Legend and the Poet* (London: Heinemann, 1960), p. 18: "he would have needed twice the time to accomplish all that he did accomplish if he had not discerned clearly and from the beginning the things that were of no use to him, or if he had not steadily ignored them."

[12] *Adam*, No. 238 (1953). See the list in J. Alexander Rolph, *Dylan Thomas: A Bibliography* (London: J. M. Dent and Sons, 1956; New York: New Directions, 1956). Three Notebook poems were considered suitable for the *Swansea Grammar School Magazine:* "The shepherd blew upon his reed," undated and thoroughly deleted in the 1930 Notebook; and poems IV and V in the 1930–1932 Notebook, both of which prompted the poet's later marginal "Ugh."

[13] From a manuscript printed in facsimile, entitled "Poetic Manifesto," *Texas Quarterly*, IV (Winter 1961).

[14] List given by Thomas in "I Am Going to Read Aloud," *London Magazine*, III (September 1956), 14. He adds: "I tried my little trotters at every poetical form. How could I know the tricks of this trade unless I tried to do them myself?"

[15] *Swansea Grammar School Magazine*, XXVII (April 1930), 25–26. Further parodies in "Children's Hour, or Why the B.B.C. Broke Down," *Swansea Grammar School Magazine* (December 1930), and "The sincerest form of flattery," *Swansea Grammar School Magazine* (July 1931).

[16] Daniel Jones, in Tedlock, *Dylan Thomas: The Legend and the Poet*, p. 17.

[17] Richard Aldington, *Exile and Other Poems* (London: George Allen and Unwin, 1923), pp. 29–30; Sacheverell Sitwell, *The Hundred and One Harlequins* (London: Duckworth, 1929), p. 27; Thomas' 1930 Notebook poems *14, 24,* and *30.*

[18] Chapter 5 of his *Dylan Thomas "A Dog Among the Fairies"* (London: Lindsay Drummond, 1949); chapter 4 of the revised edition (London: Ernest Benn; New York: John De Graff, 1956).

[19] *Portrait of the Artist as a Young Dog* (Dent edition, pp. 91–92; New Directions Paperbook No. 51, p. 62).

[20] *Letters to Vernon Watkins* (London: J. M. Dent–Faber and Faber; New York: New Directions, 1957), pp. 37, 40, and 57. The title *In Memory of Ann Jones* was first used in *Life and Letters To-day* (Summer 1938). No extant worksheet of the revision exists.

[21] Caitlin Thomas, *Leftover Life to Kill* (London: Putnam, 1957; Boston: Atlantic-Little, Brown, 1957), p. 56.

[22] See "Return Journey," *Quite Early One Morning* (Dent edition, p. 88; New Directions edition, p. 85); also Bert Trick, "Dylan—the eternal Swansea boy," *Country Quest*, I (Autumn 1960), 26–27.

[23] Marjorie Adix memoir in *Encounter*, II (January 1954), 15; included in Tedlock, *Dylan Thomas: The Legend and the Poet*, p. 66.

[24] Geoffrey Grigson remembers these two poets (along with Rossetti and Spender) as "proffered" by Thomas at his first arrival in London; "Recollections of Dylan Thomas," *London Magazine*, IV (September 1957), 40.

[25] In March 1934 Thomas wrote to a new correspondent Glyn Jones to the same effect: "My own obscurity is quite an unfashionable one, based, as it is, on a preconceived symbolism derived . . . from the cosmic significance of the human anatomy." The Glyn Jones correspondence is in the collection of Charles E. Feinberg, Detroit.

[26] "Replies to an Enquiry," *New Verse* (October 1934), p. 7.

[27] See also Claude Rawson, "Dylan Thomas" in *Talks to Teachers of English* 2 (Newcastle-upon-Tyne: King's College, 1962), pp. 51–52.

[28] To the many published testimonies concerning Thomas' apparent ill health, one can add that of his mother, given in a Canadian Broadcasting Corporation tape recording made by Colin D. Edwards in the summer of 1958: "As a young boy [Dylan] was extremely delicate. And then when he was about fifteen he had a hemorrhage rather badly too. He was always pretty weak in the chest and he had asthma very badly up until he died." Constantine FitzGibbon goes very thoroughly into the question of Thomas' health in chapter 5 of *The Life of Dylan Thomas*.

[29] The words "foster the light" were first used by Trevor Hughes in a letter to Thomas of 13 January 1934, and as used by the poet are perhaps as much a response to the troubled life of his friend as to his own.

[30] Robert Graves, "These Be Your Gods, O Israel!" in *The Crowning Privilege* (London: Cassell & Co., 1955, pp. 132–133; New York: Doubleday, 1956, p. 139). Graves' description seems rather to fit the possibly pre-Notebook poetry included in the Appendix to this volume.

[31] The Hanley collection was recently acquired by the University of Texas. Thomas exchanged many poems with Pamela Hansford Johnson, but these were invariably returned to the poet with comments. Glyn

Jones' typescript "Jack of Christ" was published in *Western Mail* (30 July 1960); see also Glyn Jones, "Dylan Thomas—The Other Man," *Western Mail* (21 April 1958).

[32] *New Verse* got poems Twenty Nine, Thirty Seven, and Thirty Nine; *Criterion* poem Twenty Four.

[33] There is no extant manuscript for *Thy Breath Was Shed;* but Pamela Hansford Johnson remembers this poem as, at one stage, having the title *The Candle* and beginning:

> Thy breath was shed
> Invisible to weave
> Around my carven head
> A carven eve.

The poem was later recast and published in *Poetry* (*London*), No. 9 (1944).

[34] It is evident that *I see the boys of summer* was not altered or lengthened for *18 Poems*.

[35] Thomas continued this work into May 1936, witness a letter to Richard Church of Dent's of the first of that month: "In less than a month I shall probably be able to let you have the other half dozen poems you need: two new ones, completing the long poem of which you have the first eight sections [the Sonnets], and four younger ones selected and revised [presumably from the Notebooks]" (quote taken from FitzGibbon typescript).

[36] For example, Henry Treece in chapter 6, "Straight Poet," of his *Dylan Thomas* (London: Ernest Benn Limited; New York: John De Graff, 1956). "C.B.S." (Bernard Spencer—I am indebted to Geoffrey Grigson for the identification) divided *Twenty-five Poems* into "sense" and "nonsense" poems in his review in *New Verse* (Christmas 1936): the nine "sense" poems are all early, revised poems.

[37] The only poems in *Deaths and Entrances* (1946) having early versions in the Notebooks are: *The Hunchback in the Park,* quite close to poem LVVV, 9 May 1932, and revised on the verso page in July 1941; and *On the Marriage of a Virgin,* doubly revised from poem Sixteen in the February 1933 Notebook, with the first revision on verso pages dated January 1941. *When I Woke* owes its opening to a discarded line in poem Fifty One in the February 1933 Notebook (see *Letters to Vernon Watkins,* p. 41); *To Others than You,* "a new short poem, nothing very much" (*Letters to Vernon Watkins,* p. 68), took one phrase from an early story and another from poem Twenty Two in the February 1933 Notebook. We can only guess how many published poems lacking worksheets are in the same category.

NOTES
TO THE POEMS

IN ORDER TO PRESENT a pleasant reading text of the Notebook poems, the poet's alterations to his early poems were not shown but relegated, along with a record of other idiosyncrasies in the manuscripts, to the following notes, which also supply a listing of the poems, their dates, the pages of the Notebook which contain them, and other pertinent information.

Footnotes are provided for (a) all Thomas' misspellings, (b) notably syntactical irregularity, and (c) alterations to words, interlinings, and other meaningful additions to the poems. No footnote is given where words have merely been deleted; square brackets enclose the deleted words or passages; sometimes, when deletion on top of deletion exists, double bracketing occurs. Occasional slips of the pen made by the poet and corrected at the time of first writing the poem are ignored both in the text and in the notes, as are also misshapen letters, careless irregularity in the verse lines, and insignificant marginal marks and stains. The ampersand has invariably been written out as "and."

After repeated failure to make any certain reckoning of the sequence in which the poet made the numerous alterations, the editor has refrained from turning the problem over to the reader; only occasional reference is made to how the alterations were done, whether in pencil or in ink, whether in green ink or in black, whether above or below the line. The date to a poem is sometimes in a different ink from the poem itself, but again these merely mystifying cases have not been noted. It was thought that anyone interested in these, and other matters of calligraphy, would, in any case, need to investigate the manuscripts themselves, available in the Lockwood Library of the State University of New York at Buffalo.

The editor has allowed some biographical illumination to enter the notes, but no explication of the poems. The notes attempt to deal concisely but fully with Thomas' utilization of lines or whole poems in other extant manuscripts and in his published books; but this is not a variorum edition. The interested reader is expected to have his *Collected Poems* available for comparison of the texts. As for manuscript versions not in the Notebooks and published poems not in the *Collected Poems,* only the more notable variants have been mentioned.

Thomas did not number the pages of the first two of the four Notebooks; for convenience in making the following notes, the editor assumes throughout the method of pagination of the later two Notebooks, where the poet numbered only the right-hand side of the page. (The verso page is here indicated by a "v.") The 1930 Notebook, by this scheme, has 104 pages numbered p. 1 to p. 52v. The leaf torn out between p. 12v and p. 13 (and correspondingly between p. 40v and p. 41)—with traces showing in the spine—is discounted in the numbering, since it does not interrupt the sequence of the poems.

The poem numbering in this first Notebook is complicated by the fact that there was a preliminary numbering up to poem 37, then a renumbering: the numbers *1* to *8* were gone over in pencil (pencil was used for all the numbering); poem 9 was thoroughly deleted, so that the original poem *10* is now *9;* old number *11* is now *10;* old *12* was deleted completely, so that old *13* was altered to *11;* old *14* was altered to *12,* which was itself deleted completely, so that old *15* was altered to *12;* old *16* to *13;* and so on (with the unexplained absence of *25* in the old sequence); old *30* was deleted completely, so that when the old sequence ends with *37* that poem is now *32,* and the new sequence continues with *33* up to *42.*

The four excised poems are in rhyme, so that the deletions and renumbering probably took place at the time Thomas added the heading to p. 1: "Mainly Free Verse Poems."

Though half the poems remain undated ("n.d." abbreviation for "no date"), they presumably all fall within the span of the first and last poem, 27 April 1930 to 9 December 1930, except for poem *21* dated 28, 29 April 1929, apparently included so that additions could be made to it.

pp. 1, 1v, 2, 2v, 3, 3v, 4　　　　　　　　　　　　　　April 27th 1930

1

Osiris, Come to Isis.
"He stands at the steaming river's edge"

The poem is illustrated in the upper margin of p. 1 by a small pencil sketch and a large ink sketch, presumably of Osiris.

This first poem is unique in having been tampered with by someone other than the poet; e.g. "sadr" (l. 9) is deleted in pencil and "sadr" (same word) interlined not in Thomas' hand. The intention was apparently to clarify the poet's calligraphy. These half-dozen intrusions have been ignored both in the text and in the notes.

[1] "Seb" is the form of the name found in Sir James Frazer. An alternative form is "Geb," but Thomas definitely uses the former.
[2] Correction of "-musled" by "c" interlined with a caret.
[3] Correction in pencil. Square brackets, here and throughout the text, indicate that the enclosed lines, words, or parts of words were deleted by the poet.
[4] Correction of "-musled" by "c" interlined.
[5] Presumably should be: "Why were you born again".
[6] Misspelling of "intercourse".
[7] Uncorrected misspelling of "muscled".
[8] Misspelling of "achieve".

pp. 4v, 5, 5v, 6　　　　　　　　　　　　　　　　　May 2[d] 1930

2

(Based upon themes from Mother Goose)
"The lion-fruit goes from my thumb"

"Poem." was added in pencil above the subtitle.
[1] Apostrophe required.

Thomas had done less metaphysical variations on "Miss Muffet" in the *Swansea Grammar School Magazine,* April 1930, parodying Ella Wheeler Wilcox and W. B. Yeats.

pp. 6v, 7　　　　　　　　　　　　　　　　　　　May 2[d] 1930

3

Poem Written on the Death of a Very Dear Illusion
"Grant me a period for recuperation,"

p. 7v   May 6th 1930.

4
"You shall not despair"
Poem also in typescript, British Museum.

pp. 8, 8v   May 10th 1930

5
"My vitality overwhelms you,"
[1] Misspelling of "muscles".

pp. 9, 9v, 10   May 17th 1930

6
And so the New Love Came.
"And so the new love came at length"

pp. 10v, 11, 11v   May 18th 1930

7
On Watching Goldfish.
"You collect such strange shapes"
[1] Misspelling of "muscles".   [2] Presumably should be "beach-comber".

pp. 12, 12v   n.d.

8
"The lion, lapping the water,"
[1] Misspelling of "unnecessary".   [3] "And" added in margin.
[2] Misspelling of "Ascetic".

p. 13   n.d.

[9]
["One has found a delicate power,"]
For further early poems in this mode, see Appendix I.

pp. 13v, 14   n.d.

9
I Am Aware
"I am aware of the rods"
The fifteen lines of the poem on p. 14 are thoroughly crossed out with the marginal note, "Omit."

pp. 14v, 15, 15v   n.d.

10
"My river, even though it lifts"

[1] Interlined: "thin".

Poem also in typescript, British Museum.

p. 16   n.d.

[12]
["The shepherd blew upon his reed"]

Thomas, as editor, published this deleted poem in *Swansea Grammar School Magazine,* July 1930, with the title *Orpheus.*

pp. 16v, 17, 17v   June 18th 30

11
"The corn blows from side to side lightly,"

[1] Interlined "As".   [3] Comma altered to period.
[2] Misspelling of "noiselessly".

p. 18   June 17th 30

[12]
[The Shepherd to his Lass.]
["He said, 'You seem so lovely, Chloe,"]

Thomas wrote this deleted poem in the autograph album of Bonnie L. James in the summer of 1930. The album is now in the National Library of Wales, Aberystwyth.

pp. 18v, 19, 19v   June 6th

12
"We will be conscious of our sanctity"

[1] Presumably should be "size of".   [2] Misspelling of "conscious".

p. 20   June 19th

13
"I have come to catch your voice,"

pp. 20v, 21, 21v   n.d.

14
"My love is deep night"

[1] Misspelling of "irretrievable".

First 24 lines of poem in typescript, British Museum.

pp. 22, 22v   July 1 1930

15
"When your furious motion is steadied,"

[1] Interlined with caret: "is".

    Poem also in typescript, British Museum.

pp. 23, 23v   July 17th

16
"No thought can trouble my unwholesome pose,"

[1] Interlined: "lightness".   [2] Question mark required.

pp. 24, 24v   July 20th

17
"The hill of sea and sky is carried"

p. 25   n.d.

18
"So I sink myself in the moment,"

pp. 25v, 26   Aug: 8th

19
"No, pigeon, I'm too wise;"

[1] Correct form "flies" found in typescript, British Museum.

p. 26v   Aug 11th.

20
"The cavern shelters me from harm;"

pp. 27, 27v, 28, 28v   28, 29 April 1929.

21
Woman on Tapestry.
"Her woven hands beckoned me,"

[1] Misspelling of "Suave".   [3] Interlined: "She".
[2] Misspelling of "believe".   [4] "Went" added in margin.

    Pencil note interlined above "So the hills": "X & Y in here" presumably indicates that the continuations of this poem, marked X and Y, should be inserted at that point.

p. 29   n.d.
>   Continuation of Woman on Tapestry.
>   This was possibly poem 25 in the old numbering, but no trace of the number remains. The caption was added in pencil, with "X" in pencil.

p. 29v   n.d.
>   Woman on Tapestry.
>   (Continued)
>   Caption in ink; "Y" added in pencil.

pp. 30, 30v   n.d.
>   *22*
>   "Pillar breaks, and mast is cleft"
> [1] Interlined: "shouldering".
>   Poem also in typescript, British Museum.

pp. 31, 31v   n.d.
>   *23*
>   "It's light that makes the intervals"

p. 32   n.d.
>   *24*
>   "Let me escape,"
> [1] Initial word capitalized in typescript, British Museum.

p. 32v   n.d.
>   *25*
>   "Oh, dear, angelic time—go on."
> [1] Word capitalized in typescript, British Museum.
>   Typescript, British Museum, lacks final deleted lines; begins "O dear, angelic Time".

p. 33   n.d.
>   [*30*]
>   ["The rod can lift its twining head"]

pp. 33v, 34, 34v   n.d.
>   *26*
>   "And the ghost rose up to interrogate:"
> [1] Possibly meant to be "distract".   though there are no quotation
> [2] Misspelling of "dahlia'll".   marks.
> [3] The speech probably ends here,   [4] Interlined: "dolphin".

[5] Word "the" capitalized after the deletion.
  First 24 lines of poem in typescript, British Museum.

pp. 35, 35v   n.d.

27
"When I allow myself to fly,"
[1] Misspelling of "echo".

pp. 35v, 36   n.d.

28
Admit the Sun.
"Admit the sun into your high nest"
[1] Misspelling of "Frankincense".   script, British Museum, which also
[2] Question mark supplied in type-   adds final period to poem.

pp. 36v, 37, 37v, 38, 38v   n.d.

29
A Section of a Poem called "Hassan's Journey into the World."
"We sailed across the Arabian sea,"
[1] Misspelling of "syncopate".   [5] Misspelling of "Believe".
[2] Misspelling of "penetrate".   [6] Interlined: "and lose".
[3] Misspelling of "incorporeal".   [7] Comma altered to period; quota-
[4] Numbers in margin: "612".   tion marks added.

pp. 39, 39v   November 3rd

30
"I know this vicious minute's hour;"
Thomas deliberately left some initial words uncapitalized, as in 24
above and some subsequent poems.

pp. 40, 40v   November 4th

31
[Claudetta, You, and Me.]
"Her voice is a clear line of light"
Typescript, British Museum, has "clean" for the Notebook's "clear"
(ll. 1 and 13).

pp. 41, 41v   November 5th 1930

32
"Come, black-tressed Claudetta, home"
[1] Interlined: "splendidly".

pp. 42, 42v   n.d.

33
"Cool, oh no cool,"

[1] Question mark required for the sentence as a whole, though the previous five lines should be taken as a speech.

Poem also in typescript, British Museum.

pp. 43, 43v, 44   n.d.

34
"They brought you mandolins"

[1] Interlined in pencil: "already".   away]".

[2] This line is followed in the Note-   [3] Possibly a mistake—"more" in-
book by a false start on the next   tended.
line: "[The garden was far   [4] Speech probably ends here.

p. 44v   n.d.

35
"The air you breathe encroaches"

Poem deliberately unpunctuated. Typescript, British Museum, follows Notebook.

p. 45   n.d.

36
"When all your tunes have caused"

[1] Apostrophe required.

pp. 45v, 46, 46v   n.d.

37
Written in a classroom.
"Am I to understand"

[1] Interlined: "hate".   omitted in typescript, British Mu-
[2] This, and also the last three lines   seum.
of the poem, deleted in pencil,

pp. 47, 47v   n.d.

38
"Hand in hand Orpheus"

The last three deleted lines are omitted in typescript, British Museum, which capitalizes the lines and adds some punctuation.

pp. 48, 48v   22ᵈ November. 1930.

39
"I, poor romantic, held her heel"

[1] Altered to "glistening".   [3] Typescript, British Museum, has
[2] Possibly should be "her".   "raise".

Typescript, British Museum, adds the title "CABARET".

pp. 49, 49v, 50   n.d.

40
"Oh! the children run towards the door,"

[1] Correct form: "barriered".

pp. 50v, 51   n.d.

41
"Tether the first thought if you will,"

A pencil figure in outer margin of p. 50v.

[1] After "It" the line was left blank, and "stays for me" added later in pencil.

[2] Misspelling of "Gratifying"; this line, and also the last line of the poem, omitted in typescript, British Museum.

pp. 51v, 52, 52v   December 9ᵗʰ 1930

42
"How shall the animal"

A female figure drawn in ink in the lower inside margin of p. 51v.

[1] Question mark required.   [4] Interlined: "lightest heel".

[2] This line is circled in pencil.   [5] A space was left, and "wingèd"
Thomas utilizes it in a letter to   added later in pencil (lacking in
Vernon Watkins dated 21 March   typescript, British Museum).
1938 (see *Letters to Vernon Wat-*   [6] Dots altered to a semicolon—per-
kins, p. 38).   haps the question mark should be
[3] Interlined: "That."   here.

Typescript, British Museum, adds final period to poem.

This poem can be taken as an ancestor of *How shall my animal,* completely redone early in 1938 (see *Letters to Vernon Watkins,* p. 37), and published in *Criterion,* October 1938, and in *The Map of Love* and *Collected Poems.*

A phone number "Royal 6034" is written in the margin of the back page of the Notebook (p. 52v), and the poet's signature "Dylan Marlais T" extending off the inner margin.

THE 1930–1932 NOTEBOOK

This Notebook continues the sequence from the 1930 Notebook up to 2 July 1932. Most of the poems are dated, some out of sequence but within the period. It has 122 pages, not numbered by the poet, but for the purpose of these notes numbered from p. 1 to p. 61v in keeping with the poet's practice later. The leaf missing between p. 20v and p. 21 does not interrupt the sequence of the poems; the corresponding leaf, pp. 41, 41v, is loose from the staple. The poems are numbered (in ink, apparently at the time of first writing) in the poet's style of Roman numeral, from I to LVVVI (i.e., sixty-six), followed by six unnumbered poems.

Following the 1930 Notebook, Thomas began this Notebook by heading it "Mainly Free Verse Poems." This caption was later deleted, though the contents of the Notebook would certainly fit that description.

pp. 1, 1v   Dec 1930

I
"This love—perhaps I over-rate it,"

As well as the date immediately below the poem, there is at the foot of p. 1v the further date: "25th Dec:" apparently unattached.

pp. 2, 2v   Dec 18 1930

II
"To-day, this hour I breathe"

[1] Presumably meant to be "prey".

A thorough revision made about January 1936 (but not extant in manuscript) produced *To-day, this insect,* published in *Purpose,* October-December 1936, and in *Twenty-five Poems* and in *Collected Poems.*

pp. 3, 3v   Dec 19 1930

III
"Sometimes the sky's too bright,"

[1] Interlined: "hot".   [2] Question mark required.

Poem also in typescript, British Museum.

p. 4   Dec 28th. 1930

IV
"Here is the bright green sea,"

[1] Pencil used for the deletion supplies new semicolon.

Inner margin contains the pejorative "Ugh". Nevertheless Thomas chose this poem for publication in the *Swansea Grammar School Magazine,* April 1931, as the first of *Two Images,* the second being the next poem.

p. 4v   December 30th 1930
V
"My golden bird the sun"
Typescript, British Museum, has title "Image".
Again a marginal pejorative, "Ogh"; and again published in the *Swansea Grammar School Magazine,* April 1931. *Adam* (1953) reproduced these *Two Images.*

p. 5   n.d.
VI
"Live in my living;"
[1] The poet left a space between the commas, which was never filled.

pp. 5v, 6, 6v   Jan 2 1931
VII
"Rain cuts the place we tread,"
[1] Misspelling of "ecstatic".   [3] Interlined: "caress".
[2] Typescript, British Museum, ap-   [4] Misspelling of "indigo".
propriately adds "not".
   Typescript, British Museum, adds final period to the poem.

pp. 7, 7v   Jan 20th. 1931
VIII
"The morning, space for Leda"
Of the two typescripts in the British Museum, one has a variant for the fourth line from the end: "Dances a measure with the swan".

pp. 8, 8v   27th Jan.
IX
"The spire cranes; its statue"
The whole poem on p. 8 is crossed through, possibly at the time the poem was revised (November 1937, see Introduction, p. 41) to become *The spire cranes* as published in *Wales,* March 1938; *Poetry,* August 1938; and in *The Map of Love* and *Collected Poems.*

T

p. 9   n.d.
X
"Cool may she find the day,"

pp. 9v, 10   22^d February 1931
XI
"Yesterday, the cherry sun"
[1] Misspelling of "Suave".

p. 10v   Feb 24th
XII
"Time enough to rot;"
[1] The apostrophe was added in pencil.

p. 11   March 20th
XIII
"Conceive these images in air,"
A rudimentary pencil sketch of a face appears in the inner margin, along with the deleted word "[Time]".

pp. 11v, 12   24th March.
XIV
"You be my hermaphrodite in logic,"
[1] Presumably should be "rip".

pp. 12v, 13   March 28th
XV
"Until the light is less,"
[1] Interlined: "growing".   [2] Misspelling of "temperament".

pp. 13v, 14   April 6th '31
XVI
"The neophyte, baptized in smiles,"
[1] Misspelling of "carelessness".   peace with you,".
[2] Interlined: "The".   [4] This line, except for the initial
[3] Pencil added the words: "of her   "And", is also written in pencil.
Poem also in typescript, British Museum.

p. 14v   10th April 1931
XVII
"To be encompassed by the brilliant earth"

pp. 15, 15v   May 18th '31

XVIII
"Who is to mar"

pp. 16, 16v, 17   March 30th '31.

XIX
"The natural day and night"

This is the first of a number of poems in this Notebook with rather chaotic syntax.

[1] Misspelling of "prerogative".

[2] Typescript, British Museum, has "beetle".

[3] Typescript, British Museum, has the probably preferable "corrupt-ing".

pp. 17v, 18   June 1st. '31

XX
"Although through my bewildered way"

p. 18v   June 1st '31

XXI
"High on a hill,"

p. 19   1931

XXII
"Refract the lady, drown the profiteer"

[1] Period required; after this point the poem is written in pencil.

pp. 19v, 20, 20v   June 10th

XXIII
"Into be home from home"

[1] Misspelling of "casuistry".   [2] Misspelling of "people".

pp. 21, 21v, 22, 22v, 23   16th June. '31

XXIV
"if the lady from the casino"

The first page of the poem, p. 21, is crossed through. This poem is certainly the closest Thomas gets to automatic writing; see Introduction, p. 17. The many irregularities are left unnoted.

pp. 23v, 24   July 3rd '31

XXV
"Through sober to the truth when"

pp. 24v, 25   July 28th '31

XXVI
"It is the wrong, the hurt, the mineral,"
[1] Apostrophe not needed.

pp. 25v, 26   Aug 2d '31

XXVII
"Even the voice will not last"

[1] Interlined: "pasture".   [3] Misspelling of "adumbratic".
[2] Interlined: "Must".   [4] Misspelling of "saillessly".

pp. 26v, 27   Aug: 8th '31

XXVIII
"True love's inflated; from a truthful shape"

pp. 27v, 28   Aug: 12th '31

XXIX
"Since, on a quiet night, I heard them talk"
[1] Misspelling of "loneliness".

pp. 28v, 29   Aug 16th

XXX
"They are the only dead who did not love,"
[1] Misspelling of "separate".

pp. 29v, 30   n.d.

XXXI
"Have old on my heart utterly,"
[1] Presumably should be "hold".   [2] From l. 13 the poem is written
                                           in pencil.

pp. 30v, 31   January 1931

XXXII
"The caterpillar is with child;"
Below the poem number is the pencil caption "[Fragment.]" deleted thoroughly. There is a pencil line after l. 9, perhaps indicating
that the fragment originally ended there. The date perhaps indicates
when the first nine lines were written, though it is placed at the end.

18ᵗʰ August '31

XXXIII
"Foot, head, or traces"

Typescript, British Museum, entitled "LITTLE PROBLEM," has "Of foot on head" (l. 4); "By toe or hair" (l. 12); and last two lines: "But only plumb such depths / As you, Original, derive."

The form of the poem, with its parentheses, is reminiscent of *How soon the servant sun* (see *Collected Poems*).

pp. 32ᵛ, 33   n.d.

XXXIV
"[When you have ground such beauty down to dust]"

Poem deleted in pencil on both pages, with an end note "further in book."—referring to the reappearance of this poem as XLVII below.

p. 33ᵛ   n.d.

XXXV
"Or be my paramour or die,"

[1] Misspelling of "lightest".

p. 34   n.d.

XXXVI
"The womb and the woman's grave"

The word "heart." in the outer margin below the poem number is deleted in heavy blue crayon.

p. 34ᵛ   n.d.

XXXVII
"Let Sheba bear a love for Solomon"

p. 35   n.d.

XXXVIII
"There was one world and there is another,"

[1] Interlined: "are".

p. 35ᵛ   Sept 11ᵗʰ

XXXIX
"For us there cannot be welcome"

[1] Correct form: "therein".

pp. 36, 36v   Sept 11th

XL
"An end to substance in decay's a sequence"
[1] Apostrophe needed.   [2] Presumably should be "born".

Pencil brackets enclosed the first ten lines. A pencil line after l. 21 perhaps acknowledges a change of pace.

pp. 37, 37v   Sept: 12th

XLI
"Why is the blood red and the grass green"
[1] Correct form: "Shan't".   [3] Correct form: "crieth".
[2] Correct form: "drieth".   [4] Question mark required.

This poem seems to be an ancestor of *Why east wind chills* (see poem Thirty Seven in the February 1933 Notebook, and *Collected Poems*).

pp. 38, 38v   21st September '31

XLII
"Have cheated constancy"
[1] Line runs to the edge of the Notebook page; period required.

pp. 39, 39v   September 24th '31

XLIII
"There's plenty in the world that doth not die,"
Manuscript, British Museum, has "Death sights and sees with great misgiving" (l. 6); lacks last two lines.

pp. 40, 40v   Sept: 30th '31

XLIV
"This time took has much"
[1] Possibly meant to be "breadth".   this does not seem to add any light
[2] Misspelling of "separate".   to the obscure syntax of the last
[3] Thomas had originally written   line.
"Breath's" but deleted the " 's";

p. 41   October 15th.

XLV
"Which of you put out his rising,"

p. 41V   17th Oct '31

XLVI
WRITTEN FOR A PERSONAL EPITAPH.
"Feeding the worm"
The title was added in pencil.

p. 42   Oct: 10th '31

XLVII
"When you have ground such beauty down to dust"
A repeat of poem XXXIV above.

p. 42V   July '31

XLVIII
"Sever from what I trust"
Below date there is a pencil note: "(Poem lost and then found.)"

pp. 43, 43V   Oct 26th

XLVIX
"Never to reach the oblivious dark"
The poet made an error in the poem number, which should be
XLIX or XLVIV.
[1] Misspelling of "pus".

p. 44   October

L
Introductory Poem.
"So that his philosophy be proven"
Title was added in pencil.
[1] Interlined: "[I]".

p. 44V, 45   n.d.

LI
"Take up this seed, it is most beautiful,"
[1] Apostrophe not needed.

p. 45V   November 3rd '31

LII
"There in her tears were laughter and tears again,"

p. 46   5th & 6th Nov '31

LIII
"How can the knotted root"

[1] Question mark required.   [2] Pencil added "way" above the
line.

pp. 46v, 47   October.
LIV
"Children of darkness got no wings,"

pp. 47v, 48   March. '31
LV
"It's not in misery but in oblivion,"

pp. 48v, 49   November '31
LVI
"What lunatic's whored after shadow,"

p. 49v   n.d.
LVII
"Here is a fact for my teeth"
    Perhaps the poem was to have been continued on p. 50, which is
blank.

pp. 50v, 51   January '32
LVIII
"Any matter move it to conclusion"
[1] "And" was altered from "Any".

p. 51v   Jan 20 '32
LVIV
"Too long, skeleton, death's risen"
[1] Misspelling of "sanitorium".

    Typescript, British Museum, has "Sly as an adder" for "Clean as a
whistle" (l. 6); "whose blood runs thick" for "whose breast hangs
low" (l. 11).

    The two lines beginning "Take now content" were used by Thomas
in a letter to Trevor Hughes in January 1934.

pp. 52, 52v   April '32
LVV
"No man knows lovliness at all,"
[1] Misspelling of "loveliness".

p. 53   (Fragment. April '32.)

LVVI
"Do thou heed me, cinnamon smelling,"

pp. 53ᵛ, 54   May 5 1932.

LVVII
"They said, tired of trafficking,"

p. 54ᵛ   May '32

LVVIII
"Be silent let who will"

pp. 55, 55ᵛ   May 7ᵗʰ '32

LVVIV
"Being but men, we walked into the trees"
[1] Misspelling of "noiselessly".   [2] Misspelling of "loveliness".

pp. 56, 56ᵛ   May 9ᵗʰ '32

LVVV
"The hunchback in the park,"

[1] Interlined: "going".
[2] Interlined: "Creates a".
[3] Interlined in pencil with caret: "wild"—then "molten" written over in ink.
[4] A preceding line, deleted at the time of first writing, was "[Calling 'Hey Mister']". "He" was added in margin before "Hears"—then deleted and "And" interlined.
[5] Apostrophe not needed.
[6] Comma altered to period.

A REVISION headed "Revised poem. July. 1941." begins on p. 55ᵛ, with note "See Opposite" and arrow pointing to p. 56, and the footnote "Continued back page" with an arrow directing us to p. 54ᵛ where the last two stanzas of the revision are headed "Continuation of Hunchback In The Park (next page)" and dated "July 16 '41".

The hunchback in the park
A solitary mister
Propped between trees and water
From the opening of the garden lock
That let the trees and water enter
Until the (church-black) bell at dark   (Sunday sombre)
Eating bread from a newspaper
Drinking water from the chained cup
That the children filled with gravel
    In the fountain basin where I sailed my ship

Slept at night in a dog kennel
But nobody chained him up.
Like the park birds he came early
Like the water he sat down
And mister they called hey mister
The (mitching) boys from the town   (truant)
Running when he had heard them clearly
[Past lake and rockery]
On out of sound[.]
Past lake and rockery
Laughing when he shook his paper
Through the (Indian ambush) of the willow groves   ([wild] loud zoo)
Hunchbacked in mockery
Dodging the park keeper
With his stick that picked up leaves.

And the old dog sleeper
Alone between nurses and swans
While the boys among willows
Made the tiger jump out of their eyes
[Apes—danced] To roar on the rockery stones
And The groves were blue with sailors

Made all day until bell time
A woman figure without fault
Straight as a young elm
Straight and tall from his crookèd bones
That she might stand in the night
After the lock and chains

All night in the unmade park
After the railings and shrubberies
The birds the grass the trees and the lake
Had followed the hunchback
And the wild boys innocent as strawberries
To his kennel in the dark.

This revision, chronologically the last to be made in the extant Notebooks, was published in *Life and Letters To-day*, October 1941, and in *Deaths and Entrances* and *Collected Poems*.

p. 57   June 7
LVVVI
"Out of the sighs a little comes,"
[1] Misspelling of "disappoint".   [2] Comma altered to period.

³ Interlined: "He'll".   ⁴ Corrected to "spilt" in *Twenty-five Poems*.

Whole poem crossed through, possibly at the time of publication, combined with the last poem of the Notebook, in *Twenty-five Poems*.

p. 57ᵛ   n.d.
          "Here is a beauty on a bough I can't translate"

p. 58   [May.]
              "At last, in hail and rain,"
¹ Interlined: "loving".   ⁶ Interlined: "love".
² Interlined: "humility".   ⁷ Interlined: "[love] work".
³ Interlined: "graveward".   ⁸ Interlined: "outrageous boy".
⁴ Interlined: "hailstoned".   ⁹ Interlined: "found" (same word).
⁵ Interlined: "Wind".
¹⁰ Semicolon altered to comma, and the stanza REVISED from this point in pencil with ink alterations overleaf on p. 58v, dated "May."

    The [rake] rage on holiday
    But now all every day
    Master goes prancing from a family malady
    [Smiling with slut and cigarette,]
    Going no place how well he knows
    And all dressed up in [sable] old skins with a pride
    For [Sheba, forbear] [moloch] forbear, outrager, and the rest.

pp. 59, 59ᵛ   June 25 '32
              "Upon your held-out hand"
¹ Correct form: "symbolize".

pp. 60, 6ov   April '32
          "Nearly summer, and the devil"
¹ Misspelling of "messengers".   ² Manuscript, British Museum, has "seasons'".

    Manuscript, British Museum, has "Poised" for "Pursed" (l. 11); and supplies final period to poem.

pp. 6ov, 61   June '32
                      Pome
        "How the birds had become talkative,"
¹ Dashes should be closed here, or   ² Presumably meant to be "Bruis-
perhaps at the end of the next line.   ing".

pp. 61, 61v   July 1
        "Were that enough, enough to ease the pain,"
[1] This line was added in pencil.
        Poem also in typescript, British Museum.
        The poem on p. 61 is crossed through in pencil, probably at the
time it was added to poem LVVVI above for publication as *Out of the
sighs* in *Twenty-five Poems*. Also see *Collected Poems*.

        Thomas signed the last page of the Notebook "Dylan Thomas" in
pencil, with the note: "End of Book July the Second 1932." and at the
foot of the page: "This has taken a hell of a time." He also experiments
with anagrams of his name; e.g. "Samot" and "Nalyd Samot".

                    THE FEBRUARY 1933 NOTEBOOK

        The working title of this Notebook is taken from the heading:
"This Book Started February 1, 1933."—though the poems are dated
up to August 1933. The poems from One to Fifty Three were written on the recto side (the exception is Thirty Eight), and the verso
side was available for the poet's drafts or revisions. The recto pages
were numbered by the poet, *1* to *139,* in pencil (the first half dozen
numbers are unaccountably erased); but a number of pages are now
missing: p. 6 (latter part of poem Three); pp. 30–32 (poem Fifteen); pp. 71–72, the middle sheet (first part of Twenty Seven);
pp. 88–99 (poem Thirty Four)—actually we can tell from the coun-
terpart pp. 41–55 that three more leaves were torn out than the page
numbering would indicate; and pp. 130–132 (poem Forty Nine).
        The poet signed his name, "Dylan Thomas." below the heading;
in pencil now erased he wrote a footnote, the name "Neuberg" (Victor Neuburg of the *Sunday Referee* "Poets' Corner") and in the
stanza gap in the middle of the page the newspaper's address: "17
Tudor St. EC4."

pp. 1, 2, 3   February 1 1933.
                              One.
                 "Sweet as [a dog's] kiss night sealed"
[1] Interlined: "the comets' kiss".   [3] Dash altered to colon in pencil.
[2] Comma apparently not needed.

p. 4   February 2 '33.
Two.
"It is death though I have died"

Pencil cross, half in the inner margin, perhaps meant to indicate deletion of the whole poem.

Poem also in typescript, Hanley collection.

This poem is a possible ancestor of *I dreamed my genesis* (*18 Poems* and *Collected Poems*).

p. 5   n.d.
Three.
"Had she not loved me at the beginning"
[1] Interlined: "Or".   meant to be "Broke").
[2] Interlined: "turn" (same word).   [4] Interlined: "bat".
[3] Interlined: "Braked" (presumably   [5] Interlined: "on".

The poem was presumably concluded on p. 6, which was later torn out. Page 5 is crossed through, with a headnote: "Used later in 'The Mouse and the Woman' "—referring to the short story of that title, where the first line of the poem appears in section 3 as: "Had she not been in the beginning, there would have been no beginning."

pp. 7, 8, 9   Feb 6, '33.
Four.
"Before the gas fades with a harsh last bubble,"

pp. 10, 11   Feb. 8. '33.
Five.
"Hold on whatever slips beyond the edge"
[1] Pencil deletion partially erased. Pencil adds punctuation to the opening lines, to read as follows:

> Hold on, whatever slips beyond the edge,
> To hope, a firefly in the veins; to trust
> Of loving; to keeping close, lest
> Words set septic, the loving thinking;

[2] Interlined: "put".   [3] Interlined: "Alone's unhurt".

Typescript, Hanley collection, (first nine lines only) has, as l. 5, "Refuse to trample in the dust".

On both pages of the Notebook the poem is emphatically crossed out. A REVISION entitled "Poem." on p. 9v is dated "December 1935."; it is the poem *Was there a time* as published in *New English Weekly*, 3 September 1936, and in *Twenty-five Poems* and *Collected Poems* (where "maggot" of l. 4 has replaced the "maggots" of the Notebook).

pp. 12, 13   Feb. 10. '33.

Six.

"After the funeral mule praises, brays,"

[1] Comma added in pencil.

[2] Comma changed to semicolon in pencil.

[3] Interlined: "him or her".

[4] "Sabbath black" circled in ink.

[5] Altered to "Dropped"—though "choke" remains unaltered.

[6] Altered to "Joined"—though "mark" remains unaltered.

[7] Interlined: "masks".

[8] Interlined: "spy".

[9] Interlined: "mewling" with an arrow indicating "mewling" to precede "masks".

[10] Interlined: "stain".

[11] Interlined: "[dart]".

[12] Interlined: "like paint in the sun." with "park" added before "sun" in pencil.

The upper margin of p. 13 has a later working: "[O] Shit on [the] his scraping tongue." Apparently at the same time Thomas added a phrase below the poem: "Birth of the womb"—circled in pencil.

Typescript, British Museum, follows Notebook, unemended version; lacks deleted l. 16.

For the circumstances surrounding this famous poem, see Introduction, pp. 20–22. A much revised version, discussed in *Letters to Vernon Watkins,* pp. 37, 40 and 57, appeared in *Life and Letters To-day,* Summer 1938, as *In Memory of Ann Jones* (also in *The Map of Love* and *Collected Poems*).

pp. 14, 15   Feb 16 '33

Seven.

"We who [are] young are old. It is the oldest cry."

[1] Interlined: "were".

[2] Interlined: "has".

[3] Interlined: "listen".

[4] Line thoroughly deleted and period supplied for line above.

Poem on both pages is crossed out. A "Conclusion of Poem Seven" appears as poem Nine below.

p. 16   n.d.

Eight.

"To take to give is all, return what given"

[1] Interlined: "blowing the [coins] quids".

[2] Comma altered to period.

[3] Interlined: "[dirt]"; semicolon

altered to period.

[4] Interlined: "quids"; this line is itself interlined.

The lower half of the page, which may have contained a continuation or a revision of the poem, is now torn off. A reworking of the last line appears just above the tear: "[Paying] [Twice the final co]".

A REVISION entitled "Poem" appears on the verso pages, pp. 15v and 16v, with note "PTO" at the foot of p. 15v, and dated "Laugharne. Sept. 1938":

	For three lean months now, no work done	
(X)	In summer Laugharne among the cockle boats	a
	And by the castle [p] with the boatlike birds	a
	On no work of words now for three lean months in the bloody	b
	Belly of the rich year and the big purse of my body	b
	I bitterly [moan to] take to task my poverty and craft:	c
		c

To take to give is all, return what is hungrily given
Puffing the pounds of manna [up] [back] up through the dew
    to heaven,
The lovely gift of the gab [flies] bangs back on a blind shaft.

	To take to leave from the richness of man is pleasing death;	
(X)	Unpleasant death will rake at last all currencies of the marked	
	breath	

To take to leave from the treasures of man is pleasing death
That will rake at last all currencies of the marked breath
And count [each] the forsaken mysteries in a bad dark.

To surrender now is to pay the expensive [phantom] ogre twice.
Ancient woods of my blood, dash down to the nut of the seas
If I take to burn or return this world which is each man's work.

The last line is repeated and circled. The first three lines and the later two lines marked "(X)" are denoted by a marginal cross in the Notebook, and are left out of the revision as it appears as *On no work of words* in *Wales,* March 1939, and in *The Map of Love* and *Collected Poems.*

pp. 17, 18, 19   Feb 17 '33
                              Nine.
                    (Conclusion of Poem Seven)
                  "No faith to fix the teeth on carries"

[1] Misspelling of "Piccadilly"; in the Notebook a line above this was left uncompleted, then deleted: "[The fanny struck, the]".

[2] Word penciled in space left for a word.

[3] Interlined: "listening".

[4] Interlined: "air;".

pp. 20, 21   February 22 '33
Ten.
"Out of a war of wits, when folly of words"
[1] Comma added in pencil.   [3] Correct form: "sympathize".
[2] Interlined: "friends' ".
  Poem also in typescript, Hanley collection.
  The Notebook poem was transcribed for *Poetry*, November 1955.

p. 22   Feb. 23 '33
Eleven.
"In wasting one drop from the heart's honey cells,"
[1] Interlined: "great".

pp. 23, 24, and 26   End of Feb. '33
Twelve.
"With all the fever of the August months,"
[1] Misspelling of "convalescence".   [4] Interlined: "hot and cold".
[2] Period added.   [5] Interlined: "burning".
[3] Interlined: "blind".   [6] Interlined: "blowing".
  The last four lines of the poem—in accordance with Thomas' note
at the foot of p. 24, " 'Twelve' Continued After 'Thirteen'."—are found
on p. 26 with the heading "Twelve (Continued)", and date "End of
Feb. '33".
  Thomas used the striking phrase "horrible desires" (l. 27) in *Then
was my neophyte* (see *Collected Poems*).

p. 25   n.d.
Thirteen.
"Their faces shone under some radiance"
[1] Interlined: "summer".
  Thomas added a title "In Hyde Park" below the poem number in
pencil, but it is deleted thoroughly in pencil and ink. The reference to
a neighboring graveyard in the poem would indicate a different locale.

pp. 27, 28, 29   March 1 '33
Fourteen.
"I have longed to move away"
  The poem on all three pages is crossed through, probably at the
time of the REVISION, which appears on p. 26v headed "Pome." and
dated "Jan 13 1936."—a fair copy of *I have longed to move away*, published in *New Verse*, December 1935 (Thomas wrote "New Verse" on
p. 27 in pencil now erased), and in *Twenty-five Poems* and *Collected
Poems*.

pp. 30, 31, 32 missing
                    Fifteen missing

pp. 33, 34, 35   March 22 '33.
                        Sixteen.
            "The waking in a single bed when light"

¹ Interlined: "famous self".

² Interlined: "cellars".

³ Interlined: "bucking".

⁴ Interlined: "he".

⁵ Interlined: "ghost".

⁶ Interlined: "[ghost] midnight sun".

⁷ Misspelling of "lovelier"; interlined: "wiser".

⁸ Interlined: "the sun".

⁹ Interlined: "wanting".

¹⁰ Interlined: "sank".

¹¹ Interlined: "all eyes and ears" with an arrow transposing the nouns; "Her" is added in margin before "Heart".

¹² Interlined: "roof".

¹³ Interlined: "Ghost".

¹⁴ Interlined: "Hidden".

¹⁵ Interlined: "undazzled"; end period added.

¹⁶ Interlined: "[sun]".

¹⁷ Interlined: "[Crowding]".

¹⁸ Interlined: "[sun]".

¹⁹ Interlined: "and his tongue".

²⁰ Abbreviation for "had".

²¹ Interlined: "just".

²² Correct form: "called".

²³ The possessive "s" needed.

²⁴ Comma added; "close" interlined.

Notable for the amount of revision which took place actually in the Notebook, this poem is further REVISED in thick pencil on pp. 29v (opposite p. 33 because of torn-out pages) and 33v:

Dog-in-a-Manger
                    For A Woman Just Married.
                    [On The Marriage Of A]

The waking in a single bed when light
Struck [luckily the palaces of her face] luckily her [mute] [mazed],
      skyscraping face
And morning's sun [trod] rode [true in the sky,] [proud]
      [like a sun] hard out of her thighs,
(The last possessor), is gone forever,
Her moonstruck self [sold] razed for one guest for good.
[Who will disturb the cellars of her blood.]
  Where there was one are two and nothing's shared
  Of love and light in all [whole holy] the hot, [su] the sunless world
[Save] But that [love-light of half love] blind shadow smeared
  Over the countenance of the bucking beast,
  And he, love knows; soon perishes the [breast] ghost,
  Reducing the midnight sun, for want of a wiser

U

Image on the ghost of paper,
Of single love to dust.

No longer
Will the vibrations of the sun desire on
Her deepsea pillow where once she sank alone,
Her heart all ears and eyes, [under]
Lips catching the [honey] avalanche of the golden
Ghost small as a farthing
Hidden behind a cloud, for where
She lies another['s] [is] lies secret at her side,
And through his circling arm she feels
The [secret] silent coursing of his undazzled blood.

It can be called a sacrifice. It can
With equal truth under the [fled] [deserted] [sun] moon
Be called the turning of sun's love to man,
And now in the [closed] double night
There can be no wild warming by sun['s] light.

Revised January 1941.

Further revision (see *Letters to Vernon Watkins*, pp. 106–107) produced the *On the Marriage of a Virgin* published in *Life and Letters To-day*, October 1941, and in *Deaths and Entrances* and *Collected Poems*.

pp. 36, 37, 38, 39, and 47, 48   Poem completed March 31 '33.
Seventeen.
"See, on gravel paths under the harpstrung [leaves]"

[1] Interlined: "trees".
[2] Interlined: "swan's" (same word).
[3] Interlined: "lake's".
[4] Interlined: "within".
[5] Interlined: "flowers' ".
[6] Comma added in pencil.
[7] Interlined: "harps"; the apostrophe of "wind's" altered to indicate plural.
[8] Added in margin: "Is".
[9] Misspelling of "people".
[10] Addition of "s" to "love" in pencil.
[11] Misspelling of "Choreographed".
[12] Interlined: "slack".
[13] End period added in pencil.
[14] Pencil capitalizes "he".
[15] Misspelling of "glowworm".

The last lines of the poem (from "O lonely among") are found on pp. 47 and 48 of the Notebook, headed "Seventeen (Continued)".
T. E. Hanley typescript omits the deleted lines.
Publication with title *Poet, 1935* in *Herald of Wales*, 8 June 1935, omits ll. 31–58 (the fourth and fifth sections). Thomas quoted

the last section in his "Reminiscences of Childhood" in *Quite Early One Morning* (only in the Dent edition, p. 4).

pp. 40, 41, and 51   n.d.
Eighteen.
"Make me a mask to shut from razor glances"

[1] Presumably unintentional repetition.
[2] The deleted lines are reworked between the lines:

> [That shall deceive the treacherous heart.]
> Turning the [bright] [cold] bold wind sick, that shall deceive
> The treacherous heart and the squat [eyes.] lies.

[3] Interlined: "squeezed through";   the".
"those" altered to "these".   [6] Interlined: "[innocence]".
[4] Interlined "chinks".   [7] Interlined: "behind the".
[5] Interlined: "Shall [hide] cheat   [8] Misspelling of "vermin".

The last section of the poem—in accordance with Thomas' note at the bottom of p. 41 "Continued Page 51"—is found on p. 51, headed in error, "Nineteen. (Continued)."

Typescript, British Museum, follows unemended Notebook version.

A DRAFT in pencil of the second section ("A snake, charmed") appears on p. 40v, and of the last section on p. 50v. The only significant variants are the third line ("Or [bad] rank breath [rising] in the booths of a bazaar,") and the sixth line from the end ("Themselves [masked] envisored from [t] men's looks,").

The REVISION on p. 39v, opposite the crossed-out first page of the poem has the heading "Poem" and is dated "Nov 1937 Blashford"; i.e., written from the house of his mother-in-law, near Ringwood, Hants. It is the version found in *Poetry,* August 1938, *Life and Letters To-day,* September 1938, and in *The Map of Love* and *Collected Poems,* with a very few variants: "[belladonna'd]" as an alternative for "enamelled" (l. 2); lines 4 and 5 read "Gag of a dumbstruck tree to [hide] block from my enemies / The bayonet tongue in [my] this undefended [mouthpiece] prayerpiece,"; and "dry" (l. 10) is underlined.

pp. 42, 43   March 28 '32 (presumably meant to be '33)
Nineteen.
"To follow the fox at the hounds' tails"

[1] Correct form: "butt-ends".   [2] Comma altered to a period.

T. E. Hanley typescript omits deleted lines. The typed "bed" (fifth line from the end) is altered to "bad" in Thomas' pencil.

pp. 44, 45, 46   March 28 '33
Twenty.
"The ploughman's gone, the hansom driver,"
[1] Interlined: "streets' stock".   [3] Interlined: "tune".
[2] Interlined: "town".

    Poem also in typescript, Hanley collection.
    A pencil DRAFT on pp. 44v and 45v has been erased.

pp. 49, 50   April 1 '33
Twenty One.
"Light, I know, treads the ten million stars,"
[1] Interlined: "from".   [3] The last two lines are in pencil,
[2] The verse line runs to the edge   deleted thoroughly in ink; omitted
of the Notebook page; period re-   in T. E. Hanley typescript.
quired.

pp. 52, 53   April 2. '33
Twenty Two.
"My body knows its wants that, often high"
[1] Interlined: "my love".   lected Poems).
[2] Interlined: "moon's canal".   [4] Interlined: "Man's".
[3] This line circled, used later in   [5] Interlined: "With".
To Others than You (see Col-
    The last four deleted lines are the origin of Twenty Three fol-
lowing.

pp. 54, 55, 56   April '33
Twenty Three.
"And death shall have no dominion."
[1] Pencil deletion later partially   [2] Interlined: "be laid".
erased.   [3] Comma added in pencil.
    As indicated in Thomas' headnote: "printed in N.E.W.", this first
version was published in New English Weekly, 18 May 1933. The
poem on all three pages was emphatically crossed through, probably
at the time of the REVISION, which appears in pencil on pp. 53v and 54v,
entitled "Poem" and dated "Feb 1936". The text is as found in Twenty-
five Poems and Collected Poems; the last line is written all in capital
letters in the Notebook.

pp. 57, 58, 59, 60, 61, 62, 63   Started April 16 '33
                                                  Completed April 20 '33
Twenty Four.
"Within his head revolved a little world"

[1] Published as "curled".   [6] Misspelling of "stiles".
[2] Published as "lightning".   [7] Interlined: "mocked".
[3] Interlined: "thro' every hole".   [8] Interlined: "Gibed".
[4] Published as "ailes".   [9] Corrected to "loneliness" on pub-
[5] Correct form: "butt-ends".   lication.

     Published with title *Out of the Pit* in *New English Weekly*, 25
January 1934.

pp. 64, 65, 66   April 20 '33
Twenty Five.
"Not from this anger, anticlimax after"

[1] Probably should be omitted.   [3] Comma altered to period.
[2] Interlined with caret: "not de".   [4] Probably meant to be "By-roads".

     The whole poem is crossed out on all three pages, probably at the
time of the copying in of the REVISED VERSION on p. 63v entitled "Poem"
and dated "January 1938 Blashford". The revision was sent to Vernon
Watkins on 21 March 1938 and published in *Poetry*, August 1938. See
Letters to Vernon Watkins, p. 40: "Before your letter came, I had cut
out the ubiquitous 'weather' from the anticlimactic poem, and am revising it all." The thorough revision apparently never occurred, but l. 4,
"In a land without weather", is deleted in the Notebook in favor of "In
a land strapped by hunger" as found in the *Not from this anger* of
The Map of Love and *Collected Poems*.

pp. 67, 68, 69, 70   April 22 '33
Twenty Six.
"The first ten years in school and park"

[1] Interlined: "to".   [4] Misspelling of "recipes".
[2] Comma altered to period.   [5] Misspelling of "people".
[3] Correct form: "discords".   [6] Misspelling of "ecstasy".

     This poem which speaks of the poet's first twenty years was
written when eighteen.

pp. 71, 72 missing
The beginning of Twenty Seven (printed here in italics) is taken from
the typescript, British Museum, entitled "PASS THROUGH TWELVE STAGES".
There is also a manuscript, British Museum, which lacks the penultimate line of the italicized section.

April 23 '33

p. 73 begins: "Although new pain, by back lane,"

[1] Question mark required (as in manuscript, British Museum).

[2] An arrow indicates transposition, as found in typescript, British Mu-seum: "The victim of grandfath-er's / Or even earlier's unwise de-sires".

This poem supplied some lines for *If I were tickled by the rub of love* (see poem Forty One in the August 1933 Notebook, and *Collected Poems*).

pp. 74, 75, 76   May 13, '33

Twenty Eight.

"First there was the lamb on knocking knees,"

[1] Misspelling of "Kingfisher's".   [3] Comma added in pencil.

[2] Abbreviation for "had".   [4] Misspelling of "knockkneed".

Some lines of this poem were used in Sonnet III of *Altarwise by owl-light* (see *Collected Poems*).

A typescript, British Museum, gives a concise version of the Note-book poem:

> First I knew the lamb on knocking knees,
> The ousel and the maniac greens of spring,
> Caught on a narrow easel metal skies,
> And on a yard of canvas inch of wing,
> Kingfisher's, gull's swooping feather and bone,
> Goodnight and goodmorning of moon and sun.
>
> Redkneed tomboy ousted ousel and lamb;
> Morning was saffron; and pink in the clouds
> Rose a pound of fair breast; I was dumb
> To say how divine were the woman moon's moods,
> And how blithe the stars as they lay
> Love scars on the woman of the sky.

pp. 77, 78   May 16 '33.

Twenty Nine.

"We lying by seasand watching yellow"

The REVISED VERSION, entitled "Poem" and dated "Sept 1937 Swan-sea.", was copied on p. 76v after publication in *Poetry*, January 1937, and *Wales*, Autumn 1937; it lacks the two lines (found also in *The Map of Love* and *Collected Poems*) beginning: "But wishes"—though those two words were written then deleted in the Notebook revision.

pp. 79, 80, 81   May 16 '33
Thirty.
BEFORE WE SINNED.
"Incarnate devil in a talking snake,"
Title added in pencil.

A REVISED VERSION, entitled "Poem" and dated "Jan 20 1936", was
copied on p. 78v after publication in the *Sunday Referee,* 11 August
1935, with the title *Poem for Sunday.* It has "heavens' hill" (l. 6) as
in *Twenty-five Poems* and *Collected Poems* where the *Sunday Referee*
has "thunder's hill".

An intermediate revision is found on a separate half-sheet in the
Buffalo collection:

                                           trinithill. crucifix

> Incarnate devil in a talking snake,
> The central plains of Asia in his garden,
> In shaping time the circle stung awake,
> In shapes of sin forked out the old-horned fruits,
> And god walked there who was a fiddling warden
> And played down pardon from a tree of ghosts.
>
> When storms struck on the tree, the [flying] stars
> And the half moon half handed in a cloud
> Spread good and evil till the [fancy] fears
> All in a fret of weathers made a word,
> [graph of] And when the moon [came] [flew] [out it was] [windily]
>   came silently she was
> Half white as wool, [half green as grass.] and greener than
>   the grass.
>
> We in our eden knew the eastern guardian
> In golden waters that no frost could harden
> And in [the hills] our time that tumbled from the earth;
> He in a horn of sulphur and the cloven myth

pp. 82, 83   May 18 '33.
Thirty One.
"Now understand a state of being, heaven"
A WORKING of the last two lines of the third stanza appears on p.
82v, as follows:

> And In [an] eternal
> Who'll long for
> Will long for home, long home, and dying.
> In an eternal state of being
> [And] All day Long for death, undying.

And in eternal state of being
[Long for the] Will long for death [that's] who's long in coming.

pp. 84, 85   May 20 '33
Thirty Two.
"Interrogating smile has spoken death"
[1] Interlined: "days".

pp. 86, 87   May 23 '33
Thirty Three.
"No man believes who, when a star falls shot,"
Publication in *Adelphi,* September 1933, with "God" capitalized throughout, and final period supplied.

pp. 88–99 missing

Thirty Four missing

p. 100   July 1. '33.
Thirty Five.
Children's Song.
"[When I lie in my bed and the moon lies in hers,]"
Title added in pencil. The whole poem is thoroughly deleted, with notation "Oh!" Also deleted is the dedication "For P.T."—Pamela Trick, the young daughter of Bert Trick (see poem One of the August 1933 Notebook).

p. 101   [July '33]
Thirty Six.
"The tombstone tells how she died."
[1] Interlined: "married".   [7] Interlined: "gold-eyed".
[2] Interlined: "some old [Welsh]".   [8] Interlined: "mirror"—with ar-
[3] Misspelling of "tombstone".   row to an additional line below the
[4] Interlined: "mad Welsh".   poem: "[Her legs] That showed
[5] Interlined: "[clean] girl".   death coming in."
[6] Interlined: ", milk and clean".
        The poem is crossed out, and a REVISION appears on p. 100v en-
titled "Poem." and dated "Sept 1938. Laugharne." (The last three lines
of the revision run over on to the foot of p. 101.) There is a small drawing of a tombstone in the upper margin.

The tombstone told when she died.
Her two surnames stopped me still.

A virgin married at rest.
She married in this [raining] pouring place,
That I struck one day by luck,
Before I heard in my mother's side
Or saw in the looking-glass shell
The rain through her cold heart speak
And the sun killed in her face.
More the thick stone cannot tell.

Before she lay on a stranger's [farmer's] bed
With a hand plunged through her hair,
Or that [small wet] raining tongue beat back
Through the [small] devilish years and innocent [great] *deaths*
To the room of a [quiet] secret child,
Among men later I heard it said
She cried her white-dressed limbs were bare
And her red lips were kissed black,
She wept in her pain and made *mouths,*
Talked and tore though her eyes smiled.

I who saw in a [hurried] [winding] hurried film
Death and this mad *heroine*
Met once on a mortal wall,
Heard her speak through the chipped beak
Of the [angel] stone bird guarding her:
I died before bedtime came
But my womb was *bellowing*
And I felt with my bare fall
A [strange and] blazing red harsh head tear up
And the [great] dear floods of his hair.

Some form of this revised poem was sent to Vernon Watkins in
September 1938, with the query: "In the ballad-like poem I'm not *quite*
sure of several words, mostly of 'great' floods of his hair. I think it's
right, though; I didn't want a surprisingly strong word there. Do tell
me about it, soon" (*Letters to Vernon Watkins,* pp. 43–44). In the next
letter, dated 14 October 1938, he gives an extended account of his re-
thinking of his "Hardy-like" poem: "I considered all your suggestions
most carefully. A 'strange and red' harsh head was, of course, very weak
and clumsy, but I couldn't see that the alliteration of 'raving red' was
effective. I tried everything, and stuck to the commonplace 'blazing',
which makes the line violent enough then, if not exactly good enough,
for the last. In the last line you'll see I've been daring, and have tried to
make the point of the poem softer and subtler by the use of the danger-
ous 'dear'. The word 'dear' fits in, I think, with 'though her eyes smiled',

which comes earlier. I wanted the girl's *terrible* reaction to orgastic death to be suddenly altered into a kind of despairing love. As I see it now, it strikes me as very moving, but it may be too much of a shock, a bathetic shock perhaps, and I'd like very much to know what you think. No, I still think the womb 'bellowing' is all right, exactly what I wanted; perhaps it looks too much like a stunt rhyme with heroine, but that was unavoidable. 'Hurried' film I just couldn't see; I wanted it slow and complicated, the winding cinematic works of the womb. I agree with your objection to 'small'; 'innocent' is splendid, but 'fugitive' and 'turbulent' are, for me in that context, too vague, too 'literary' (I'm sorry to use that word again) too ambiguous. I've used 'devilish', which is almost colloquial" (*Letters to Vernon Watkins*, pp. 44–45).

   The revised poem was published in *Seven*, Winter 1938, and *Voice of Scotland*, December 1938–February 1939. In *Poetry*, November 1939 (typescript, The Harriet Monroe Collection, University of Chicago Library) the poem is entitled (on the cover) *A Winding Film*. In *The Map of Love* (and *Collected Poems*) the "winding film" (l. 21) was changed to "hurried film"; and "Her tombstone" (l. 1) changed to "The tombstone". Thomas Taig has a typescript of the final version.

pp. 102, 103, 104   July 1. 33

Thirty Seven.
"Why east wind chills and south wind cools"
¹ Misspelling of "nighttime".   in pencil and then deleted.
² Misspelling of "Isinglass".   ⁴ Interlined: "the valley".
³ Quotation marks were supplied

   The question "What colour is glory?" was originally asked of Thomas by Pamela Trick, aged four (see poem Thirty Five above), according to A. E. Trick in conversation with the editor, which prompted a new attempt at the theme broached in poem XLI above. The specific question was dropped out of the revision, but was used later in *My world is pyramid* (see *18 Poems* and *Collected Poems*).

   The first page of the poem (p. 102) is crossed through, and a REVISION, untitled, appears on p. 101v, with the date "Jan 21 1936."—a fair copy of the version published in *New English Weekly*, 16 July 1936 (and in *Twenty-five Poems* and *Collected Poems*), but lacking the l. 14 of the published poem. The Notebook has a little drawing within the poem, apparently illustrating "the towers of the skies" (l. 19)—this phrase has a variant in the *New English Weekly* printing: "houses of the sky".

pp. 105, 105v, 106   July 4 & 5. 33
Thirty Eight.
"This is remembered when the hairs drop out:"
[1] Possibly should be "windy"; this   circled in pencil.
phrase and the following line are   [2] Question mark required.

Thomas is later (poem Fifteen in the August 1933 Notebook) to make much use of "In the beginning / Was the word".

Thomas mentioned this poem to Pamela Hansford Johnson in a letter of 20 July 1934: "Ha! 'Teredo' is an old one on me. I wrote a poem in 1933 beginning . . ."—he then quotes the last two lines of the Notebook poem.

See *Poetry,* November 1955, for a previous transcription of this poem.

pp. 107, 108   July 33
Thirty Nine.
"In me ten paradoxes make one truth,"
[1] Interlined: "among".   [2] Interlined: "in [the] two".

pp. 109, 110, 111   July 7. 33
Forty.
(After the performance of Sophocles' Electra in a garden. Written for a local paper)
"A woman wails her dead among the trees,"
The poem is crossed through on all three pages, possibly at the time of publication in the *Herald of Wales,* 15 July 1933, entitled *Greek Play in a Garden.* Thomas mentions this poem in "Return Journey": ". . . used to have poems printed in the *Herald of Wales*; there was one about an open-air performance of *Electra* in Mrs Bertie Perkins's garden in Sketty" (see *Quite Early One Morning*: Dent edition, pp. 75–76, 177–178; New Directions edition, p. 71). The performances were on the 5th and 6th July 1933; production by Thomas Taig, music by Daniel Jones.

p. 112   July 7. '33
Forty One.
"Praise to the architects;"
For discussion of this poem, see Introduction, pp. 23–24.

pp. 113, 114   July 9 '33
Forty Two.
"Here in this spring, stars float along the void,"
[1] Comma altered to semicolon in   below were in pencil later partially
pencil.   erased.
[2] This deletion and that a few lines   [3] Plural "s" added in pencil.

[4] Interlined: "winter's".

[5] Interlined: "teach"—in pencil, later erased; end period altered to semicolon in pencil (not erased).

[6] Question mark altered to period in pencil.

[7] Interlined: "teach".

[8] Deletion in pencil, later erased; interlined: "[timeless insect] timeless insect / Says the world".

[9] Comma altered to colon in pencil.

The first page of the poem (p. 113) is crossed through in pencil (now partially erased); two arrows in the inner margin of p. 114 seem to refer back to the REVISION, untitled, on p. 112v, with the date "Jan 1936". This is the version as published in *Twenty-five Poems* and *Collected Poems*.

p. 115   July 9 '33
Forty Three.
"A praise of acid or a chemist's lotion"
[1] Period altered to exclamation mark in pencil.

[2] Misspelling of "chloroform".

[3] Interlined: "coward".

The whole poem is crossed through in pencil.

p. 116   July 9 '33
Forty Four.
"Too many times my same sick cry"
[1] Interlined: "rattled".

The whole poem is crossed through in pencil.

pp. 117, 118, 119   July 14 '33
Forty Five.
"We have the fairy tales by heart,"
[1] Interlined: "garden".

[2] Interlined: "evening".

[3] Phrases "children's stories" and "the nursery of fairies" are circled in ink.

[4] Interlined: "characters".

[5] Interlined: "know".

pp. 120, 121, 122   July 15 '33
Forty Six.
" 'Find meat on bones that soon have none"
The REVISION of this poem, dated below the first date by the addition of "and January 1936", took the form of interlinings, as follows:

[1] "The merriest marrow and the dregs" (with comma added to the line above).

[2] "Before the ladies' breasts are hags".

[3] "And the limbs are torn".

⁴ "ladies are".
⁵ "wicked".
⁶ "word of the blood".
⁷ "wily".
⁸ "merry".
⁹ Interlined revised lines for this

and the next three lines are:
And the man no rope can hang
Rebel against my father's dream
That out of a bower of red swine
Howls the foul fiend to heel.
¹⁰ Interlined: "sweet".

The interlinings compose a revised version found in the Thomas Taig manuscript, and published in *Purpose,* April-June 1936, and in *Twenty-five Poems* and *Collected Poems.* (The first page of the poem, p. 120, is crossed through in pencil.)

The penultimate line, "Doom on the sun!" was to have been the title of Thomas' early novel, written prior to this time.

pp. 123, 124   July 17, '33.
                        Forty Seven.
                "Ears in the turrets hear"
¹ Interlined: "Ships".
        A pencil sketch of a face on p. 122v is a possible illustration of the poem.

        The first page of the poem, p. 123, is crossed through in pencil. The poem is also in a Thomas Taig manuscript. A version lacking the second stanza was published in *John O'London's Weekly,* 5 May 1934, with the title *Dare I?* Thomas referred to the poem as a "terribly weak, watery little thing" in a letter to Pamela Hansford Johnson during the week it appeared. The full poem appeared in *Twenty-five Poems* and *Collected Poems.*

pp. 125, 126, 127, 128, 129   July 33.
                        Forty Eight.
                      (From A Play)
            The Woman Speaks:
            "No food suffices but the food of death;"
¹ Correct form: "strewed".   ³ Published as "A mouse it was
² Misspelling of "greenness".   played".
        Manuscript, British Museum, is entitled "From A Play To Be Called, 'Ravens.'"; and the publication in *Adelphi,* March 1934, *The Woman Speaks.* Thomas contemplated revising this poem for *18 Poems* (see Introduction, p. 40), but it was never republished.

pp. 130, 131, 132 missing
                        Forty Nine missing

pp. 133, 134   August 33
                              Fifty.
                 "Let the brain bear the hammering,"
[1] Misspelling of "people".   and the gun."
[2] Interlined: "Beware the treaty

   "Domdaniel" is apparently used here (l. 6) as a person, as in a letter to Trevor Hughes about this time. "Daniel Dom" appears as a
character in the prose piece "Prologue to an Adventure," in *Adventures
in the Skin-Trade* (New Directions Paperbook No. 183, 1964), p. 212.

pp. 135, 136   August '33
                            Fifty One.
                 "The minute is a prisoner in the hour,"
[1] Interlined: "Now".   line was used later in *Love in the
[2] Interlined: "the [striking] chim-   Asylum* (see *Collected Poems*).
ing".   [6] Misspelling of "stivvy".
[3] Comma added in pencil.   [7] Word added in pencil in a space
[4] Interlined: "arrow".   left in the line.
[5] Interlined: "[year] [stars]"; the

   After the first stanza was an interlined line, deleted before it was
finished: "[You woke and the dawn spoke and the]". On 1 April 1938
Thomas wrote to Vernon Wakins: "I've got one of those very youthfully-
made phrases, too, that often comes to my mind and which one day I
shall use: 'When I woke, the dawn spoke'." One sees him, some time
during the following months, trying out the phrase inside the back
cover of *Wales,* March 1938 (in the Thomas Taig collection), as follows:

                 [The lonely]   webbed down the
           [The Lonely Owl My Marrow]   [feathery,] shell
            When I woke, the dawn spoke
            The lonely owl's my marrow. I walk

For final poem, see *When I Woke* in *Deaths and Entrances* and *Collected Poems.*
   Two attempts at REVISION of the first stanza appear on p. 134v,
along with scattered words in the upper margin, as follows:

            Loud with   Bu   Its
                     like slate   [R] red
                                              feathered
           script   Its young   Or

         This minute's locked to learn me in the hour,
      [O] [And] Who sees it burn to break the chiming cell
         And play the truant in the den of days

Chock   Loud   burn and break
   [Chock] with my [written heart and slate-grey hair] [scrib-
      bling blood] fringed rod and talking script
[Chock-loud] in the   chimed the ground

This minute's locked to learn me in the hour,
Who sees it burn to break the scriptured cell
And play the truant on the tip of days?
I, [said] rang the lock[s] at my temple, [but]
But [sentinel the] burn and break no [cap] marked boy, or
   beast, or taper

First vision that set fire to the air
In a [square] room [with] above the [final] town.

pp. 137, 138   August.
                    Fifty Two.
          "Shall gods be said to thump the clouds"
[1] Probably meant to be "dye".   "wood".
[2] Arrow transposes "brass" and
   The first page of the poem, p. 137, is crossed through. The last
stanza is written in pencil and is omitted, along with the third stanza,
in the published version in *Twenty-five Poems* and *Collected Poems*.

p. 139   August 16.
                    Fifty Three.
          "Matthias spat upon the lord"
   The poem is written in pencil, crossed through in pencil. Thomas
later added a heading "Rev David Rees", the name of his mother's
sister's husband, a clergyman on whose retirement Thomas as a reporter
had written a eulogy "End of a Great Ministry" in the *Herald of Wales*,
5 November 1932. A letter to Trevor Hughes, written about this time
and sharing some of the phraseology with this poem, indicates Thomas'
mood as he ends this Notebook: "Look at the notices in tramcars:
Spitting on Christ prohibited. In the parks: Do not walk on God. What
shall it be? Jew's mucus or gentile's praise? Ripeness is all—all balls.
We're over-ripe."

p.139v   Pencil note at the foot of the page: "Finished—'33".

THE AUGUST 1933 NOTEBOOK

Thomas wrote the poems of this Notebook in sequence between August 1933 and April 1934. He numbered them as he wrote them, One to Forty One; and, with the exception of Twenty Seven, they are in ink on the recto pages, which are numbered from *1* to *90* in pencil. (The numbers up to *66* were later partially erased.) Missing pages are: p. 29 (poem Fourteen); pp. 46–47 (the conclusion of Twenty One); and the last two leaves of the Notebook, which possibly contained the first draft of the conclusion of poem Forty One.

At some point Thomas added a motto as a heading to the first page:

To others caught
Between [Twixt] black and white

and appended his signature below it.

pp. 1, 2   August 17 '33.
One.
"The hand that signed the paper felled a city;"
[1] Misspelling of "sovereign".

The lower half of p. 2 is torn off. The last stanza was thoroughly scrawled through in pencil and does not appear in the New York Public Library manuscript nor in the published version in *New Verse*, December 1935 (Thomas wrote "New Verse" in pencil, now erased, beside the poem number) nor in *Twenty-five Poems* and *Collected Poems*. It does, however, receive a form of reinstatement in the Notebook in that Thomas attempted to erase the pencil deletion and go over the whole stanza in ink. The poem on both pages was later crossed through in ink.

This acknowledgedly political poem is dedicated "To A.E.T."—Bert Trick of the Swansea Labour Party; see Introduction, p. 23.

p. 3   August 20, 33.
Rayner's Lane.
Two.
"Let for one moment a faith statement"
Dedicated "To T.H."—Trevor Hughes—this poem was presumably

written during Thomas' visit to his ex-Swansea friend's house on Per-
well Ave., Rayners Lane, Harrow, Middlesex.

Poem also in typescript, Hanley collection.

p. 4   August 22 '33.
Three.
"You are the ruler of this realm of flesh,"
T. E. Hanley typescript has "thudding head" (l. 7).

p. 5   August 24 '33.
Four.
"That the sum sanity might add to nought"
[1] Misspelling of "apparelled".   [2] Unattached word "Girl" in margin.
[3] In first writing this poem, Thomas apparently left this line blank; he
later gave himself two alternatives written in pencil, bracketed together:

> I would make genuflexion with the sheep
> I would reverse my collar to the sheep

—the second was deleted and the former gone over in ink.

A DRAFT or more probably a REVISION (an attempt rather like that
for poem Thirty below) appears on p. 4v as follows:

> That the sum sanity might add to nought
> And [wom] matrons ring their harebell-lips
>   the harebells on their lips
> Girls woo the weather through long Sabbath night
> And rock twin floods upon their starry laps,
> I would enforce the black apparelled flocks[,]
> And raise a hallelujah to the *Lamb*
> Cut on my breast a secret crucifix;
> I wd be woven at the sabbath loom.

T. E. Hanley typescript is arranged in couplets.

The poem was thoroughly revised (manuscript not extant), and
published in *Swansea and West Wales Guardian*, 8 June 1934, with the
title *Twelve*:

> That the sum sanity might add to nought
> And words fall crippled from the slaving lips,
> Girls take to broomsticks when the thief of night
> Has stolen the starved babies from their laps,
> I would enforce the black apparelled cries,
> Speak like a hungry parson of the manna,
> Add one more nail of praise on to the cross,

X

And talk of light to a mad miner.
I would be woven a religious shape;
As fleeced as they bow lowly with the sheep,
My house would fall like bread about my homage;
And I would choke the heavens with my hymn
That men might see the devil in the crumb
And the death in a starving image.

Thomas intended this revision for *18 Poems* (see Introduction, p. 40), but apparently decided to exclude it.

pp. 6, 7   August 26, '33.
Five.
"Grief, thief of time, crawls off"

From this poem came the first stanza of *Grief thief of time* as published in *Comment*, February 1936, and in *Twenty-five Poems* and *Collected Poems*. The REVISION appears on p. 5v with the heading "Five"; has "bones of youth" (l. 11) for "bone of youth" (in *Collected Poems*). A footnote to the revision, "Written and copied in later, August 1935. Glen Lough. Donegal.", indicates that the revision was made during the poet's summer holiday in Ireland in 1935. For the second stanza of *Grief thief of time*, see poem Eighteen below.

pp. 8, 9, 10, 11   August 29 33.
Six.
"Shiloh's seed shall not be sewn"

[1] Pencil deleted the "e" of "sewn" in both the first and last stanzas, supplying an "o"; also deleted the second unnecessary "n" of "Anointed" in the last stanza. These pencil markings were later erased.
[2] "A" added in margin.

[3] Would normally be "labour"; the "o" here was apparently written over an "e".
[4] Interlined in pencil then in ink is an added line: "With falling night a saviour,"; a comma is added in pencil after "day".

Thomas' own footnote refers us to Johanna Southcott (1750–1814), a domestic servant who identified herself with the "woman clothed with the sun" of Revelations. Although sixty-four she promised to give birth to a son, the Shiloh of Genesis 49:10; see Introduction, p. 28.

The seed-at-zero, published in *Twenty-five Poems* and *Collected Poems*, derived its form and some of its phrasing from this Notebook poem.

Previously transcribed for *Poetry*, November 1955.

pp. 12, 13, 14, 15   September 6
                          Seven.
          "Before I knocked and flesh let enter,"
[1] Corrected by the deletion of the "b" in pencil.

Typescript, British Museum, capitalizes "Father," "His," and "Him"
throughout; a variant in the last line is "my mother's womb."

For discussion of the poem, see Introduction, pp. 28–30. Thomas submitted it to *Criterion* soon after it was written; it did not, however, get
into print until *18 Poems,* when stanzas five and nine were omitted
(also in *Collected Poems*).

An important little prologue to this poem appears on p. 11v with
an arrow indicating its applicability to poem Seven:

> If God is praised in poem one
> Show no surprise when in the next
> I worship wood or sun or none:
> I'm hundred-heavened   rainbow sexed
>   and countless

pp. 16, 17   September 8.
                          Eight.
          "We see rise the secret wind behind the brain,"
[1] Abbreviation for "the".

pp. 18, 19, 20, 21   September 12.
                          Nine.
          "Take the needles and the knives,"
[1] Interlined: "beggar".   [4] Line written below, itself deleted:
[2] Interlined: "wind".   "[Like a wren through the trap
[3] Interlined: "fall".   land]".
A DRAFT of the last four stanzas is found opposite them on p. 20v
with no significant variant. Sending the poem to Pamela Hansford Johnson in November 1933, Thomas wrote: "For some reason, I don't think
you will like the needles and the knives. I don't think I do either, but
there you are!"

pp. 22, 23   September 15. '33
                                                  Llangain Carms.
                          Ten.
          "Not forever shall the lord of the red hail"
[1] Interlined: "stamp".   [2] Interlined: "one".

Dedicated "To B.C."—not at present identified, but perhaps associated with the poet's trips to Blaen Cwm, a house belonging to his mother's family, near Fern Hill farm in the village of Llangain, Carmarthenshire.

The beginning of a REVISION appears on p. 21v:

> As fire falls, two hemispheres divide,
> Shall drown the boys of battle in their swill,
> The stock and steel that bayonet from the mud,
> The fields yet undivided behind the skull.
> Both mind and matter at the scalding word
> Shall drop their stuffs and scatter like a shell
> Your world and mine, one venom as they blew
> > hail

Thomas intended a revision of this poem to be included in *18 Poems* (see Introduction, p. 40) but perhaps the revision was never completed.

pp. 24, 25   September 16. 33.
                                                              Llangain

Eleven.
"Before we mothernaked fall"
[1] Interlined: "build".

Lacking the last four lines, but with punctuation added, the poem was published in *New English Weekly*, 30 July 1936. The Notebook poem was transcribed for *Poetry*, November 1955.

p. 26   September 16.
                                                              Llangain.

Twelve.
"[Our] sun burns the morning, a bush in the brain;"

[1] Interlined: "The".   present l. 4 was interlined.
[2] An original l. 4 "[And the wail-   [3] Semicolon altered to comma.
ing heart is screwed to my side]"   [4] Interlined: "[stable][m]".
was deleted and used as l. 5; the
[5] This line was interlined above a rejected line "[A mother in labour pays twice her pain.]" from which the last line was apparently formed. The last two lines were later deleted in pencil with arrows indicating alternative lines on p. 25v:

> A mother in labour pays twice her pain,
> Once for the Virgin's child, once for her own

T. E. Hanley typescript follows the revision.

pp. 27, 28   September 17 '33.
                                                      Llangain

Thirteen.
"My hero bares his nerves along my wrist"

[1] Interlined: "Praising".

Typescript, British Museum, has no punctuation at all; omits the last deleted stanza—this stanza provided the basis for poem Eighteen below. The truncated version appeared in *18 Poems* and *Collected Poems*.

p. 29 missing

Fourteen missing

pp. 30, 31   September 18 '33
                                                      Llangain.

Fifteen.
"In the beginning was the three-pointed star,"

[1] Abbreviation for "the".   [2] Line circled in pencil.
[3] The deleted lines are reworked in pencil opposite on p. 30v:

> In the beginning was the three-tongue star
> Translating into light, that is all-tongued,
> The secret word spelling a single name.

These three lines are then repeated in ink immediately below.

Thomas' penciled note at the head of the poem "See 40" refers us to the rewritten version, poem Forty below.

p. 32   September 18. '33

Sixteen.
"Love me, not as the dreamy nurses"

[1] Interlined: "midnight"; published version has "dreaming".   [2] Interlined: "two"; "lover" is altered to "loves" in pencil.

Published with title *Song* in the *Sunday Referee,* 7 January 1934.

pp. 33, 34, 35, 36   September 25 33.

Seventeen.
"For loss of blood I fell where stony hills"

[1] Corrected to "lack" in pencil.   space left for a word; Charles E.
[2] Comma added in pencil.   Feinberg typescript has "raging".
[3] Word inserted with caret in a   [4] Misspelling of "chequered".

Thomas' penciled heading "In three Parts" indicates his intention to link this poem and the two following; the three were typed by Thomas under the title "Jack of Christ" and sent to Glyn Jones in 1934. The typescript, now in the collection of Charles E. Feinberg, was published in the *Western Mail,* 30 July 1960. This printing generally follows the Notebook, omitting the fourth and the last stanzas of Seventeen, with the notable variant in the last line of the third stanza: "A frozen lie upon the rising land."

The first line of the poem was adapted for Sonnet V of *Altarwise by owl-light* (see *Collected Poems*).

pp. 37, 38, 39   September 26. '33.
Eighteen.
"Jack my father, let the knaves"
[1] Misspelling of "victual".

A pencil arrow between the second and third stanzas points to an additional stanza on p. 36v, written first in pencil and then gone over in ink:

> Let them escape, the living graves
> Be bared of lovliness [and lorn] and shorn of sex,
> Let sense be plundered and the dryboned wrecks
> Of words perplex the sad tides of the brain.

This extra stanza appears in the Charles E. Feinberg typescript and *Western Mail* printing; but the first two lines of stanza six are omitted, and some of the stanzas have the last line printed as two in recognition of the internal rhyming.

Also on p. 36v are the first four lines of a REVISION:

> Now Jack my fathers let the time-faced crook,
> Death flashing in his sleeve,
> With swag of bubbles in a bony sack
> Sneak down the century's grave,

These lines appear with some changes as the beginning of the second stanza of *Grief thief of time*—for first stanza, see poem Five above. For the origin of these lines, see poem Thirteen above.

pp. 40, 41, 42   September 29 '33.
Nineteen.
"The girl, unlacing, trusts her breast,"
[1] Interlined: "move".   [3] Interlined: "surgeon wrist".
[2] Pencil supplies semicolon.   [4] Interlined: "the bride".

"End" in pencil indicates the completion of the poem "In three Parts". Charles E. Feinberg typescript (and the *Western Mail* printing) has variant, the second stanza, l. 5: "Their many-pointed charms would drop".

pp. 43, 44   September 30. '33.
                          Twenty.
           "Through these lashed rings set [in] their hollows"
¹ Interlined with caret: "deep in-   talized.
side".   ⁵ Interlined: "this"; " 's" interlined
² "M" written over "m".   between "heart" and "pit".
³ Misspelling of "Whereon".   ⁶ Capitalized in pencil.
⁴ The original line "[God who   ⁷ Interlined: "from".
springs and fills the tidal well]"   ⁸ Interlined: "tongue-plucked".
was deleted and used as the follow-   ⁹ Interlined; "draws".
ing line; "And," was added in the   ¹⁰ Interlined: "[tiny] awkward".
margin, and "With" left capi-

    T. E. Hanley typescript has Thomas' alteration of "isle" (l. 8) to
"island" in pencil on the typescript, and the reworking of stanza two
in pencil:

    Through, I tell you, your two [cursing] midnight lips I pray
    To that unending sea around my island
    The water-spirit moves as it is bidden,
    And with not one fear-beggared syllable
    Praise him who springs and fills the tidal well.

p. 45   n.d.
                        Twenty One.
              "Ape and ass both spit me forth,"
    The poem was presumably continued on pp. 46 and 47, which, be-
ing the middle pages of the Notebook, became loose and are missing.

pp. 48, 49, 50   Oct 5 '33.
                        Twenty Two.
          "The eye of sleep turned on me like a moon,"
¹ Quotation presumably ends here.   ³ The phrase "the hours' ladder"
² Interlined: "lights".   fills a space left in the line.
    Thomas sent this poem to Pamela Hansford Johnson in October
1933, and stressed in his following letter: "It is *not* the best I have sent
you. Only superficially is it the most visionary. There is more in the
poem, 'Before I knocked', more of what I consider to be of importance
in my poetry." His correspondent had apparently remembered the
phrase (l. 3) "wound his horn" in William Collins, and Thomas
countered: "So the poor old snail has wound his horn before. It is a long

time since I read the 'Ode to Evening,' so long that my memory refuses all responsibility." In a later letter he considered the poem "very
bad indeed": "I have rewritten 'The Eye of Sleep' almost entirely, and
it is now a little better" (see Introduction, p. 40). The rewriting, a fus-
ing of this poem with Thirty One below, produced *I fellowed sleep* of
18 Poems and *Collected Poems*.

pp. 51, 52   October 12. '33
Twenty Three.
"The force that through the green fuse drives the flower"
[1] Interlined: "How time has ticked a heaven round the stars."—which
line appears in *18 Poems* and *Collected Poems*. Publication in the *Sunday Referee,* 29 October 1933, has: "And I am dumb to tell the timeless clouds / That time is all." Charles E. Feinberg typescript omits this
fourth stanza.
　　The later inscription (written over the erased page number) "To
E.P." has not been identified. The "12" of the date was added in pencil
over a dash.
　　The DRAFT was crossed through in pencil, which added the note
"Referee" plus a few other words now unintelligible because of erasure.

pp. 53, 54   October 14 '33
Twenty Four.
"From love's first fever to her plague, from the soft second"
[1] Initially written: "as two meeting   ."—with space left for a word.
But "mountains" is interlined after "two" in pencil and a period supplied
after "meeting".
[2] Abbreviation for "had".
　　Completed as poem Twenty Six below.

p. 55   October 16. 33
Twenty Five.
"The almanac of time hangs in the brain;"
　　T. E. Hanley typescript follows Notebook poem, which was previ-
ously transcribed for *Poetry,* November 1955.

pp. 56, 57   October 17 '33
Twenty Six.
(Continuation of Twenty Four)
"And from the first declension of the flesh"
[1] Abbreviation for "had".   [3] Corrected from "me" to "be"
[2] Comma supplied in pencil.   in pencil.

The last three lines are added in pencil. These and the previous eight lines were omitted in the publication in *Criterion,* October 1934, and in *18 Poems* and *Collected Poems*. It is presumably concerning the Notebook ending that Thomas wrote to Pamela Hansford Johnson in November 1933: "Your remark about the end of my Feverish poem is entirely justified. I plead guilty to bathos, but offer in excuse the fact that I copied out the poem as soon as I had written it, wanting to get it off to you and too hurried to worry about its conclusion. In the ordinary way I would never have passed it." See also Introduction, p. 31.

pp. 57v, 58v   n.d.
Twenty Seven.
"All that I owe the fellows of the grave"
¹ Correct form: "bequeath".   ³ Corrected from "me" to "be" in
² Correct form: "a".   pencil.

In pencil on the verso pages (pp. 58 and 59 are blank), this poem probably has the status of a first draft, never reworked. The first line of the second stanza was used later in *I dreamed my genesis* (*18 Poems* and *Collected Poems*).

p. 60   October 25 33.
                                                          Llangain.
Twenty Eight.
"Here lie[s] the [worm] of man and here I feast,"
¹ Interlined: "beasts".   ³ Interlined: "angels".
² Interlined: "beast".   ⁴ Interlined: "slips".
     T. E. Hanley typescript follows emended Notebook version.

pp. 61, 62, 63, 64   November 11. 33.
Twenty Nine.
"When once the twilight locks no longer"
¹ Misspelling of "Sargasso".   ⁴ Apostrophe needed.
² Correct form: "bequeaths".   ⁵ An arrow transposes "cypress" as
³ This and the next line are circled   adjective for "dead".
in pencil.   ⁶ Syntax not clear.

     Thomas wrote to Pamela Hansford Johnson about this poem in November 1933: "I'm enclosing one poem, just finished. It's quite my usual stuff, I'm afraid, and quite probably you won't like it. But, honestly, the one 'cancer' mentioned *is* necessary."
     A much revised version was published in *New Verse,* June 1934, and in *18 Poems,* with "dammed" (l. 3). *Collected Poems* reverts to "damned" and omits a stanza, stanza six of the *18 Poems* version:

> The hanged who lever from the lines
> Ghostly propellers for their limbs,
> The cypress lads who wither with the cock,
> These, and others in sleep's acres,
> Of dreaming men make moony suckers,
> And snipe the fools of vision in the back.

pp. 65, 66   November 20 33.
Thirty.
"Light breaks where no sun shines;"
¹ Misspelling of "glowworms".   ³ The same line interlined above
² Comma added in pencil.   the deletion.

Poem also in typescript, British Museum.

A hardly serious attempt at REVISION appears on p. 64v, stopping with the eighth line, and providing no variant except "with great glow-worms in their heads" (l. 4).

Thomas wrote "Listener." in pencil now erased on p. 65, indicating the poem's publication in the *Listener,* 14 March 1934, entitled *Light;* reprinted in *18 Poems* and *Collected Poems*. See Introduction, pp. 36–37, 39, 40.

p. 67   November 27th 33.
Thirty One.
"I fellowed sleep who kissed between the brains;"
Poem also in typescript, British Museum.

Fused with poem Twenty Two above for publication as *I fellowed sleep* in *18 Poems* and *Collected Poems*.

pp. 68, 69   December 13 '33
Thirty Two.
"See, says the lime, my wicked milks"
Thomas' pencil note in the margin of p. 68 "See 28" might refer to poem Twenty Eight above, with which this poem has affinities.

Typescripts are in the British Museum and Hanley collection.

Thomas wrote to Pamela Hansford Johnson soon after completing this poem: "A new poem accompanies this. I suppose it's my usual stuff again, and even a little more death-struck. But don't be put off by my anatomical imagery . . . Because I so often write in terms of the body, of the death, disease, and breaking of the body, it doesn't necessarily mean that my Muse (*not* one of my favorite words) is a sadist. For the time at least, I believe in the writing of poetry from the flesh, and, generally, from the dead flesh." See Introduction, p. 37.

p. 70   Dec: 24 '33
                        Thirty Three.
            "This bread I break was once the oat,"
[1] Error for "bread".

    A DRAFT on p. 69v entitled "Breakfast Before Execution." was also
dated "December 24 '33."; has variant last line: "God's bread you break,
you drain His cup." The last line was further revised for publication in
New English Weekly, 16 July 1936, and in *Twenty-five Poems* and *Collected Poems.*

pp. 71, 72   January 12. '34.
                        Thirty Four.
            "Your pain shall be a music in your string"
[1] Interlined: "[Mansion] [The house of bone]"; then the original line
repeated in the margin.

pp. 73, 74   February 2. '34
                        Thirty Five.
            "A process in the weather of the heart"
[1] In an interesting slip of the pen, Thomas first wrote "tomb" then corrected it immediately to "womb".

    Thomas' headnote "Referee" in pencil now erased indicates publica-
tion in the *Sunday Referee,* 11 February 1934; also in *18 Poems* and
Collected Poems.

    A DRAFT with same date and entitled "Poem." appears on pp. 72v
and 73v:

        A process in the weather of the heart
        Turned Turns damp to dry. The golden shot
        Bolts [in] down the freezing grave.
        A weather in the process of the veins
        Turns night to day: blood in the suns
        Lights up the [burning] living worm

                Storms down.   in the quarter

        A process in the eye forewarns
        The bones of blindness; and the womb
        Drives in a death as life leaks out.

        A darkness in the weather of the eye
        Is half its light. The fathomed sea
        Breaks on the unplumbed land.
        The seed that makes a forest of the loin

> Forks half its fruit; and half drops down,
> Slow in a sleeping wind.
>
> And weather in the [blood] flesh and bone
> Is damp and dry: The quick and dead
> Move like 2 ghosts before the eye
>
> A process in the weather of the world
> Turns ghost to ghost; each mothered child
> Sits in their double shade.
> A process blows the moon into the sun,
> Pulls down the hanging curtains of the skin.
> [Let] And the heart gives up its dead.

pp. 75, 76   February 23. '34.
Thirty Six.
"Foster the light, nor veil the bushy sun,"

[1] Abbreviation for "the".

Thomas apparently took the opening phrase of this poem from a letter he received from Trevor Hughes, dated 13 January 1934, a letter concerning Thomas' father's illness, and containing the sentence: "Foster the light and God be with you" (carbon copy in Lockwood Library, Buffalo).

First publication was in *Sunday Referee,* 28 October 1934. It was revised thoroughly (worksheet not extant) for *Contemporary Poetry and Prose,* May 1936, which version is found in *Twenty-five Poems* and *Collected Poems.*

pp. 77, 78, 79, and 82   March '34.
Thirty Seven.
"The shades of girls all flavoured from their shrouds,"

[1] These two lines were written in pencil, and deleted in ink; the following lines are interlined: "Groom the dark brides, and widows of the night / Fold in their arms."

[2] Interlined: "When love, awoken, hungers in her womb."—*New Verse* has variant: "When love awakes her delver to the worm."

[3] Interlined: "The sunny gentlemen, the Welshing rich".

[4] Thomas had apparently copied in the next poem, Thirty Eight, when he became dissatisfied with the ending to Thirty Seven. He deleted the last stanza and the date, and continued the poem for four lines on the same page, p. 79, with a footnote "(Continued)"; on p. 82 under the heading "Thirty Seven (Continued)" are the last two stanzas, with date.

[5] Interlined: "from rag to bone".

[6] Interlined: "Suffer this world to spin."

The revisions in the penultimate stanza were made after the poem, truncated in its first section, had been accepted for publication in *New Verse* (Thomas wrote "New Verse" in pencil above the poem number), and were proposed to the editor in a letter from Thomas to Geoffrey Grigson, in which the poet feared the "jarring optimism" of the original lines: "I suggest that this revised stanza sounds far less false." He was not in time to effect the change; the unemended version appears in *New Verse,* April 1934, and in *18 Poems* and *Collected Poems* as *Our eunuch dreams.*

pp. 80, 81   March 18. '34.
                        Thirty Eight.

                "Where once the waters of your face"
[1] Probably meant to be "source" (as in typescript and publication).
    Charles E. Feinberg typescript has "Grim" for "Sage" in the last stanza, l. 3.
    Thomas wrote "Referee" in pencil now erased above the poem number, indicating publication in the *Sunday Referee,* 25 March 1934; also in *18 Poems* and *Collected Poems.*

pp. 83, 84, 85, 86   April '34.
                        Thirty Nine.

                "I see the boys of summer in their ruin"
[1] Period written over a comma;   [2] Period altered to exclamation "Oh" in the next line is written   mark. over "I".

    A marginal number "24" appears toward the end of the first and the second sections, perhaps indicating the number of lines.
    Thomas wrote headnote "New Verse" in pencil now erased, referring to publication in *New Verse,* June 1934, which has a variant in the fourth stanza, l. 5: "Of doubt and dark" in place of "Of love and light". The *18 Poems* and *Collected Poems* printings revert to the Notebook phrase.
    An ineffectual DRAFT or REWORKING of the first three lines appears on p. 82v, with one variant: "Lay the gold tithings low".

pp. 87, 88   [March] April. '34.
                        Forty.

                "In the beginning was the three-pointed star,"
[1] Interlined: "forked".

Thomas' headnote on p. 87 "See Fifteen" refers us to the first version of this poem, poem Fifteen above.

The last two lines were reworked for *18 Poems;* also in *Collected Poems.*

pp. 89, 90, 90v   April 30, '34.

Forty One.

"If I was tickled by the rub of love,"

[1] Published version has "were" throughout.

[2] Interlined: "walls".

[3] Interlined: "girls".

[4] Interlined: "men"; "the" altered to "their".

[5] Interlined: "manhood"; "falling" altered to "fallen".

[6] Interlined: "The sea of scums could drown me as it broke / Dead on the sweethearts' ".

Parts of this poem were derived from poem Twenty Seven in the February 1933 Notebook, especially the deleted third stanza, reworked as the sixth. Perhaps reworking took place on pp. 91 and 92, which were torn out, and the poem finished on p. 90v, now the last page of the Notebook.

Thomas sent the poem to Pamela Hansford Johnson in May 1934, with the comment: "The poem is, I think, the best I've written—I've said that to you about a lot of mine, including all sorts of wormy beasts. It may be obscure, I don't know, but it honestly was not meant to be. It's too—I can't think of the word—for anything but *New Verse* to print." Thomas wrote "New Verse" in pencil now erased on p. 89, and the emended poem was published in *New Verse,* August 1934; and in *18 Poems* and *Collected Poems.*

APPENDIX

APPENDIX

ADDITIONAL POEMS 1930−1934

THIS APPENDIX *gathers together twenty poems not found in the extant Notebooks but contemporaneous with them. The first eight, transcribed from manuscripts in the British Museum (see Introduction, page 39), were probably written just prior to the 1930 Notebook, or, since they are not "Mainly Free Verse Poems," from the rhymed Notebook that we postulate was a companion to the 1930 Notebook. The deleted poem 9 in the 1930 Notebook seems especially close in mode to the "They" series below; the first poem here has strong similarities to the poem that opens the 1930 Notebook.*

i

He turned his forehead to the trooping air,
And stood there breathing like a god;
He had sought them with a slender rod,
Calling out to them, "I am Azelea". He is there
Who walks upon the clouds with coral eyes;
They whom he calls upon are many; "I am Azelea of the loud sun".
He stands preparing incense for their feet.
"I am Azelea". His call is sweet.

ii

You hold the ilex by its stem
And touch its petals one by one;

Y   [337]

You make them glad and tender them
With lifted fingers to the sun.

The flower will not join the sky;
It was the oracle that told
You how the stem and leaves should lie,
Stem close to white, and leaf to gold.

And now the sun denies it rest,
You will have tears to carry, bearer.

The ilex has a snowy breast;
There is not any flower fairer.

The first of the third person plural poems below is quoted by Daniel Jones in E. W. Tedlock, ed., Dylan Thomas: The Legend and the Poet *(London, 1960), p. 17, as an example of his collaboration with Thomas: "I had the odd-numbered lines and Dylan the even-numbered, and we made it a rule that neither of us should suggest an alteration in the other's work." Each line of the version printed by Daniel Jones is made up of two lines of the typescript, British Museum; e.g., the first line is "They had come from the place high on the coral hills".*

iii

They had come from the place
High on the coral hills
Where the light from the white sea fills
The soil with ascending grace.

And the sound of their power
Makes motion as steep as the sky,
And the fruits of the great ground lie
Like leaves from a vertical flower.

They had come from the place;

They had come and had gone again
In a season of delicate rain,
In a smooth ascension of grace.

iv

They come with their soft white hair
In a power of candid motion;
Silver birds and flowers are there
In the depth of the deep-olive ocean.

They gather the fruit of the grass
And the soil of the hills of the sea;
They will talk like tall trees when they pass,
And carry wise beauty to me.

v

They enter the gates of the temples of light,
Laden and carefully sweet;
The stars in their mouths are folded and white,
And the dust is like dew for their feet.

They enter unfolding their robes of delight,
And kiss the old women with love;
The curve of their mouths is so perfect and bright,
And the moon is so gracious above.

vi

They are so much without sound
That their coming is calm and unheard,
And their feet are as soft on the ground
As the feet of a clear-coloured bird.

The nightingale branches his song
And the delicate leaves become notes,
And the sounds of its splendid voice throng
A path to the rose of their throats.

vii

They wait full of love
At the shores of the lotus sea;
Like rain from the wings of a dove
They mingle fair magic with me.

They wait in the light
Of a single anemone tree;
Like flowers that sing in the night
They bring many sorrows to me.

viii

They will climb to the edge of the earth
And kneel on the beautiful soil;
They will fill their fair bosoms with mirth,
In a curious image of toil.

The sea is not sweeter than they,
Nor the little white birds of the air,
And their bodies are brighter than day,
And they cover the earth with their hair.

Poem iv was printed by Thomas himself as editor in the Swansea Grammar School Magazine, *July 1931, as the first of* Two Decorations, *the second of which is printed below from the* Swansea Grammar School Magazine, *followed by* The Callous Stars *from the same issue, both poems signed "D.M.T."*

ix

They do not approach my care
   In a filigree coming of death,
But move like a moon in the air,
   Or shape a white cave of their breath.
And I cannot see their true pain
   Carved in a dainty surprise,
Because of the wind and the rain
   That blows like a cloud to their eyes.

x

The clear-eyed, callous stars look down
On darkened field and lighted town;
Slow moving through unmeasured space,
Or set in their appointed place,
From whence they shed impartial light
On sin and sorrow of the night,
Unstained, untouched by all they see,
Too bright and cold for sympathy.
We gaze upon the stars, and they
Behold us with a chilly ray,
In hard indifference to the sight
Of all we suffer in the night.
But could they feel as well as see,
The sky would droop from misery;
And hidden in a cloudy veil
The light of all the stars would fail.

   *The following poem, written within the period of the 1930-
1932 Notebook but not included in it, was published in the* Herald
of Wales, *23 April 1932, accompanying an article Thomas wrote as*

a working journalist on the Swansea poet James Chapman Woods.
The poem, entitled Youth Calls To Age, *is apparently addressed*
to the older poet.

xi

You too have seen the sun a bird of fire
Stepping on clouds across the golden sky,
Have known man's envy and his weak desire,
Have loved and lost.
You, who are old, have loved and lost like I
All that is beautiful but born to die,
Have traced your patterns in the hastening frost.
And you have walked upon the hills at night,
And bared your head beneath the living sky,
When it was noon have walked into the light,
Knowing such joy as I.
Though there are years between us, they are nought;
Youth calls to age across the tired years:
"What have you found," he cries, "what have you sought?"
"What you have found" age answers through his tears,
"What you have sought."

The remaining eight poems to be presented here from the
British Museum manuscripts were probably typed copies of poems
in the Notebook not extant which covered the period July 1932 to
January 1933. They can be considered adolescent rather than juven-
ile, and one of them has the distinction of being an early version
of the famous Especially when the October wind, *revised for the*
Listener, *24 October 1934; also in* 18 Poems *and* Collected Poems.

xii

Walking in gardens by the sides
Of marble bathers toeing the garden ponds,

Skirting the ordered beds of paint-box flowers,
We spoke of drink and girls, for hours
Touched on the outskirts of the mind,
Then stirred a little chaos in the sun.
A new divinity, a god of wheels
Destroying souls and laying waste,
Trampling to dust the bits and pieces
Of faulty men and their diseases,
Rose in our outworn brains. We spoke our lines,
Made, for the bathers to admire,
Dramatic gestures in the air.
Ruin and revolution
Whirled in our words, then faded.
We might have tried light matches in the wind.
Over and round the ordered garden hummed,
There was no need of a new divinity,
No tidy flower moved, no bather gracefully
Lifted her marble foot, or lowered her hand
To brush upon the waters of the pond.

xiii

Now the thirst parches lip and tongue,
The dry fever burns until no heart is left,
Now is decay in bone and sinew,
When heaven—open wide the gates—has taken flight,
Searing the sky for thunderbolts to fall
On man and mountain,
Is treason's time and the time of envy.

The acid pours away, the acid drips
Into the places and the crevices
Most fit for lovers to make harmony,
To catch the lovers' palsy,
And on the sweethearts' bed to lie and grin,

To smirk at love's undress,
Make mock of woman's meat,
And drown all sorrows in the gross catastrophe.

xiv

Lift up your face, light
Breaking, stare at the sky
Consoling for night by day
That chases the ghosts of the trees
And the ghosts of the brain,
Making fresh what was stale
In the unsleeping mummery
Of men and creatures horribly
Staring at stone walls.
Lift up your head, let
Comfort come through the devils' clouds,
The nightmare's mist
Suspended from the devils' precipice,
Let comfort come slowly, lift
Up your hand to stroke the light,
Its honeyed cheek, soft-talking mouth,
Lift up the blinds over the blind eyes.

Out of unsleeping cogitations,
When the skeleton of war
Is with the corpse of peace,
(Notes not in sympathy, discord, unease),
The only visitor,
Must come content.
Therefore lift up, see, stroke the light.
Content shall come after a twisted night
If only with sunlight.

xv

Let it be known that little live but lies,
Love-lies, and god-lies, and lies-to-please,
Let children know, and old men at their gates,
That this is lies that moans departure,
And that is lies that, after the old men die,
Declare their souls, let children know, live after.

xvi

The midnight road, though young man tread unknowing,
Harbouring some thought of heaven, or haven hoping,
Yields peace and plenty at the end. Or is it peace,
This busy jarring on the nerves yet no outbreak?
And this is plenty, then, cloves and sweet oils, the bees' honey,
Enough kind food, enough kind speaking,
A film of people moving,
Their hands outstretched, to give and give?
And now behind the screen are vixen voices,
The midnight figures of a sulphurous brood
Stepping in nightmare on a nightmare's edges.
Above them poise the swollen clouds
That wait for breaking and that never break,
The living sky, the faces of the stars.

xvii

With windmills turning wrong directions,
And signposts pointing up and down
Towards destruction and redemption,
No doubt the wind on which the rooks

Tumble, not flying, is false,
Plays scurvy tricks with values and intentions,
Guides and blows wickedly, for larks
Find hard to dart against a cloud,
To London's turned, and thirsty loads
Of men with flannel shirts
And girls with flowered hats
Intent on visiting the famous spots,
Ride in their charabancs on roads
That lead away to dirty towns
Dirtier with garages and cheap tea signs.

Faith in divinity would solve most things,
For then the wrong wind certainly
Would be the devil's wind, and the high trinity
Be guiltless of the windy wrongs.

But ways have changed, and most ways lead
To different places than were said
By those who planned the obvious routes
And now, mistaking the direction,
On miles of horizontal milestones,
Perplexed beyond perplexion,
Catch their poor guts.

The wind has changed, blown inside out
The coverings of dark and light,
Made meaning meaningless. The wrong wind stirs,
Puffed, old with venom, from a crusted mouth.
The changed wind blows, and there's a choice of signs.

To Heaven's turned, and pious loads
Of neophytes take altered roads.

xviii

The gossipers have lowered their voices,
Willing words to make the rumours certain,

Suspicious hands tug at the neighbouring vices,
Unthinking actions given causes
Stir their old bones behind cupboard and curtain.

Putting two and two together,
Informed by rumour and the register,
The virgins smelt out, three streets up,
A girl whose single bed held two
To make ends meet,
Found managers and widows wanting
In morals and full marriage bunting,
And other virgins in official fathers.

For all the inconvenience they make,
The trouble, devildom, and heartbreak,
The withered women win them bedfellows.
Nightly upon their wrinkled breasts
Press the old lies and old ghosts

xix

Especially when the November wind
With frosty fingers punishes my hair,
Or, beaten on by the straight beams of the sun,
I walk abroad, feeling my youth like fire
Burning weak blood and body up,
Does the brain reel, drunk on the raw
Spirits of words, and the heart sicken
Of arid syllables grouped and regrouped with care,
Of the chosen task that lies upon
My belly like a cold stone.

By the sea's side hearing the cries of gulls,
In winter fields hearing a sheep cough
That wakes out of tubercular oblivion
Into a wet world, my heart rebells
Against the chain of words,

Now hard as iron and now soft as clouds,
While weighted trees lift asking arms far off.

Shut in a tower of words, I mark
Men in the distance walk like trees
And talking as the four winds talk,
Children in parks and children's homes
Speaking on fingers and thumbs,
And think, as drummed on by the sun,
How good it is to feel November air
And be no words' prisoner.

To view the changing world behind
A pot of ferns, lifting the sunblind
See gilded people walking on hindlegs
Along the pavement where a blind man begs
Hopefully, helplessly, feeling the sun's wings,
To trim a window garden with a shears,
To read front pages, fall asleep,
Undreaming, on a linen lap
This, when the heart goes sick
And ears are threatened in the spring of dawn
By the triumphant accents of the cock,
Is more to be longed for in the end
Than, chained by syllables at hand and foot,
Wagging a wild tongue at the clock,
Deploring death, and raising roofs
Of words to keep unharmed
By time's approach in a fell wind
The bits and pieces of dissected loves.

*The final extant, unpublished poem within the 1930–1934 period
is a typescript in the Pamela Hansford Johnson papers in Lockwood
Library, Buffalo, of an early version of* Do you not father me, *which
was revised for publication in* The Scottish Bookman, October 1935
(*also in* Twenty-five Poems *and* Collected Poems). *The typescript
accompanies a similar typescript of the revised version of* Especially

when the October wind; *it was therefore probably made in September 1934, with a view to including it in* 18 Poems.

XX

Do you not father me, nor the erected arm
For my tall tower's sake cast in her stone?
Do you not mother me, nor, as I am,
The lover's house, lie suffering my stain?
Do you not sister me, nor the erected crime
For my tall turrets carry as your sin?
Do you not brother me, nor, as you climb,
Adore my windows for their summer scene?
Do you not foster me, nor the hailfellow suck,
The bread and wine, give for my tower's sake?

Am I not father, too, and the ascending boy,
The boy of woman and the wanton starer
Marking the flesh and summer in the bay?
Am I not sister, too, who is my saviour?
Am I not all of you by the erected sea
Where bird and shell are babbling in my tower?
Am I not you who fronts the tidy shore,
Nor roof of sand, nor yet the towering tiler?
Am I not all of you, nor the hailfellow flesh,
The fowl of fire and the towering fish?

This was my tower, sir, where the scaffolded coast
Walls up the hole of winter and the moon.
Master, this was my cross, the tower Christ.
Master the tower Christ, I am your man.
The reservoir of wrath is dry as paste;
Sir, where the cloudbank and the azure ton
Falls in the sea, I clatter from my post
And trip the shifty weathers to your tune.
Now see a tower dance, nor the erected world
Let break your babbling towers in his wind.

Books by Dylan Thomas mentioned.

18 Poems. London: The Sunday Referee and the Parton Bookshop, 1934.

Twenty-five Poems. London: J. M. Dent & Sons, 1936.

The Map of Love. London: J. M. Dent. & Sons, 1939.

Portrait of the Artist as a Young Dog. London: J. M. Dent & Sons, 1940; New York: New Directions, 1940, paperbook No. 51, 1955.

Deaths and Entrances. London: J. M. Dent & Sons, 1946.

Collected Poems 1934-1952. London: J. M. Dent & Sons, 1952.

Collected Poems of Dylan Thomas. New York: New Directions, 1954.

Quite Early One Morning. London: J. M. Dent & Sons, 1954; New York: New Directions, 1954.

Letters to Vernon Watkins. London: J. M. Dent and Faber & Faber, 1957; New York: New Directions, 1957.

Adventures in the Skin Trade. New York: New Directions Paperbook No. 183, 1964.

INDEX

INDEX

THE INDEX lists the titles and/or first lines (sometimes abbreviated) of the poems in the text and Appendix. It also lists the works and names mentioned in the Introduction, in the footnotes to the Introduction, in the Notes to the Poems, and in the commentary in the Appendix.